MW01030297

COVER

Elvis and Nashville

To Pat & Bob —
and a great
Rhodes Scholar

Don Cusic

Don Cusic
5/28/15

Copyright 2012 by Don Cusic

Brackish Publishing
P.O. Box 120751
Nashville, TN 37212

All rights reserved. Printed in the United States of America.
No part of this book may be reproduced in any manner
whatsoever without written permission except in the case of
brief quotations embodied in critical articles and reviews.

Cover photo licensed from Elvis Presley Enterprises.

Cover Design & Layout:
Wendy Mazur, Oddball Group
www.theoddballgroup.com

Production Coordinator:
Jim Sharp, Sharpmanagement

Contents

Preface

There was no Music Row when Elvis first came to Nashville. The music business was centered in the downtown area, specifically the WSM Studios on Commerce Street, the Ryman Auditorium on Fifth Avenue, and the Cumberland Lodge Building on Seventh Avenue North. By the time Elvis died, Music Row was established as the heart of the country music business in Nashville and the city was firmly established as "Music City U.S.A."

Elvis played a role in this development. Because of the income generated by the sales of Elvis' records, RCA established a permanent office and a studio on Music Row. During the 1960s and 1970s Elvis spent a lot of time in Nashville, primarily at the RCA Studio where he recorded over 260 songs during his career. Elvis' career was tied to Nashville; in November, 1955, he attended the Disc Jockey Convention at the Andrew Jackson Hotel, where he first announced that he was signing with RCA. Elvis was booked by Jamboree Productions, owned by Hank Snow and Colonel Tom Parker and most of these tours were package tours with country artists.

Elvis' manager, Colonel Tom Parker, lived in Nashville and that became the headquarters for the Elvis Presley Fan Club as well as the ventures that launched Elvis. When Elvis signed with RCA, he was part of the Country Division, headquartered in Nashville under the leadership of Chet Atkins.

The local newspapers in Nashville covered the music industry because Nashville was emerging as a music center, led by the Grand Ole Opry and the annual Disk Jockey Convention held each November. The Country Music Association emerged out of this organization. Elvis received significant coverage from Nashville newspapers because Colonel Parker actively courted the press. From his days as manager of Eddy Arnold, through his management of Hank Snow, Parker knew the value of press coverage, especially in his home town and made sure that reporters had access to him and the star he managed. This gave Nashville newspapers a unique advantage during the early years of Elvis' career, because they had access during his early visits to Nashville and during his recording sessions.

During the 1950s when there were so many attacks on Elvis by the national media, the Nashville newspapers often seemed to go out of their way to present favorable coverage. After all, Elvis was a fellow Tennessean with strong links to the local community who brought attention to the city and its music industry.

Since Elvis died, there have been a number of books written that have exposed his private life; however, during his lifetime, there was a huge mystique surrounding Elvis. He did not give in-depth interviews to reporters, attend industry functions or make himself visible to outsiders. Most people wondered what he was doing and where he was. His social life centered around the tight knit group known as the "Memphis Mafia" who were, for the most part, relatives and friends who dated back to Elvis' childhood and early years. There was a huge barrier set up between Elvis and the public out of necessity; an appearance by Elvis at a public event inspired pandemonium. It was nearly impossible to gain access to Elvis and this lent an air of mystery to him.

In this book, I have concentrated on Elvis' connection to Nashville and used local media articles to tell his story. This is not a biography; Peter Guralnick's masterful two volume work and Alanna Nash's book on the women in Elvis' life have covered that territory much better than I could. Instead, it's the story of Elvis' connection to Nashville.

I am indebted to Ray Walker and Gordon Stoker of the Jordanaires, Elvis' first guitar player, Scotty Moore, session guitarist Jerry Kennedy, singer Millie Kirkham, pianist and member of the Imperials Joe Moscheo, Tony Brown, Peter Guralnick, Norbert Putnam, David Briggs, Jerry Chesnut, Eddy Arnold, Mike Curb and others who knew Elvis for sharing their stories with me.

I am indebted to Mike Curb and the Mike Curb Family Foundation for providing me a Professorship as well as several trips to Memphis, which enabled me to do this book. The world owes a great debt to Mike Curb and the Curb Foundation for purchasing and restoring RCA Studio B and making it available to those who come to Nashville and want to see where Elvis recorded. The studio is administered by Belmont University and the Country Music Hall of Fame. Mike also purchased the first home that Elvis owned in Memphis, which is administered by Rhodes College.

I must thank my former assistant, Molly Shehan for all her help as well as the librarians in the Tennessee Room at the Nashville Public Library and John Rumble and Michael Gray at the Frist Research Library at the Country Music Hall of Fame. Many thanks also to Sue Perkins, who read the manuscript and made valuable suggestions.

Chapter 1: 1954

On Saturday morning, October 2, 1954, Elvis, Scotty Moore, and Bill Black loaded their instruments into Sam Phillips big black 1951 Cadillac–Black's bass was strapped to the roof of the car–and headed east on Highway 70 towards Nashville, a little over 200 miles away. It was Elvis' first trip to Nashville and it was special: his first appearance on the Grand Ole Opry was scheduled that evening. Marion Keisker, Sam's secretary and the woman who really "found" Elvis stayed in Memphis until she closed the studio, then took a bus to Nashville.[1]

Since Elvis did not own a suitcase, he borrowed one from Marion; in that suitcase were almost all the clothes he owned.

Although this was the first time Elvis had been to Nashville, he grew up listening to the Grand Ole Opry, broadcast live on 650 AM from his radio. First in Tupelo, Mississippi, then Memphis, Elvis' parents, Vernon and Gladys Presley, loved listening to the Opry and Elvis grew up hearing Ernest Tubb, Hank Snow, Eddy Arnold, Roy Acuff, Red Foley, Minnie Pearl, Lonzo and Oscar, Rod Brasfield, Grandpa Jones, Uncle Dave Macon, Pee Wee King, Whitey Ford ("The Duke of Paducah") and Hank Williams. And now Elvis was going to Nashville to appear on the very same Grand Ole Opry where those giants of country music appeared.

Just a couple months before–on July 5–Elvis had recorded his first Sun Records release, "That's All Right, Mama" b/w "Blue Moon of Kentucky." Elvis recorded with guitarist Scotty Moore and bassist Bill Black–Elvis played rhythm guitar–and that record was doing well in and around Memphis. Sam Phillips, who owned Sun Records, called Jim Denny, manager of the Opry, a number of times to get a booking for Elvis on that show. Finally, Denny agreed to book the young singer and his group on October 2.

"Blue Moon of Kentucky" was a streak of luck, just like "That's All Right, Mama." Scotty Moore had a group, the Starlite Wranglers, who released a record on Sun, but it had gone nowhere. Moore was an ambitious young man who wanted a career in the music business; having coffee with Sam Phillips one day at Miss Taylor's restaurant, next door to the Memphis Recording Studio at 706 Union, Phillips gave him the name and phone number of Elvis Presley, a young man who had been in Sam's studio a week before to record "Without You," a song Sam found in Nashville. Sam knew Elvis because the young man had been in the studio twice to make a custom record and kept dropping by the studio to chat with Sam's secretary, Marion Keisker. Marion kept his phone number and called him for a session on Saturday, June 26. That session didn't work out; the song didn't quite fit Elvis and, although he stayed for about three hours, singing everything he knew to Sam, nothing came out of the session except a hunch that Sam Phillips had that there was something special in this young man.

The first time Elvis came to the Memphis Recording Studio he recorded "My Happiness" and "That's When Your Heartaches Begin." The second time, he recorded two country songs, "I'll Never Stand In Your Way" and "It Wouldn't Be the Same Without You." These songs represent the wide array of influences on young Elvis Presley. "My Happiness" had been a pop hit in 1948, released by five different acts: Jon and Sondra Steele, the Pied Pipers, Ella Fitzgerald, the Marlin Sisters and John Laurenz. "That's When Your Heartaches Begin" was recorded by the Ink Spots in 1941 but was never a national chart hit for them. "I'll Never Stand in Your Way" and "It Wouldn't Be the Same Without You" were both co-written by Nashville songwriter and publisher Fred Rose, who had written "Be Honest With Me" and "Tweedle O'Twill" for Gene Autry and "Blue Eyes Crying in the Rain." "I'll Never Stand in Your Way" was recorded by pop singer Joni James, but had never been a national chart hit, while "It Wouldn't Be the Same Without You" was recorded by Jimmy Wakely but it, too, had never reached the national charts.

Scotty Moore, who worked at the dry cleaners owned by his brother, did not know that Elvis had been in the studio the week before when he called him that evening after supper. Mrs. Presley answered and told him Elvis was at the movies; Scotty said he represented Sun Records and Gladys Presley promised to track down her son. Within an hour, Elvis called and they arranged to meet at Scotty's apartment the next day.

On Sunday, July Fourth, Elvis came to Scotty's apartment to "audition," wearing pink pants with a black stripe, a black shirt, and white shoes; his hair was long and greasy. Bass player Bill Black, who played in Scotty's band, worked at Firestone and lived just three doors down. Scotty invited him to join him and listen to the young man sing a number of ballads. Scotty was surprised at the wide range of material that Elvis knew, everything from pop songs to country to gospel. But there were no up tempo songs; they were all ballads.

Later Scotty called Sam and the label owner asked if Scotty felt it was worth an evening in the studio to try out the young singer; Scotty said he thought it was. Not wanting to make a big production out of the evening, Scotty did not invite his group, the Starlite Wranglers, to come along; instead, it was only him, Bill Black and Elvis who gathered in the studio with Sam that evening.

The small group recorded several songs; first they tried "Harbor Lights," which had been a chart record for seven different acts in 1950: Sammy Kaye had the biggest hit, followed by Guy Lombardo, Ray Anthony, Ralph Flanagan, Bing Crosby, Ken Griffin and Jerry Byrd & Jerry Murad's Harmonicats. Then they did "I Love You Because," which had been a country hit for two artists in 1949: Leon Payne (who wrote the song) and Ernest Tubb. Finally, around midnight—with all of them having to tackle day jobs the next morning—they decided to call it quits. That's when Elvis started "clowning around," banging out "That's All Right, Mama"—an old R&B (Rhythm and Blues) number written and recorded by Arthur "Big Boy" Crudup—on his guitar. Scotty and Bill joined in; Sam, who was in the control room, stuck his head in the door of the studio and asked, "What are you doing?" According to Scotty Moore, they said, "We don't know." Sam replied "Well, back it up, try to find a place to start and do it again." [2]

That's how "That's All Right, Mama" was recorded. Listening to those early recordings today, on "Harbor Lights" and "I Love You Because" there are glimpses of the future Elvis but the singer has a tight throat, holding back emotions and his voice was mostly in the tenor range. But on "That's All Right, Mama," Elvis cuts loose, his voice is lower and the song pours out of his heart. The first two songs sound uptight and tentative; the last one sounds relaxed and confident. Elvis Presley had found his voice and his future in that old R&B song.

The next day, Tuesday, the group re-assembled in the studio; they needed a second song for the "B" side of a record. They tried "Blue Moon," a pop hit from 1935 that had been recorded by Glen Gray, Benny Goodman, Al Bowlly with Ray Noble, Mel Torme and Billy Eckstine, but it didn't seem to click. (That song later became a number one pop hit by the Marcels, a doo wop group, in 1961.)

On Wednesday evening it was the same thing, but they finished early. After Elvis, Scotty and Bill left, Sam Phillips called Dewey Phillips–no relation–a disc jockey who had the "Red, Hot and Blue" show on WHBQ (which played rhythm and blues), broadcast from a studio in the Hotel Chisca in Memphis. Dewey was one of the early DJs who played R&B; the most famous was Alan Freed in Cleveland, but there were others. Dewey ruled night-time R&B radio in Memphis, playing R&B records from nine until midnight six nights a week. Sam invited Dewey over to the studio after he finished his show. When Dewey arrived at the office, he opened a beer and then sat and listened as Sam played him the tape of "That's All Right, Mama." Dewey had played the original record by Arthur "Big Boy" Crudup on the air but he listened, intrigued by the new version.

The next day Dewey called Sam and told him he wanted two copies of that song to play on his show that night. Sam made the acetates and called Elvis to let him know the record might be played on Dewey's show that evening. Elvis set the radio dial on WHBQ and then went to the movies. Sometime around 10 o'clock Dewey played the record seven times in a row while phone calls came into the station; Dewey dialed Elvis' home and told Mrs. Presley he wanted Elvis in the studio. Gladys and Vernon Presley went to the movie theatre, found Elvis and delivered the message; Elvis then went to the WHBQ studio for his first interview.

On Thursday evening, July 8, they still didn't have a "B" side so on Friday evening they came back into the studio to try again. After several days of dead ends, as they tried song after song, bass player Bill Black started clowning, singing "Blue Moon of Kentucky"—which had been recorded as a waltz by bluegrass pioneer Bill Monroe in 1946—in a falsetto voice (Monroe sang in a high tenor). Elvis jumped in and then Scotty joined and Sam got it down on tape, adding "slapback" or an echo that came to be a defining sound from the Sun Studio.

The single was officially released on Monday, July 19. Elvis began to perform in Memphis; on two Saturdays he played his two songs at the Bon Air Club where the Starlite Wranglers performed. On Friday, July 30, Elvis performed at the Overton Park Band Shell where the crowd went wild when Elvis–as he did in the studio–raised up on the balls of his feet, his legs shaking, while performing. This would be the start of the movements that shook a nation.

The next night, a Saturday, Elvis performed again at the Bon Air Club. On August 7, his single was reviewed in *Billboard*, and on Wednesday, August 18 "Blue Moon of Kentucky" was at number three on *Billboard's* regional Country and Western chart for Memphis.

At this point, Elvis was a country artist. He was "country" because he was white and southern; the rhythm and blues acts were all black in the segregated United States. He was not a "pop" artist because his sound was too raw, he was a country boy and the record was made in the South. Pop acts were cultured, sophisticated and connected to Tin Pan Alley and the Big Band sound, although by this point most of the Big Bands were gone and singers like Perry Como, Rosemary Clooney, Nat "King" Cole, Frank Sinatra and Tony Bennett dominated the charts.

The big pop hits of 1954 were "Little Things Mean a Lot" by Kitty Kallen, "Sh-Boom" by the Crew-Cuts," "Wanted" by Perry Como, "Oh! My Pa-Pa" and "I Need You Now" by Eddie Fisher, "Make Love to Me" by Jo Stafford, "Mr. Sandman" by The Chordettes, "Hey There" and "This Old House" by Rosemary Clooney, "Secret Love" by Doris Day and "Three Coins in the Fountain" by the Four Aces.

When the Cadillac arrived at the Ryman Auditorium on Fifth Avenue, the group went inside the building and looked around. Elvis was disappointed; "You mean this is what I've been dreaming about all these years?" he said to those around him.

Jim Denny was also disappointed and confronted Sam. "I wanted the full band that's on the record. Our agreement was that we were gonna have the performance just like it is on the record," said Denny.[3] Sam informed Denny that the record contained the same three musicians standing in the Ryman–and nobody else. It was a "big" sound they got out of Sun's

Studio and it fooled a lot of people, who thought there were more musicians involved.

Backstage, Elvis met Buddy Killen, who played bass and pitched songs for the new Tree Publishing Company. Elvis was filled with insecurity; he introduced himself to Chet Atkins, then introduced Scotty to Chet, who was one of his heroes. They were nervous about seeing Bill Monroe; after all, they had goosed up his song quite a bit. They were surprised when Monroe complimented them on their version. (Monroe had already recorded an up tempo version of "Blue Moon of Kentucky" based on their record—although Elvis, Scotty and Bill did not know this.)

The group was known as "The Blue Moon Boys" and before they went on stage, Bill Black peeked from backstage and was surprised to see his wife, Evelyn, and Scotty's wife, Bobbie, on the front row. The two young ladies were supposed to stay in Memphis and wait for the musicians to return; instead, after the group left Memphis, Evelyn went over to Bobbie's house and the two drove to Nashville, arriving around eight that evening. Somehow they managed to obtain front row seats. When Bill saw them sitting out front, he managed to get them backstage. Marion Keisker had also managed to get backstage.

The Grand Ole Opry was broadcast in 15 minute segments, hosted by a member of the Opry, who generally did an opening song, then invited a guest to appear before closing with a song. Elvis appeared on the 10:15 segment hosted by Hank Snow and sponsored by Royal Crown Cola; before they went on stage, Snow asked Elvis "What name do you go by?" "Elvis Presley" came the reply. Then the trio performed "Blue Moon of Kentucky" and left the stage.

Scotty Moore remembered the reaction from the audience was polite and warm—but not overwhelming. At this point, Elvis was a virtually unknown artist playing before an audience used to hearing the likes of Snow, Ernest Tubb and Roy Acuff. There was no hint of R&B in the Opry acts at that time.

After their performance, Opry manager Jim Denny stood with Sam and Elvis and, according to Scotty Moore, told the young man, "You'd better keep driving the truck."[4] The "truck" was the Crown Electric Truck that Elvis was driving on weekdays, hauling building supplies to industrial construction sites.

However, Sam Phillips told Peter Guralnick that Denny said "Elvis just did not fit the Opry mold" but "This boy is not bad."[5]

After the Opry, the "Midnight Jamboree" was held across Broadway at the Ernest Tubb Record Shop. Elvis, Scotty and Bill went over and performed "Blue Moon of Kentucky" again for that audience, who were also polite and appreciative.

After the show, Bill, Scotty and their wives drove back to Memphis. Sam Phillips wanted to listen to a piano player he'd heard about so he, Marion and Elvis secured rooms at a motel and went to the club to hear the piano player. Elvis only stayed in the club a short while, then went outside and paced on the sidewalk. Marion went outside and asked if anything was the matter. Well, yes–it wasn't the kind of place his parents wanted him to be, Elvis told her. And so he waited on the sidewalk until Sam finished listening.

The next day, Sunday, as Sam, Marion and Elvis drove back to Memphis, Sam pulled into a service station to fill up with gas. Elvis took the suitcase with his clothes into the gas station's bathroom to change and then left the suitcase in the bathroom. It wasn't until they were back in Memphis that they realized the suitcase was missing. Phone calls ensued and "it took three or four days for them to retrieve the suitcase, which contained Elvis's entire wardrobe" said Scotty.[6]

The Grand Ole Opry could make "stars" out of unknown performers during the 1940s and early 1950's so Elvis' failure to connect with Opry management was a major setback. The Opry was part of WSM, which was owned by the National Life and Accident Insurance Company. WSM went on the air on October 5, 1925 and shortly after that first broadcast the station, whose call letters stood for the insurance company's advertising slogan, "We Shield Millions," hired George D. Hay as program director. Hay had been with "The National Barn Dance," on WLS in Chicago, which was the top radio show for country music at that time.

On Saturday night, November 28, 1925, Hay invited fiddler Uncle Jimmy Thompson to play on WSM for an hour. This led to the formation of "The WSM Barn Dance," patterned after the show in Chicago. In 1927 the name was changed to "The Grand Ole Opry."

The owners and executives of the insurance company were community leaders and prominent in the social, cultural and political circles of Nashville so they were determined that WSM should be a first class radio station. During the 1930s the station was given "clear channel" status, which meant that it eventually broadcast 50,000 watts at 650 on the AM dial with no other radio station on that frequency. In 1939 the Opry obtained a major sponsor, Prince Albert Tobacco, and became a network show, broadcast for a half hour on Saturday nights. The popularity of the Grand Ole Opry grew as it attracted top name country artists and, because of its 50,000 watt clear channel status, it was heard over most of the United States.

Jim Denny began his career in 1929 in the mailroom of the National Life and Accident Insurance Company. He loved the Opry and during the 1930s was authorized to run the concession and souvenir stand at the Opry and keep the profits, which soon became substantial. In 1946, Denny was named head of the Grand Ole Opry's Artist Bureau, which booked Opry acts on "packages" for fairs, auditoriums and arenas.

By the time Elvis Presley performed on the Grand Ole Opry, Jim Denny was the most powerful man in country music. Not only could he determine who became a member of the Grand Ole Opry, he also determined the bookings of Opry performers who depended on their performances to generate the bulk of their income. Getting turned down by Jim Denny and the Opry was a major setback for Elvis in the Fall of 1954.

Chapter 2: 1955

During the next ten months, Sun released "Good Rockin' Tonight" b/w "I Don't Care if the Sun Don't Shine" in September, 1954 and "Milkcow Blues Boogie" b/w "You're a Heartbreaker" on December 28. In 1955 Sun released "Baby Let's Play House" b/w "I'm Left, You're Right, She's Gone" in April and Elvis' fifth and last Sun Single, "I Forgot to Remember to Forget" b/w "Mystery Train" in August.

The Blue Moon Boys performed at the Eagle's Nest in Memphis and then, on Saturday, October 16, performed on "The Louisiana Hayride" in Shreveport, Louisiana.

A key to a country performer achieving success in the mid-1950s was obtaining a regular spot on a "barn dance," which was the term used for a live country music show on radio. The Grand Ole Opry was the top radio show with its signal so strong that it was almost like appearing on a national show each week. The Louisiana Hayride, which was formed in 1948, was a competitor to the Opry, although it was often viewed as a farm club for the Nashville show. A number of artists proved themselves on the Hayride before they were invited to the Opry; among the artists who became stars on the Hayride before going to Nashville were Jim Reeves, Webb Pierce and Johnny Horton.

Elvis became a regular on the Louisiana Hayride, which gave him regional exposure each week, although by the time he finished with the Hayride, he had leapfrogged the Opry and become a national star.

Bob Neal, a radio DJ in Memphis, was Elvis' first manager and on Friday, October 29, Neal introduced Elvis to Oscar Davis at the Eagle's Nest in Memphis. Davis worked with Colonel Tom Parker, who had managed Eddy Arnold; Davis was in Memphis to do advance work for an Eddy Arnold concert. This "advance work" consisted of putting up posters, visiting disc jockeys and the media in order to gain publicity for the show and attract a paying audience.

At WMPS, disc jockey Bob Neal played Davis "Blue Moon of Kentucky" and that Saturday evening they watched Presley perform at the

Eagle's Nest. The next day, Sunday, October 31 was the Eddy Arnold concert. After this concert, Davis was introduced to Elvis, who first met Eddy Arnold and the Jordanaires, who appeared with Arnold.

Legally, Scotty Moore was Elvis' manager at this point, but Scotty was more interested in being the guitar player in the band. Still, he knew the young, inexperienced Elvis needed management and, in order to protect him, agreed to manage the young singer. However, Bob Neal, a popular disc jockey in Memphis who regularly promoted shows, became Elvis' manager on January 1, 1955.

After the October concert at Ellis Auditorium, Oscar Davis drove back to Nashville and went to Tom Parker's house at 1225 Gallatin Pike in Madison, Tennessee, where the promoter was having lunch with journalist Charlie Lamb. Oscar Davis told Colonel Tom Parker about Elvis and how impressive the young performer was. After listening to Davis describe the young performer, Parker got in his car and drove off. He may have gone to Memphis but soon returned to Nashville.

On Saturday, January 15, 1955, about two weeks after Bob Neal had taken over Presley's management, Parker and his assistant, Tom Diskin, drove to Shreveport to watch Elvis perform on the Louisiana Hayride. During this time, Parker approached Neal with an offer to book Presley on some country music package shows.

The connection with Colonel Tom Parker was a key Nashville connection for Elvis. Colonel Tom Parker was actually Andreas Cornelis van Kuijk, born June 26, 1909 in Breda, Holland and an illegal immigrant in the United States, but these facts did not emerge until after Elvis died. What was known about Colonel Tom Parker was that, while living in Tampa, Florida, he had worked with Gene Austin and some Grand Ole Opry acts, promoting their shows, then moved to Nashville where, beginning in 1945 he managed Eddy Arnold—the most commercially successful act in country music during the late 1940s and early 1950s.

During his time managing Eddy Arnold, Parker obtained a weekly radio show for Arnold on the Mutual Network, sponsored by Purina. This led to a daily network show, "Checkerboard Jamboree," and Arnold's popularity led him to leave the Grand Ole Opry in 1948. Eddy Arnold was on RCA Victor, and Parker developed a relationship with Steve Sholes, head of the country division of Victor and Arnold's producer.

During his time with Arnold, Parker became a "Colonel," thanks to a decree from Louisiana Governor Jimmie Davis, who was also a country singer and songwriter ("You Are My Sunshine").

Tom Parker lived, breathed, ate and slept Eddy Arnold; seven days a week, twenty-four hours a day he devoted himself to Arnold's career. Managing Eddy Arnold, Parker worked closely with Steve Sholes at RCA Victor, Jean and Julian Aberbach, owners of Hill and Range Publishers (Arnold was signed to them), and the William Morris Agency, which obtained network radio and television bookings for Arnold and placed him in two Hollywood movies, *Feudin' Rhythm* and *Hoedown*.

However, in September 1953, Eddy Arnold dismissed Tom Parker as his manager. The dismissal came, in part, from Parker's involvement in Hank Snow's career. Snow, who was also on RCA Victor, needed a booking agent in the fall of 1954 and, seeing the success of Eddy Arnold, met with Parker. Parker formed a booking agency, Jamboree Attractions, and booked Whitey Ford ("The Duke of Paducah"), Minnie Pearl, Cowboy Copas and Tommy Sands. Parker agreed to book Snow and became his manager, effective January 1, 1955. A short time later, Parker suggested a 50-50 partnership, Hank Snow Enterprises-Jamboree Attractions with Snow to appear as a headliner on package shows.

Tom Diskin, owned 25 percent of Jamboree Attractions at the time, which Snow bought for $1,225. Snow then invested $1,775 for 50 percent ownership in the agency. Parker set up several tours with Snow as the headliner.

In 1955, Bill Haley and the Comets reached the top of the pop charts with "Rock Around the Clock." Parker booked Bill Haley and the Comets on a tour with Snow through Jamboree Attractions in 1955 and the shows were sell-outs. Also in 1955 Parker told Snow about Elvis Presley and arranged to have Elvis on some shows headlined by Snow.

According to Hank Snow, on the opening night of their first tour together, "I was truly amazed at the reaction Elvis received after his first performance on stage. The crowd went wild. For a completely unknown artist to capture an audience in this manner was unbelievable. Since I was the headline act of the show, it was customary for me to close each performance. Since Elvis preceded me on stage, I soon found I was walking out on his applause. This can be a little embarrassing to any performer, and I mentioned this to Parker and told him of the difficulty I was having. We both agreed, on the strength of this, we should have Elvis close the shows."

Snow contended that Parker enlisted him to help convince Elvis to sign with the Jamboree Agency. "I would talk with Elvis at every opportunity in the dressing rooms, in the car, or backstage, and sometimes we would talk for hours at a time. I didn't try to force him to sign with us, but I told him from time to time that I thought he had a great future under the proper guidance...I firmly believed if he signed with our agency, we could be a great asset to his future."[7]

Snow insisted that he talked to Steve Sholes about signing Elvis to RCA Victor and "mentioned and promoted Elvis everywhere I went."

According to Snow, a conference call between him, Parker, Bob Neal and Tom Diskin proposed that Jamboree Productions book "26 TV guest appearances on Snow's TV show, 26 radio and TV appearances on 26 Saturday nights, one hundred personal appearances to be made by Elvis Presley at locations designated by Col. Parker, $10,000 in cash to be paid by Hank Snow/Col. Parker towards obtaining full and absolute release of Elvis Presley artist service from the Sun Recording Company and signing to a label-recording company selected by Col. Tom Parker...on the following terms: three percent royalties to Elvis Presley, two percent royalties to Hank Snow/Col. Parker. Total package price for the above: $40,000. The acceptance of this tentative proposition would be contingent upon a complete and absolute break with the Sun Recording Company, leaving Elvis Presley free and clear of all recording commitments and enabling Col. Tom Parker to negotiate a contract with another company."[8]

On July 24, 1955, Elvis signed a contract stating that Colonel Tom Parker and Hank Snow Attractions would provide exclusive representation; Bob Neal continued as manager. On August 15 Elvis, with his father, Vernon, and Bob Neal met with Parker in Memphis. Presley signed a contract that named Parker as "special advisor" who would control every aspect of Elvis' career.

Parker continued to act as Snow's manager and negotiated a new five-year contract with Steve Sholes for Snow to continue on RCA Victor.

After these contracts were signed, Parker contacted Julian Aberbach with Hill and Range and informed him that a deal with a major label was close. Parker solicited Hill and Range to help arrange a contract with RCA Victor.

During the next several months Elvis continued to tour; he played the Louisiana Hayride each Saturday night as well as a number of dates in Texas, Arkansas, Mississippi, Virginia, North Carolina, Tennessee and Missouri. On Friday, September 2, Elvis was in an auto accident when his pink and black Fleetwood Cadillac, driven by Scotty Moore, had a head-on collision near Texarkana, Arkansas. During this period Elvis appeared in a movie starring Cleveland disc jockey Bill Randle which was never released; the movie was *A Day in the Life of a Famous Disc Jockey*.

During his tour of Texas Elvis met June Carter, who was married to Carl Smith at the time, and she invited him to stop by her house the next time he was in Nashville. Not long after that invitation Elvis and Red West, his friend from high school, decided to take her up on the offer and went to Nashville for that visit. Unfortunately, when they arrived at her house nobody was home. Since the two were tired and hungry they broke a window, went in the house, fixed themselves a snack and then crawled into the double bed in the master bedroom. Carl Smith came home the next day and saw the broken window, then saw the mess in the kitchen and headed to the master bedroom. Elvis heard his footsteps and when Smith opened the door Elvis sat up in bed, rubbed his eyes and said, "Hi, Carl." This woke up Red who, afraid that Carl would think the body under the covers was his wife, slowly uncovered himself, poked his head out and said, "How're you doing, Carl?" Smith then broke out laughing at the two in his bed. Being a good sport, Smith then showed them around the house and that night, when June came home, they had a big meal and sat around singing and talking.[9]

Colonel Tom Parker intended to manage Elvis so he went to New York, checked into the Warwick Hotel and told the RCA executives that he represented the singer. He backed this up with a long telegram from Vernon and Gladys Presley as well as an agreement with Bob Neal that he presented to the label. There was still no exclusive management contract or even a firm agreement between Elvis and Parker but this did not dissuade the Colonel from acting like the management agreement was a done deal. He began negotiations with RCA and Hill and Range, both whom he knew and had dealt with while managing Eddy Arnold.

On October 28, Parker received a telegram from RCA's singles division manager, W.W. Bullock, which stated that RCA was only willing to offer $25,000 for Elvis' Sun contract. The next day he and his assistant Tom Diskin went to Memphis and met with Sam Phillips and Bob Neal. Ben Starr, the attorney for Hill and Range, arrived the same day to work out a publishing agreement.

Phillips was adamant that he wanted $35,000 for Presley's contract and did not like dealing with Tom Parker no matter what the amount; however, Parker gave Phillips a check for $5,000 as a non-refundable deposit and Phillips agreed to give Parker two weeks to raise the final amount. Parker gambled that he could find another $35,000 without knowing where the money would come from.[10]

During the Fall of 1952, Murray Nash, who worked for music publisher Acuff-Rose promoting recordings of Acuff-Rose songs to radio, approached Jim Denny about bringing disc jockeys to Nashville to socialize and develop personal relationships as part of helping get radio airplay. Since many DJs also worked as concert promoters, booking country acts into their area, the Opry Artists Bureau, which booked Opry artists on personal appearances, would benefit but Denny, who was head of the Bureau, as well as Jack Stapp, WSM's program director, turned down the idea. However, Murray Nash decided to send out invitations and Harrianne Moore, secretary of Bill Daniel, head of public relations for WSM, worked to pull the event together.

There was only two weeks from the time the invitations were sent until the event but on November 22, 1952 a group of disc jockeys—less than 100—came to the Andrew Jackson Hotel in Nashville. There was a birthday cake for the Grand Ole Opry cut by "The Solemn Ole Judge," George D. Hay, followed by much socializing. According to author Craig Havighurst in his history of WSM, "By the time the day was over, the DJs had met dozens of Opry stars, walked the halls and studios of WSM, seen the mysterious city of Nashville for the first time, and met one another. A Fraternity was in the making."[11]

During 1953 WSM helped disc jockeys obtain new record releases from Opry artists, sent out a newsletter to inform DJs about upcoming releases and appearances and arranged for Opry acts to visit DJs. In November, 1953 the second "Disc Jockey Festival" was held and over 400 DJs came. BMI gave out its first songwriting awards that year, organized by Frances Williams, a receptionist and "mail girl" at WSM. This became an annual event where disc jockeys who played country music came to Nashville to be treated to parties and social gatherings where they met country stars. It was the major business convention for country music and the single event where those involved in country music needed to attend.

On November 10, 1955, Elvis attended the Fourth Annual Country Music Disc Jockey Convention in Nashville and stayed at the Andrew Jackson Hotel. The Country and Western Disc Jockey Association had named Elvis "Most Promising Country Artist." During his stay he heard "Heartbreak Hotel" for the first time when songwriter Mae Boren Axton played it for him. The next day Elvis met DJs before he went back to Memphis. During his visit with DJs, Elvis told them he was signing with RCA, although the deal had not been finalized.

At the DJ Convention Parker spent time with Steve Sholes, hoping RCA would raise their offer. Outside the Andrew Jackson hotel, Colonel Parker tied a sign on an elephant that said, "Like an elephant Hank Snow never forgets. Thanks Dee Jays."

After Elvis left Nashville for Memphis, he went to Shreveport for an appearance at the Louisiana Hayride and on Sunday afternoon was back in Memphis where he performed on the "Western Swing Jamboree" as a headliner, over Hank Thompson, Carl Smith and Carl Perkins. Parker and Hank Snow were both there and Snow was sure the time he spent with Vernon and Gladys Presley would seal the deal that would benefit him and the Colonel.

Ten days after he left Nashville, on November 21, 1955, Elvis was at Sun's Studio to sign a contract with RCA Victor. Also at the studio were RCA executives Steve Sholes and Coleman Tilley, Ben Starr, the attorney for Hill and Range, Hank Snow, Tom Diskin and Colonel Tom Parker. Sam Phillips, Vernon and Gladys Presley and Bob Neal were also there. On that date, Elvis received a check for $4,500. The Colonel received $1,500 of the original $6,000 check, a 25 percent commission.

Bob Neal agreed to a buy-out of Elvis' contract which meant that Neal received 15 percent of Elvis' income until March 15, 1956. As part of that buy-out agreement, Sun Records agreed to hand over all of Presley's recordings to RCA and not sell or distribute any more of Elvis' records on Sun effective the last day of the year.

The final money reportedly came from the publisher, Hill and Range, who compiled a song folio of the songs Elvis had recorded. As part of that agreement Hill and Range set up two publishing companies; Elvis Presley Music (BMI) had Elvis owning 50 percent of the company while Jean and Julian Aberbach, the owners of Hill and Range, each owned 25 percent. Gladys Music (ASCAP) was set up with the same arrangement. Further, the Aberbachs required that Hill and Range own at least one side of every Elvis Presley single released.

After this contract was signed, Parker sent a letter to Harry Kalcheim at the William Morris Agency, asking Kalcheim to pursue a deal for a movie with Elvis and Hank Snow.

That Christmas, Elvis was at home with his parents. Steve Sholes sent ten songs on demonstration records for Elvis to listen to and consider recording for his first RCA Victor session in January in Nashville.

Chapter 3: January - July, 1956

On Tuesday morning, January 10, 1956, Elvis drove to Nashville and arrived at the Methodist TV, Radio and Film Commission at 1525 McGavock, where RCA had its studios. The session was scheduled to begin at 2 p.m.

There was no "Music Row" in Nashville when Elvis arrived. The previous year RCA established its first permanent office in Nashville with Chet Atkins as head. Less than a mile south of the Methodist's studio was a recording studio in the basement of a house at 804 16th Avenue South. Owen and Harold Bradley had set up that studio the previous year in a residential neighborhood; the future "Music Row" had no other music-related businesses in the area. At this point, the music industry was located downtown, close to WSM's offices on Union Avenue, near the State Capitol.

Steve Sholes sent Elvis acetates of "I'm Counting on You" written by Don Robertson, and "I Was the One," written by Aaron Schroeder, Hal Blair, Bill Pepper and Claude DeMetrius, that Sholes felt would be good for Elvis to record.

The first song recorded that day was "I Got a Woman," followed by "Heartbreak Hotel," and "Money Honey." The musicians on the session were Elvis, Scotty Moore and Chet Atkins on guitars (but Chet did not play on "I Got a Woman"); Bill Black on bass, D.J. Fontana on drums, Floyd Cramer on piano, with backing vocals by Gordon Stoker, Ben Speer and Brock Speer. That first session ended at 10 p.m. The next day, the group recorded "I'm Counting On You," and "I Was the One" in a session that lasted from 4 till 7 p.m. Producer Steve Sholes oversaw the session and the engineer was Bob Ferris.

Nashville sessions were different than those done at Sun in Memphis. Nashville was the home of the country music industry and the musicians and producers had developed a structured system of recording. The musicians heard a demo, ran through the song a time or two, then recorded it. In this way, a three-hour session generally yielded four songs. The musicians and producers watched the clock; time was money and the more songs they could get in a three-hour session, the better off they were. There were rules from the Musician's Union to guide them about the number of songs, time spent recording and breaks.

Elvis was used to working differently. At Sun, they never watched the clock. The group went into the studio, searched for a sound, tried out songs and let the creativity flow. That was how "That's All Right Mama" and "Blue Moon of Kentucky" were recorded. And that's how Elvis recorded in Nashville.

After the Nashville sessions, Elvis and his band went back to Memphis then, on Saturday, performed on the Louisiana Hayride, followed by shows in Texas. On Wednesday morning, Elvis and Colonel Parker flew from Nashville to New York City where Elvis appeared on "Stage Show," a television show hosted by big band leaders Tommy and Jimmy Dorsey. On this show, broadcast live on a Saturday evening, Elvis performed "Shake, Rattle and Roll" (with a bit of "Flip, Flop and Fly" inserted) and "I Got a Woman."

On Monday, January 30, Elvis recorded at RCA's New York Studio, doing "Blue Suede Shoes, "My Baby Left Me," "One Sided Love Affair," and "So Glad You're Mine." The next day Elvis recorded "I'm Gonna Sit Right Down and Cry (Over You)," and "Tutti Fruitti." On February 3 he returned to that studio and recorded "Lawdy, Miss Clawdy" and "Shake, Rattle and Roll."

The next day, Elvis made his second "Stage Show" appearance, singing "Tuitti Frutti" and "Baby, Let's Play House." The following day he began a three-week tour headlining over Nashville acts Justin Tubb, the Louvin Brothers and the Carter Sisters. The tour covered North Carolina, South Carolina, Virginia and Florida. On Saturday nights Elvis flew back to New York to perform on "Stage Show"; on the eleventh he performed "Heartbreak Hotel" and "Blue Suede Shoes" and on the eighteenth he performed "Tuitti Frutti" and "I Was the One."

On March 3, Elvis made a down payment for his first house for himself and his parents, at 1034 Audubon Drive in Memphis. That same day, "Heartbreak Hotel" debuted on the *Billboard* chart at number 68 pop and number nine on the country chart. Of RCA's top 24 best selling records, six were by Presley–four originally on Sun.

On March 5, Elvis and his cousin, Gene Smith, flew into Nashville and met with Colonel Parker to sign a new contract, then flew back to Memphis that evening. The new contract meant that Bob Neal and Hank Snow were no longer part of the management and booking of Elvis.

Elvis continued to tour and made his fourth appearance on "Stage Show," performing "Heartbreak Hotel" and "Blue Suede Shoes." On his fifth "Stage Show" appearance he performed "Money Honey" and "Heartbreak Hotel" and the next day he flew to Hollywood for a screen test. During the time in Hollywood, Elvis and Colonel Parker signed a formal agreement whereby Parker would act as "sole and exclusive Advisor, Personal Representative, and Manager in any and all fields of public and private entertainment."[12]

In April, Colonel Parker paid the Louisiana Hayride $10,000 for Elvis' release from their contract. Hollywood producer Hal Wallis signed Elvis to a contract that resulted in two movies. Also in April, Elvis appeared on the "Milton Berle Show" telecast from San Diego aboard the USS Hancock.

On April 13, 1956, Elvis flew from Amarillo, Texas, where he had performed, to Nashville for a session the next day where he recorded "I Want You, I Need You, I Love You." Musicians were Elvis' regular band—Elvis, Scotty Moore, Bill Black and D.J. Fontana—with Chet Atkins on guitar and Marvin Hughes on piano supplementing the sound. That same day he was presented a special "Gold Record" for "Heartbreak Hotel."

Elvis played dates in Texas and Oklahoma, then appeared in Las Vegas for two weeks at the New Frontier Hotel, but did not go over well. However, he saw a number of shows and heard Freddie Bell and the Bellboys version of "Hound Dog," which had been a rhythm and blues hit for Big Mama Thornton. Elvis learned the song and incorporated it into his live performances.

"Heartbreak Hotel" reached number one on the *Billboard* pop charts on April 28. The following week his first album, *Elvis Presley*, reached number one on the *Billboard* album charts; it stayed in that position for ten weeks and spent 48 weeks on the chart.

Elvis continued touring in May, including an appearance at Ellis Auditorium in Memphis on Bob Neal's "Cotton Pickin' Jamboree" where he headlined over Hank Snow and the Jordanaires. He made his second appearance on the Milton Berle Show, and sang "I Want You, I Need You, I Love You" and "Hound Dog." The performance of "Hound Dog" created a backlash as newspapers, preachers and local officials reacted to what they considered to be an "obscene performance." The New York *Times* stated "Mr. Presley has no discernible singing ability" while other reporters noted that Elvis' performance was "a display of primitive physical movement difficult to describe in terms suitable to a family newspaper" and that pop music "has reached its lowest depths in the 'grunt and groin' antics of one Elvis Presley."[13]

On July 1 Elvis appeared on "The Steve Allen Show," broadcast on Sunday evenings, and performed "I Want You, I Need You, I Love You" and "Hound Dog," backed by the Jordanaires, who had flown in from Nashville. For his performance of "Hound Dog," Elvis wore a tuxedo and sang to a basset hound in what, to Elvis, was a rather humiliating experience, although he tried to make light of it during the telecast.

Associated Press writer Charles Mercer, under the headline, "Elvis the Pelvis Belongs in Jungle, New York Writer Tells Steve Allen," wrote an open letter to Allen after the booking was announced which appeared in the Nashville Banner. In this public letter Mercer stated that "until now I've refrained from joining in the chorus of public and critical condemnation of Presley's primitive exhibition on the Milton Berle show a couple of weeks ago" before observing that "you apparently plan to bring Elvis the pelvis back to a national television network to titillate teenage girls and cause numbskull boys to imitate him." Mercer continued, "Certainly Presley embarrasses mature sensibilities and enflames–to judge from effects of rock'n'roll throughout the country–the immature" but cautioned "I'm not taking a moral stand in this case." Instead, Mercer told Allen, "Your television career has been marked by a high sense of humor and a great respect for talent...My argument against his appearance is simply lack of talent. I can't for the life of me see why you want to have such an untalented guy on your program."

Mercer continued that "A very small but very noisy minority of the immature have been infected in recent years by the digga-boom convulsions known as rock'n'roll. There is no talent involved in their rigorous efforts at self-torture."

Mercer concluded his attack on Elvis and rock'n'roll by informing Allen that "if, however, you insist on having somebody do rock'n'roll on your program, I can tell you where to get one. There's a little red tape involved, but you can manage it. After making arrangements with the Belgian government, fly a guy to Irumu in the Congo, which is in almost the exact center of Africa. There have him rent a car, driver and interpreter. Take the southwest fork out of Irumu and drive down across the plains to the Ituri Forest. Toward nightfall, as fires light up in the villages, you will hear the beat of drums, the bleat of gourds, the honk of conch shells. They're playing rock'n'roll, Steve. No kidding. I've heard them many times and it's the same beat. Any one of those singers and shufflers will be happy to fly over and appear on your program. And you won't have to give him a Cadillac. He'll settle for a bicycle."[14]

On the day after his TV performance on "The Steve Allen Show," Elvis went into the RCA Studios in New York and recorded "Hound Dog," "Don't Be Cruel" and "Any Way You Want Me," with the Jordanaires providing background vocals. Interestingly, on "Don't Be Cruel," Scotty Moore played the opening guitar riff, then did not play again until he played a chord at the end of the song; the rhythm was carried by the Jordanaires "omm bop bop," the piano and Bill Black's bass.

Another Associated Press writer in New York, Saul Pett, could not refrain himself from expressing his cultural superiority when writing about Presley after the appearance on Steve Allen's show. Pett began his article, which was printed in the Nashville Tennessean, "Elvis (The Pelvis) Presley consulted his mother back in Memphis. This, he reports, was the conversation: 'Momma,' ah said. 'Momma, do you think ahm vulgah on the stage?' 'Son,' she said. 'You're not vulgah, but you're puttin' too much into your singin.' Keep that up, you won't live to be 30.' 'Momma,' ah said, 'Ah can't help it. Ah just have to jump arown' when ah sing.'"

Pett noted that Presley "wore long sideburns and his thick brown hair rose high over his forehead in a grand, suspenseful wave. You kept wondering when it would break." The top button on his sport shirt was open and this "was less décolletage than usual. Normally, he's in a three-button mood, at least." The writer stated that Elvis owned "a fat recording contract, four new Cadillacs (canary yellow, white, pink and blue) a motorcycle, a three-wheeled Messerschmidt, a new ranch home in Memphis with swimming pool, and a wardrobe including 30 sport coats and 40 sport shirts."

During the interview Elvis "wore some impressive jewelry. A ring with four big, black star sapphires swimming in a pool of small diamonds adorned his right hand. On the left, a horseshoe ring with 14 diamonds and horse head. On his wrist, a watch in which each of the hours was symbolized by a diamond."

"First, there was Rudy Vallee moaning into a megaphone," stated Pett. "Then Frank Sinatra, with his trembling, intimate phrasing. Then, Johnny Ray, the most agonized singer since Al Jolson. And now, Elvis Presley, the rock and roll sensation, jerking his arms, snapping his knees, wiggling, swaying, gyrating, 'puttin' too much into it.' 'But it ain't vulgah,' said Presley. 'It's just the way ah feel. And ah don't feel sexy when ahm singin'. If that was true, ah'd be in some kind of an institution as some kind of a sex maniac.'"

Asked if his exuberant fans frighten him, Elvis answered, "No, cuz ah know they're not going to hurt me real bad. Oh, ah've lost a few shirts. Girls break into mah dressin' room, tear at mah shirt, bust my lip a couple of times tryin' to kiss me, pull on mah hair. They do a little bit of everythin' but ah enjoy it."

Regarding his singing style, Elvis told the writer about his family belonging to the First Assembly of God church in Memphis. "We used to go to these religious singin's all the time. There were these singers, perfectly fine singers, but nobody responded to 'em. Then there were these other singers—the leader wuz a preacher—and they cut up all over the place, jumpin' on the piano, movin' every which way. The audience liked 'em. I guess I learned from them singers." (Elvis was referring to Hovie Lister and the Statesmen Quartet.)

His first ambition, Elvis said, according to the writer, "All ah wanted to do wuz drive a truck. Ah used to see them drivers with their shirts off, handkerchiefs around their neck, a little cap on their head. They looked darin' to me. Ah always dreamed of being a real wild truck driver."

When asked about the controversy swirling around him, the article stated "Nobody raised much fuss about his style, Elvis says, until he appeared on the Milton Berle show. That brought a flood of complaints about overly suggestive movements. Two weeks later he appeared on the Steve Allen show and this time, he said, he toned down his style 'by 85 per cent.' The teenagers in the studio audience screamed as usual but after the show Elvis appeared glum, unfulfilled. 'Those kids wuz wantin' some blood—some action. Ah sure wanted to give it to 'em, but ah like workin' on television and didn't want to raise another fuss.'"

After the Allen show, according to the article, there were "40 or 50 females, mostly teen-agers...waiting on the street [who]...moved in, yelling. But the cops would have none of it. They rushed the singer into a waiting, open convertible. One woman—and this one was at least 30—kept screaming semi-hysterically, 'Just one kiss, Elvis! Just one!' But the cops ordered the driver to get rolling. The car moved away as Elvis climbed up and perched on the top of the back seat. He sat there waving to his admirers as the car moved off."[15]

In a black-bordered box in the newspaper, outside the article were these quotes:

Says the Rock'n Roll King: After a performance in New Orleans: "Ahm in this business to make money. And if the kids like the way ah sing and are willing to pay to hear me, then ah'll go right on doin' it."

After biting a girl reporter on the hand after a performance in North Carolina: "You've gotta be different to get ahead nowadays."

Before he attained success: "Ah used to lie awake at night wondering what to do with mahself."

Chapter 4: August - December, 1956

On August 22, production began on Elvis' first movie, originally titled The Reno Brothers but later changed to Love Me Tender. Elvis sang four songs in the movie: "Love Me Tender," "Poor Boy," "We're Gonna Move" and "Let Me."

During the filming Elvis went to RCA's Hollywood studio, Radio Recorders on Santa Monica Boulevard and recorded "Playing For Keeps," "Love Me," "How Do You Think I Feel," "How's the World Treating You," "When My Blue Moon Turns to Gold Again," "Long Tall Sally," "Old Shep," "Paralyzed," "Too Much," "Anyplace is Paradise," "Ready Teddy," "First in Line" and "Rip It Up." Some of these were new songs from Brill Building writers in New York, who wrote early rock'n'roll hits in the tradition of Tin Pan Alley, but some had Nashville connections. "How Do You Think I Feel" was written by Wayne Walker and Webb Pierce and published by Nashville-based Cedarwood; "How's the World Treating You" was written by Chet Atkins and Boudeleaux Bryant. "When My Blue Moon Turns to Gold Again" was a former country hit, as was "Old Shep" by Red Foley.

While in Los Angeles, Elvis made his first appearance on "The Ed Sullivan Show," broadcast on Sunday nights over CBS. During this first appearance, on September 9, the show was hosted by actor Charles Laughton because Sullivan had been in an auto accident. The show was broadcast live from New York but Elvis' performance was in L.A. via remote. He performed "Don't Be Cruel," "Love Me Tender," "Ready Teddy" and an abbreviated version of "Hound Dog" while 80 percent of Americans watching television tuned into his performance.

The single, "Love Me Tender" was shipped to radio and retailers; however, before it was released it had been certified "Gold" because of pre-release orders of over a million copies following his performance of the song on the Sullivan show. An EP, "Any Way You Want Me," which contained that song, the B-side of "Love Me Tender," and three Sun singles was released on September 21, the same day he finished filming.

On Wednesday, September 26 Elvis appeared at the Mississippi-Alabama State Fair in Tupelo on the stage where he made his first public appearance at age 12. The Nashville *Tennessean* sent reporter John Seigenthaler to cover the event and Seigenthaler opened his article with "A surging, screaming crowd of thousands of frenzied teenagers yesterday welcomed a jerking, jumping, guitar-thumping Elvis Presley back to the town where he was born...The young prince of rock'n'roll...turned two grandstand show appearances at the Mississippi-Alabama state fair into a near riot with his singing and accompanying twitches and gyrations."

Seigenthaler noted that Elvis sang "Heartbreak Hotel," "Long, Tall Sally," "I Got a Woman," "Don't Be Cruel," and "You Ain't Nothin' But a Hound Dog" while "a cigar-chewing press agent" observed "I haven't seen anything like this since Sinatra used to wow 'em at the Paramount during the '40s."

The *Tennessean* reporter stated that the two shows brought Elvis $5,000 plus 60 percent of the gate, with tickets $1 each for the two shows.

During the show, 16-year-old Judy Hopper of Alamo, Tennessee broke through the crowd, leaped on the stage and "startled Elvis while he was singing 'I Got A Woman.'" According to the reporter, Elvis "fell backwards laughing" while two police officers "carried her kicking from the stage. Asked why she attempted the rush, she replied 'I love him and I need him and I want him.'"

Reminiscing about the time he appeared on stage at the Fair in Tupelo and sang "Old Shep," Elvis said "I'm 21 now and my family left Tupelo when I was 12 but I still remember that night. I sneaked in with my guitar and asked the man to let me on the stage. They finally let me sing."[16]

When Elvis made his second appearance on "The Ed Sullivan Show," he performed "Don't Be Cruel," "Love Me," "Love Me Tender" and "Hound Dog."

At the end of October, Evangelist Billy Graham appeared in Nashville and weighed in on Elvis Presley. According to an article in the *Tennessean*, Graham "admits he has never met rock and roll star Elvis Presley and doesn't know much about him, but says: 'From what I've heard, I'm not so sure I'd want my children to see him.'"[17]

In November, the annual Country and Western Disk Jockeys Convention was held in Nashville; the previous year, an unknown Elvis Presley appeared at the convention just before he signed his recording contract with RCA Victor.

Nashville *Tennessean* reporter Jacqueline Sharborough wrote "the ghost of Elvis Presley haunted WSM's Fifth Annual Disc Jockey festival... as screaming teen-agers crammed into hotels, squealing for the man who wasn't there."

The article continued "Rumors that Elvis would and wouldn't show traveled faster than the rock'n'roll star's motorcycle, and hotels cleared their lobbies only by announcing that The Pelvis had checked in somewhere else in town. But Elvis wasn't to be found."

Sharborough reported that "disk jockeys whose only resemblance to the idol was long sideburns" were mobbed because fans mistook them for Elvis.

In a bit of one-upsmanship practical joking, someone came on the public address system at the Andrew Jackson hotel and "informed the teen-agers that Elvis was signing autographs at the Hermitage. The rush was on, and the Hermitage was invaded." Then, a short while later, an announcement was broadcast at the Hermitage, "'Elvis Presley has just checked into Room 18 of the Andrew Jackson.' And the scramble went into reverse."

The reporter noted that Elvis was en route to Las Vegas at that time while Colonel Tom Parker was also out of town although Elvis' guitar player, Scotty Moore, was there and "got his share of mobbing by the teen-agers as did a bewildered Miami musician, who was mistaken for a member of Elvis' band."

Elvis won the *Billboard* magazine award for most programmed artist, which was scheduled to be presented at the event, and rumors of his appearance there apparently began when disk jockey George Williams announced over local station WMAK that Elvis was coming. The result was a "confusion" that had "reached such a scale by mid-afternoon that the policemen at the Andrew Jackson and Hermitage hotels adopted the policy of keeping all teen-agers except those wearing festival identification tags out of the lobbies."

Local school principals stated that a number of their students had skipped school during the convention. W.E. Lowe, principal of Central High School was quoted saying "We've had about 100 more students out today than usual" and he had "just learned from talking with other principals where these students spent the day—at the disk jockey convention looking for Elvis Presley." The reporter found a Highland Heights Junior High School student who proclaimed "Go to school today? Are you crazy? Elvis is going to be here. I know he is!"[18]

An article in the Nashville *Banner* asked "Will another 'Heartbreak Hotel'—1956 version—come from the Fifth Annual Country Music Disk Jockey Festival?" The article observed that the previous year a 20-year-old promising singer named Elvis Presley "heard a 'dub' record of 'Heartbreak Hotel' at the insistence of its co-author, Mrs. Mae Boren Axton, then of Jacksonville, and Bob Neal of Memphis, then Presley's manager. Presley heard the dub 10 times and agreed to make it his next release. On the wings of this song that became the 'hit of the year' was launched the fabulous 'Presley Year' in music of the nation."

The article stated that this year "Mrs. Axton and Neal are attending the festival, but Presley is reported to be in Las Vegas, Nevada despite rumors that brought hundreds of teenagers to the Andrew Jackson Hotel Friday. However, Glenn Reeves, now of Nashville, who cut the original 'dub' of 'Heartbreak Hotel,' is on hand. He records for Atlantic."[19]

In the Nashville *Tennessean*, syndicated writer Dick Kleiner stated that "To the boys in the advertising dens of Madison Avenue, Elvis Presley is just a statistic...They see in Elvis Presley a way to reach the teen-age market, an ever-increasing group that has an average of $12.71 spending money each week." Kleiner noted that "Elvis Presley's appeal is often hard for some people to figure. There have been attempts to explain it psychologically—he represents, this reasoning has it, the freedom from adult supervision that many teen-agers subconsciously hunger for. And there have been attempts to explain it economically—cold publicity bought him his fame and fortune. And some people shrug and say that it's just one of those crazy things."

Kleiner observed that "A TV show with Presley on it zooms into the wild high-ratings yonder; a new Presley record sells almost a million copies before it comes out; a Presley movie, sight unseen, is booked into the biggest theaters across the nation; Presley-sponsored hats and bracelets and scarves dot the counters in stores and are snapped up by adoring fans [in the] 13-19 year old bracket [and] every day... 10,000 more children qualify...He sells to the same age group that used to buy Rudy Vallee megaphones and Russ Columbo shirts and Frank Sinatra bow-ties. He sells to the vast teen-age horde that buys, according to estimates, a little more than half of all the phonograph records."[20]

On Thursday, November 15, Elvis' debut film, *Love Me Tender,* opened at the Paramount Theatre in New York City; it was released nationally the following Wednesday and Elvis was now a movie star. One week later, the film debuted in Nashville accompanied by "mild squeals from the junior female set and catcalls from their male counterparts." The Nashville *Tennessean* reported that "The scene was anything but bedlam, though, as Presley stepped to the front of the wide-screen at the Paramount and flashed his toothpaste smile. And his first real punchy dramatic line was dampened somewhat when, right at the gripping climax, a youngster in the audience squalled: 'Stop the world! I want off!'"

Reporter Gene Graham observed "the crowd was orderly and the auditorium was but half filled when the first showing of *Love Me Tender* started unreeling at 11 a.m." although "a few teen-aged girls, who apparently felt it was expected of them, made the noises they were expected to make."

Graham wrote that "to objective observers, it seemed like a half-hearted effort, at best, though. The Pelvis drew scattered shrieks when he first appeared on the screen as an obscure blur following a mule and a plow far, far in the background."

At the first afternoon showing "the crowd had increased somewhat. It was a full house at the mid-afternoon session. School was out, the squeals and catcalls increased proportionately." This was on the Wednesday before Thanksgiving and the theater manager stated that youngsters will have "Thursday and Friday off for Thanksgiving. I don't know where we'll put them tomorrow."

Although the theater manager "wasn't expecting any boisterous behavior" he was "taking no chances. The Paramount's plush lobby furniture was quietly stowed away in an upstairs storage room shortly before the doors opened."

The *Tennessean* article stated that "Duck tail haircuts and long bushy sideburns were a dime-a-dozen as Presley shook his long locks for the first time on a Nashville screen." In the lobby of the theater was an Elvis souvenir booth, which did a brisk business.[21]

Nashville *Tennessean* theater and film critic Clara Hieronymus reviewed the movie and wrote "My considered judgment: as an actor Elvis Presley is a houn' dawg. He's Elvis playing Elvis, and playing him strictly to type. If the setting is slightly archaic, Elvis is still late '56, performing with all the subtlety and tender restraint of a half-grown Saint Bernard having a romp in the snow. He has scenes in which he must look sorrowful, sincere, troubled or half-crazed with jealousy. His expression is the same for all–just sullen. The droop of the eyelids slides down to become the juttingly compressed lips of a little boy mad at his mama."

The critic did observe that "Elvis is the only member of Randall's Confederate raiders who sounds like a Southerner. If he's a stranger to the flexible beautifies of the spoken word, he's a least in character when he exclaims: 'Somebody's rode up!'" She concluded her review with the observation that "as one who has always valued easy arrogance as a quality of the male, I must in fairness admit that when Elvis cut loose on the front porch with a hot guitar and plenty of legroom, I was just another 'sore-eyed kitten with a whole saucer of milk.'"[22]

On Monday, five days after the premier of *Love Me Tender* in Nashville, Elvis was in town at Colonel Tom Parker's house sleeping. The Nashville *Banner* reported that "Yup, the two-fisted, sideburned, be-diamonded, pink-cadillaced motorcycled male Monroe with erratic pelvis who wants all the gals to 'Love Me Tender' was in town ...while the gals sighed and cried and their dates pretended not to be chartreuse with envy as they watched this sex dynamo in action on the screen at the Paramount Theater." The article observed that "the closest thing to a real-live H-bomb was snoozing comfortably on the sofa at the Madison home of his manager, Col. Tom Parker" after leaving a sell-out engagement in Louisville on his way to Memphis.

Tennessean reporter George Barker wrote that Elvis drove his "long, sleek, pink Cadillac" on to Colonel Parker's driveway around 7:30 that evening. Elvis took a nap on the couch in Parker's home and then talked to reporters and photographers who showed up, alerted by Parker. Reporter Barker observed that "when we walked in, his feet were propped upon the sofa's soft arm. His hands were clutched behind his head. His eyes were shut. His guitar was tucked away in the trunk of the Cadillac, outside. 'Elvis,' Col Parker whispered, 'someone is here to see you.' Elvis batted his long eyelashes several times, scratched his sideburns and swung his number 12s to the floor. 'Hi, fellas,' he said.'"

Presley had driven into town with Bitsy Mott, who worked for Parker and served as Elvis' security officer on this date, and Tom Diskin, who was Parker's administrative assistant.

Elvis wore "gray flannel slacks, a black and gray sports jacket and a sport shirt which would have been considered too low-cut for his admirers" as he "groused lightly at the Nashville weather. 'Maybe it will be warmer in Memphis,' he said."

Elvis admitted he was tired, saying "These quickie stops around the country and bucking the crowds do it." Talking about the crowds he attracted Elvis observed that he thought the crowd at the State Fair in Tupelo was big "But we played for 30,000 folks at the Dallas Cotton bowl. Now there was a crowd." As he twisted a diamond horseshoe ring on his left hand he said, "I love crowds. People have sure been wonderful to me. I am as grateful as I can be."

Elvis told the reporters that he planned to stay close to home until later in December when he was scheduled to sing at a Christmas benefit. He said he'd probably just stay close to home because "I don't think much of hunting, fishing, golfing or that sort of thing."[23]

After he left Parker's home, Elvis drove to the Tic Toc Restaurant at 133 Seventh Avenue North, but it was closing. Seventeen-year-old Dorothy Stevens and Ed White were sitting in the restaurant when Elvis drove up in his pink Cadillac and "Dorothy started pulling her hair and almost went wild," White told a *Tennessean* reporter. Dorothy borrowed a piece of paper and pencil, chased Elvis outside the restaurant, and got his autograph.

Elvis didn't get too far from the restaurant when the water pump in his car stopped working and he had to get the car to a garage, then he checked into the Andrew Jackson Hotel, where he spent his time in room 940—the hotel's largest suite—until his car was repaired and he could continue his trip to Memphis.[24]

At the end of November, Elvis performed three dates in Ohio and then a date in Louisville, Kentucky, where his grandfather, Jessie, lived and attended the show. The day after the show Elvis stopped in Nashville at Colonel Parker's home on the way back to Memphis.

In Memphis, Elvis stopped in at the Sun Studios on December 4 where he sat at the piano and jammed with Carl Perkins, Jerry Lee Lewis and Johnny Cash in a session known later as "The Million Dollar Quartet." During this session, the group did a number of songs–many only partially–but Elvis showed both his love for gospel as well as the influence of Nashville. The group did "Peace in the Valley" by Thomas A. Dorsey, the Ernest Tubb song, "I'm With a Crowd But So Alone," the gospel standard "Farther Along," several songs by bluegrass pioneer Bill Monroe ("Little Cabin On the Hill," "Summertime Is Past and Gone," "I Hear a Sweet Voice Calling" and "Sweetheart You Done Me Wrong"), the Ray Price hit, "Crazy Arms" (which had knocked Elvis off the top of the country charts that year), and a Hank Snow song, "I'm Gonna Bid My Blues Goodbye."

During 1956 Elvis sold over ten million single records or about two thirds of the total of RCA's single sales that year. It was the year that Elvis—and rock'n'roll—exploded in America.

Near the end of the year an Associated Press story, written by Ed Creach and datelined "Washington" appeared in the Nashville *Banner*. The writer lamented, "Maybe this will become known as the Elvis Presley century. It's whinney, sneering, trembly in the legs and it makes a lot of money. Its voice is discordant to everybody except teenagers. It reeks of sex instead of romance, but it runs like a hare from serious commitments. Maybe, like the groaning post-adolescent from Tennessee, the 20th century is more a fad than a reality."

The writer observed "We don't have, as the post World War I days had, a lost generation. We've lost a whole century. We split the atom and opened the door to power and riches undreamed of. Instead we used this new tool to blast two cities level with the earth and raced on, idiot fashion, finding bigger and better ways to blow ourselves to pieces. We invented radio, and used it, in some instances, to broadcast either syrupy nonsense or rate propaganda. We built a standard of living that put two cars in many a garage–four, for that matter, in a certain male canary's entourage—but we begrudged the money to build the schools to educate our kids. Yep. An Elvis Presley century. Brash and childish. Rich and whimpering. History may say this sideburned youth who wiggles his hips while singing popular songs was a symbol of this time—that this century does a lot of wiggling and squirming without ever getting anywhere."[25]

Chapter 5: 1957

In January, 1957, RCA released "Too Much" b/w "Playing for Keeps" and the third Elvis EP, "Strictly Elvis." On January 6, Elvis made his third appearance on "The Ed Sullivan Show" and performed "Hound Dog," "Love Me Tender," "Heartbreak Hotel," "Don't Be Cruel," "Too Much," "When My Blue Moon Turns to Gold Again" and finished with "Peace In The Valley." During this performance, Elvis was filmed from the waist up; the outcry in America against Elvis was such that Ed Sullivan wanted to play it safe.

That evening, Elvis was hung in effigy on the Vultee Boulevard overpass on Murfreesboro Road in Nashville. The next morning, rush hour traffic saw the dangling dummy, dressed in blue jeans, light colored leather sandals, a brown duck-bill cap and a red shirt with "Elvis" in white paint on the back, hanging from about twenty feet of rope. The pockets of the pants were stuffed with play money. Police were contacted—some thought it was a dead man hanging from the overpass —and a group of motorists gathered, halting traffic, to watch. As the trooper hauled him down the crowd shouted "Lift him tender," "Don't be cruel" and "Y'ain't nothin' but a houn' dog." Since initial reports indicted an actual person was hanging by that rope, an ambulance was called to the scene and the dummy Elvis was taken to the basement of a funeral home in Donelson, where it attracted curious onlookers throughout the day.

Although this incident may seem mild today, it demonstrates that many people felt threatened by Elvis and rock'n'roll. It is not known whether this was a playful prank or a hate filled incident, but it does prove that in 1957 Elvis inspired strong feelings.[26]

Following the Sullivan Show, Elvis went to Los Angeles where he recorded "I Believe," "Tell Me Why," "Got A Lot O'Livin' To Do," "All Shook Up," "Mean Woman Blues," "Peace in the Valley," "I Beg of You," "That's When Your Heartaches Begin" and "Take My Hand, Precious Lord."

He filmed his second movie, originally titled *Lonesome Cowboy* but released as *Loving You*. Elvis' parents, Vernon and Gladys Presley, visited Elvis on the set of *Loving You* and can be seen in the audience while Elvis performed "Loving You" and "Got a Lot O' Livin' To Do." Elvis recorded the soundtrack to the movie, which included the songs "(Let's Have A) Party," "Lonesome Cowboy," "Got A Lot O' Livin' To Do," "Teddy Bear," "Loving You," "One Night," "Blueberry Hill," "Hot Dog," and "Mean Woman Blues."

On January 19 Elvis went back to Radio Recorders and recorded "It Is No Secret (What God Can Do)," by Stuart Hamblen, "Blueberry Hill," the Scotty Wiseman classic "Have I Told You Lately That I Love You," and the Faron Young song, "Is It So Strange."

In February Elvis recorded "Don't Leave Me Now," "I Beg of You," "One Night," "True Love," "I Need You So," "Loving You" and "When It Rains, It Really Pours." The recordings were for RCA to release; until this time, Elvis had not been satisfied with his performance of "Loving You" for a single release.

Elvis' home at 1034 Audubon Drive in Memphis soon attracted legions of fans, one of whom wanted the street renamed "Presley Drive." Carol Frazier, a 14-year old from New Orleans, wrote a letter to Henry Loeb, commissioner of public works (whose job dealt with street names) as well as residents of Audubon Drive about changing the name of the street. Readers of the Nashville *Banner* read a story of the proposed street re-naming in February. A newspaper reporter called several residents of the trendy neighborhood (houses sold for $40,000 and up!) and received these responses:

"From housewives: 'Over my dead body!' 'This is very silly.' 'I wouldn't think of it.' From a husband: 'I have come to the conclusion we have a cross to bear here on this street. The cars come and go all the time. It was hard to take for awhile but we have gotten somewhat resigned to it.' From another husband, who started his argument with cool logic and wound up shouting: 'I have nothing against him, nothing personal that is. I dislike the commotion and the traffic, of course, but that is getting better lately. The police have co-operated beautifully by posting 'No Parking signs.' The newspapers have been considerate by not running Presley's address as much as they did at first. It's getting better all right. But to name the street for a singer (louder). Under no condition would I favor that. I think I speak for all my neighbors and they would fight it tooth and nail."

Young Carol was an avid fan; she had reportedly collected 5,000 pictures of Elvis and saw *Love Me Tender* 100 times (not counting watching the preview 94 times) but she was unsuccessful in her quest.[27]

Elvis finished filming *Loving You* in early March, then returned to Memphis and on Tuesday, March 19, made a down payment on a new home, Graceland; on June 16 Vernon and Gladys Presley moved from their home on 1034 Audubon to Graceland.

Elvis went back on tour for eight dates in late March and early April. In March RCA released "All Shook Up" b/w "That's When Your Heartaches Begin." Also that month Nashville readers saw a picture of the new home Elvis had just purchased for $100,000. The headline "No Cottage in the Pines for Elvis" appeared over a picture of Graceland.

A nationally syndicated column by Eugene Gilbert, "Director, Gilbert Research" appeared in a Nashville newspaper under the headline "He's Nothing Anymore,' Girls Say; Pat Boone Moving Up Strongly." In this article Gilbert states "Singer Elvis Presley's phenomenal popularity among the nation's teenagers seems to have taken a dive. As recently as last October, our country-wide survey showed that a whopping 35 per cent of all youngsters questioned considered the guitar-strumming squirmer their favorite male vocalist. But going over the same territory again, we find that his rating has skidded to 21 per cent....Moreover, a full 35 per cent of the teeners admitted liking Elvis less now than they did last year."

The article featured quotes from unnamed teenagers about Elvis. A 16-year-old girl proclaimed "He's nothing anymore. Last year he was news. Today he's just another wiggler." Another young female was reported saying "Last year I used to think Elvis was the sexiest male alive, but I can see now that he'll become just another commercial singer, like the rest." A young man was quoted saying "Hollywood's got him, the personal appeal he had for all of us teenagers is gone forever."

Gilbert's article acknowledged that Elvis, "who has managed to inspire almost as much antagonism in adults as he produced veneration in the younger set—still reigns supreme in the affection of 21 per cent of the teenagers covered by our survey. Moreover, 12 per cent, predominately in the 13-15 age group, declared they found their hero even more resplendent than before."

Gilbert then asked: "Who's threatening to fill his shoes? Our survey shows Pat Boone moving up strongly. He now ranks tops with nearly 13 per cent of the youthful balloters." He quotes a Pat Boone fan who states, "You can take Elvis and give him back to the Indians. I'll take Pat any day" while a teenage boy is quoted saying that Pat Boone is "really quite a guy. Look at him supporting a family and going to school as well as being a successful singer...He's terrific."

According to Gilbert's survey, "Thirty-nine percent of the boys and 33 per cent of the girls thought the Elvis craze would run its course within less than a year. Forty-two per cent of the girls and 31 per cent of the lads gave him from one to two years of peak popularity, 8.5 and 17 per cent respectively, figured two to four years more, while the rest thought the side-burned rock'n'roller wouldn't fade for another four years yet."[28]

In the next day's Nashville *Banner* there was a sharp rebuttal by Red O'Donnell, whose article stated, "If Elvis Presley's star is in descendency, as some critics contend, it isn't evident in his box office appeal or record sales. The dissenter is Col. Tom Parker, Madison, Presley's manager, who arrived home Thursday from Hollywood, where his money-making protégé has been performing in front of the cameras. 'All right,' grunted Parker, 'so I'm prejudiced. I also got facts and figures to back my argument in favor of Elvis.'"

O'Donnell stated that Parker had just put Elvis on a train for Memphis where the singer planned to vacation for a week with his family and friends. Parker warmed up to the challenge of answering the assertion of Elvis' decline. "Lookee here: Elvis starts a personal-appearance tour in Chicago March 28. He also is booked for one nighters in Fort Wayne, Ind., St. Louis, Philadelphia, Buffalo, Toronto and Ottawa," said Parker. "Five of those towns already are sellouts—and he's playing auditoriums which seat 10,000 people. Does that look like the boy is losing public favor?"

Parker continued, "Take the records...Elvis hasn't been out with a record in three months until the past Monday when 'All Shook Up' was released. Guess what happened to 'All Shook Up' in three days? —Sold 750,000 copies. The kid's sacred album, 'Peace in the Valley' also is selling okay.'"

O'Donnell noted that Elvis had just finished filming *Loving You* for 20th Century and would return to Hollywood on May 1 to start a picture for MGM.[29]

In Sunday's Nashville *Tennessean* reporter David Halberstam quoted Vanderbilt psychologist Dr. George Copple who stated, "Reluctant parents—who prefer that Elvis stay out of their living room–may unwittingly have boosted the rock and roller's popularity. This may be a way of letting the parents know that the children can make up their own minds. It's not a crucial issue in the home but it shows that the adolescents have to be treated as individuals."

Referring to Thursday's article by Gilbert in the *Tennessean*, Halberstam noted that "record stores and public opinion polls checked by THE TENNESSEAN showed that Presley still ranks high and has lost little in this area." Halberstam then quoted Dr. Copple, who said about the Presley phenomena, "It seems to me that this is symbolic of a breaking away from parental authority. There are few parents who like Presley very much. Other than that it's hard for me to tell about Presley's appeal–I haven't got any teenagers, but it seems that this is a snow balling thing. It starts with a few and suddenly it becomes important to belong and go along with the crowd. I think a lot of the youngsters get this feeling from their friends, rather than directly, and don't feel too strongly themselves. A few leaders can influence a whole group like that."

The article stated that Elvis had announced he would appear at the annual Alabama-Mississippi Fair and Dairy show in September in his hometown of Tupelo, with all proceeds going to a youth recreation center.[30]

The same day that Halberstam's article appeared there was news that an 18-year-old Marine had accused Elvis of threatening him with a pistol while the singer was making a movie in Hollywood. The pistol, which turned out to be a stage prop, was brandished by Presley during an exchange of words.

In the latter part of April, Elvis returned to Los Angeles to film *Jailhouse Rock*. Also in April, RCA released a four song gospel EP with "Peace In The Valley." Beginning on April 30 Elvis recorded the soundtrack for the movie, which included the songs "Jailhouse Rock," "Young and Beautiful," "Treat Me Nice," "I Want to Be Free," "(You're So Square) Baby I Don't Care," and "Don't Leave Me Now."

These songs were all written by Jerry Leieber and Mike Stoller, a songwriting team based in Los Angeles at the time of this movie. Steeped in blues and R&B, Leiber and Stoller were the "hep cats," the "coolest" by any measure during the 1950s and early 1960s. They loved rhythm and blues and formed an immediate connection with Elvis because they wrote songs for him connected to their R&B roots.

The hit songs of Jerry Leiber and Mike Stoller include rock and roll classics such as "Hound Dog," "Charlie Brown," "Stand By Me," "Spanish Harlem," "Yakety Yak," "Along Came Jones," "This Magic Moment," "Bossa Nova Baby," "Don't," "Girls, Girls, Girls," "His Kiss," "I (Who Have Nothing)," "Is That All There Is?," "Jailhouse Rock," "Kansas City," "Little Egypt," "Love Me," "Love Potion #9," "Loving You," "On Broadway," "Poison Ivy," "Ruby Baby," "Searchin'," "Smokey Joe's Cafe," "There Goes My Baby," "Treat Me Nice," "(You're So Square) Baby I Don't Care" and "Young Blood."[31]

In mid-June, Elvis finished filming *Jailhouse Rock*. RCA released "Teddy Bear" b/w "Loving You" and the four song EP "Loving You," which contained "Mean Woman Blues." On Tuesday, June 25, Elvis left Los Angeles by train for Memphis; on Wednesday he spent his first night at Graceland, his new home.

In July RCA released the album *Loving You*, which reached number one on the charts and a four song EP, "Loving You," which went Gold. On July 30 the film *Loving You* was released nationally. At the end of August, Elvis began a tour which included dates in Spokane, Vancouver, Tacoma and Portland on the West Coast and RCA shipped the four song EP "Just For You."

That same month a news report from Iran stated that rock'n'roll music had been banned in that country "as a threat to civilization." Police launched a "Hate Elvis" campaign and announced "This new canker can very easily destroy the roots of our 6000 years' civilization." The decision to ban rock'n'roll and Elvis "was founded on Moslem custom which forbids undignified behavior of women in public. It also was based on doctors' reports that young people had been sustaining serious injury in the hip-jerking motions of rock'n'roll." The newspaper article reported that "some youngsters had been hospitalized with broken limbs. Two boys were known to have bitten off their tongues. And one broke a knee, his neck and spine during one spin."

A photographer published photos of youngsters in a nightclub dancing to rock'n'roll, which prompted Tehran's most prominent magazine *Teherean-I-Mossaver* to print a story describing the "decadent, degrading, immoral, dangerous and lascivious new dance." Radio Tehran then ceased playing rock'n'roll.[32]

In September, Elvis went into Radio Recorders and recorded "Treat Me Nice," "Blue Christmas," "My Wish Came True," "White Christmas," "Here Comes Santa Claus," "Silent Night," "Don't," "O Little Town Of Bethlehem," "Santa Bring My Baby Back (To Me)," "Santa Claus Is Back in Town" and "I'll Be Home for Christmas."

On this session, which contained songs for Elvis' first Christmas album, producer Steve Sholes, at Elvis' request, hired Nashville studio singer Millie Kirkham.

Millie Kirkham grew up in Nashville, worked at WSM as Jack Stapp's secretary and sang with the original Anita Kerr Singers when they were an eight member group—four men and four women. Millie began doing sessions with the Anita Kerr Singers and when Ferlin Huskey recorded "Gone" in 1955, Millie Kirkham sang the high soprano part. Producer Ken Nelson had called Gordon Stoker of the Jordanaires and told him that he wanted a female soprano on the session, so Stoker called Kirkham, who replied, "that's not much of a vocal group—four guys and a female." Stoker agreed, but that's what the producer wanted so she joined them for that session. Kirkham noted that Nelson's suggestion probably came because in Los Angeles, where Nelson was from, a female singer, Lula Jean Norman, often worked with a male vocal group.[33]

The Jordanaires told Elvis about Millie so he flew her out to be on the sessions that produced his first Christmas album.

Millie was six months pregnant at the time and it was an all day trip on a prop plane to get to Los Angeles. When she arrived, "my ankles were swollen, and I looked like I had elephant leg and just as I walked in the phone rang and Gordon Stoker said 'we're going over to Paramount to see a screening of Elvis' new movie *Jailhouse Rock*. Do you want to go?' I said, 'yes,'" remembered Kirkham. "So here I come waddling in and I had never met Elvis and he had never seen me and they said, 'Elvis, this is Millie' and he looked at me sort of puzzled and then he grinned and said, 'Somebody please get this woman a chair.'"

During those sessions Millie had a stool to sit on. The producers wanted Elvis to record "Blue Christmas," but he resisted. Finally, knowing he had to eventually do the song, he told the background singers to "do something really stupid" behind him. That's when Millie did her famous "whoo oo oo oo" as Elvis sang "Blue Christmas." When the recording was over, the singers looked at each other and agreed, "The label will never release that!"[34]

There were some problems in the Elvis Presley camp that surfaced in September; both Scotty Moore and Bill Black resigned because of the low pay they were receiving. Elvis hired Nashville session guitarist Hank "Sugarfoot" Garland to replace Scotty and bass player Chuck Wigginton to replace Bill Black. Along with drummer D.J. Fontana—who remained with Elvis during this period–this group was in Tupelo, Mississippi in a concert to benefit the Elvis Presley Youth Center on September 27.

In September RCA released the single "Jailhouse Rock" b/w "Treat Me Nice." On Friday, October 11, Elvis drove from Memphis to Nashville to confer with Colonel Tom Parker; he drove back to Memphis the same day.

In October *Elvis' Christmas Album* was released; the next day a four song EP "Elvis Sings Christmas Songs" was released and at the end of October the five song EP "Jailhouse Rock" was released. On November 8, the movie *Jailhouse Rock* was released nationally.

In October, singer Frank Sinatra publicly criticized rock'n'roll, saying the music "is phoney and false, and sung, written and played for the most part by cretinous goons." Rock'n'roll fans—and Elvis defenders—rushed into the breech.

In Nashville, 16-year Jane Hieronymus was quoted saying "I think Frankie just doesn't have it. I like his acting, but he misses it as a singer. Elvis hasn't lost anything as far as the kids are concerned, he's easily the most popular—we can really dance to the beat. And I can't understand all this interest in Frankie."

Tennessean reporter David Halberstam contacted Col. Tom Parker and the Jordanaires in Hollywood and stated that "Presley was unharmed by Sinatra's jab. Elvis himself was unavailable for comment, but his feelings were believed to be hurt." Col. Parker stated "Elvis can't understand why Frank said that. He admires Frank. I think he's very disappointed. Elvis would never had said something like that about Frank or any other singer."

The article noted that in Nashville "record salesmen and disc jockeys reported an age factor as a key in the battle. 'You can almost spot the Presley fans when they walk in,' said Mrs. Mary Charmella, saleslady in a Nashville record store, 'whereas Frank's span all ages." Mrs. Charmella admitted that she often can't spot a difference between Sinatra fans and devotees of classical music. She noted that "Sinatra sells particularly well among Nashville musicians." Bob Lamm, who played and sang "Near You," the first million seller recorded in Nashville, stated, "I think Sinatra's appeal to a large degree comes because he sings songs musicians like. His success is a combination of taste, good choice of songs, and an easy relaxed manner."[35]

A tour of the West Coast was followed by concerts in Honolulu, Hawaii on Sunday, November 10 and at Pearl Harbor the next day. These were the last public performances by Elvis for many years because he dedicated himself to doing films.

Touring would also cease because Elvis was drafted; on Friday, December 20, Elvis stopped by the Memphis Draft Board and picked up his draft notice. That evening he drove a rental truck to Nashville carrying a red Italian sports car—an Isetta—valued at $1,800 to present to Colonel Parker as a Christmas gift.

Elvis also handed checks of undisclosed amounts to members of the Jordanaires. "Now, isn't he a sweet kid," Colonel Parker was quoted as saying. "He could have just sent something in the mail."

Red O'Donnell went to Parker's house and interviewed Elvis about his imminent induction into the service, which was scheduled for January 20.

"I am not the least bothered," said Elvis and O'Donnell noted that he always said "Yes, Sir" and that "for the record, Elvis is most courteous to his elders." Presley kiddingly told O'Donnell "Maybe they will send me to sing in Russia. I would either cure them or kill them with my singing," before adding "Frankly...I might have been in uniform before this if my mother hadn't wanted me to wait for the draft. You know how mothers are. They don't want their boys to leave home. I am looking forward to the experience."[36]

Tennessean reporter George Barker also interviewed Presley, who stated that he just might become a career soldier. "The way I feel about it now, I may just re-enlist after my two-year hitch is up," he said. "Naturally, I may change my mind once I'm in–who can tell?" Presley was obviously kidding with the reporters, trying to put a brave face on an event which potentially threatened his successful career.

Elvis stated "My induction notice said for me to leave my car at home. Transportation will be provided. They tell me just to bring a razor, toothbrush, toothpaste, a comb and enough money to hold me two weeks. I'll probably show up broke."

A photographer from the Tennessean brought along some Army fatigues and enticed Elvis to wear them for a picture.

Elvis was in the midst of filming a movie for Paramount and producer Hal Wallis had a reported $350,000 already invested in the picture; if Elvis did not get a deferment from his January 20 induction date, that money would be lost.

"Naturally, the picture work will stop when Elvis goes into the army," said Parker. "But he will still be able to cut records. It just takes a few hours to make a record and we can time recording sessions to Elvis' free time."

Parker stated that "We sent out 10,000 Christmas cards this year, and we had some mats rolled of the card. It will appear as an advertisement in a dozen newspapers here, in England and in France and in a whole bunch of show business magazines during Christmas week. I figure our total audience will be 15,000,000 people."

"It was just three years ago Elvis and I met each other," added Parker. "Just three years."[37]

Elvis spent the rest of the day in Nashville with Gordon Stoker of the Jordanaires and the two went to a clothing store where Elvis purchased a tuxedo for a visit to the Grand Ole Opry that evening. At the Opry, Elvis came on stage and waved to the crowd, but did not perform. He spent time visiting backstage and had his picture taken with country stars Ferlin Huskey, Faron Young, Hawkshaw Hawkins and WSM DJ Tom Perryman. When it was time to leave, Elvis changed back into his regular clothes, threw his tux into a trash can, and, according to Stoker, drove back to Memphis.

Stoker said he always regretted not reaching into that trash can and pulling out the tux that Elvis threw away but "the only reason I didn't is because I knew Neal Matthews would say 'are you queer on him?'" Stoker did not like that accusation so he left the clothes in the trash can.[38]

Although Stoker thought Elvis drove back to Memphis that night, Billy Smith, Elvis' cousin who was with him on that trip said that after leaving the Grand Ole Opry they went to a party at the Governor's Mansion. Smith remembers that, at the party, "I got tired and Governor Clement's wife told me to go on in the bedroom and go to sleep. She told Elvis, 'Just leave him here. I'll put him on the bus tomorrow" but Elvis said "No, I'll wake him up when we get ready to go.'" Smith said that "I never did go to sleep. I was afraid I'd miss something. I always followed Elvis around like a little puppy dog."[39]

Chapter 6: 1958 - 1959

On January 7, 1958—the day before Elvis' twenty-third birthday—
"Don't" b/w "I Beg of You" was released. On the twentieth, filming began
on *A Stone for Danny Fisher*, based on the novel by Harold Robbins; how-
ever, the title was changed to *King Creole*. During January and February
Elvis made the soundtrack recordings for *King Creole*, which included the
songs "Hard Headed Woman," "Trouble," "New Orleans," "King Creole,"
"Crawfish," "Dixieland Rock," "Lover Doll," "Don't Ask Me Why," "As
Long as I Have You," "Steadfast, Loyal and True," "Young Dreams," and
"Danny." These were done in Los Angeles.

He also recorded "My Wish Came True," "Doncha' Think It's Time,"
"Your Cheatin' Heart" and "Wear My Ring Around Your Neck." It is interesting that he recorded a Hank Williams song ("Your Cheatin' Heart") on
this session; that song was originally released in early 1953 and remained
number one on the country charts for six weeks that Spring–the year Elvis
graduated from Humes High School.

In early March, location filming was done in New Orleans before the
film crew returned to Hollywood. On Friday, March 14, Elvis returned
to Graceland then, on Monday, March 24, reported for induction into the
Army. The inductees were taken to Fort Chaffee, Arkansas, where they
were processed before Elvis was sent to Fort Hood in Killeen, Texas,
where he was assigned to the Second Armored Division.

That same month, the album *Elvis' Golden Records*, consisting of
14 of Elvis' top hit singles, shipped. The next month, "Wear My Ring
Around Your Neck" b/w "Doncha' Think It's Time" shipped. This left
RCA Victor with almost no new material to release while Elvis faced two
years of Army duty.

Elvis had been granted an eight-week deferment by the Memphis
Draft Board in order to complete his movie, which caused an outcry from
both fans and critics. Milton Bowers, Sr., Chairman of the Memphis Draft
Board, was "fed up to the teeth with the outcries of those who think Elvis
is the greatest and those who think he is the least ...With all due respect

to Elvis, who's a nice boy, we've drafted people who are far, far more important than he is. After all, when you take him out of the entertainment business what have you got left? A truck driver." Bowers told a newspaper reporter "One woman in a letter called us a bunch of damn southern goons...I talk about Elvis Presley more than I sleep. A crackpot called me out of bed last night and complained that we didn't put Beethoven in the army. Considering the fact that Beethoven was not an American and had been dead for some time, I don't see how he felt we were discriminating against rock and roll music. I told him we put Mr. Eisenhower in the army and that ought to count for something. Then I asked him how old he was and when he told me he was 52 I asked him how he got so stupid in 52 years."[40]

Shortly before he entered the Army, an article by Norman Weiser, headlined "Elvis Not Sure He Has It Made" appeared in the Nashville *Banner*. In this article Weiser stated, "Unquestionably Presley is the most controversial figure to hit the popular music field since Johnny Ray, and, like Ray, he is confused, and still retains a humbleness which, after being exposed, tends to soften the first impressions."

Weiser quoted Elvis saying "I'm not so sure I've really got it made" and Weiser observed that "it is this constant controversy, and the constant sniping by critics, which brings about this indecision in Presley. Taciturn by nature, he is now more sparing with his words than ever before in his 23 years of life. He realizes that every time he speaks, there are listeners who are ready to pick up his every word, often twisting them."

Weiser talked to Colonel Parker about Elvis entering the service and Parker stated, "We're going in the Army to be soldiers." When he was asked if Elvis would do Special Service work during his stint Parker replied "We'll do television if they'll pay us our price" which he stated was "$100,000 for an hour show–maybe we'll do a half-hour for $75,000." When asked "What do you think of the critics?" Parker replied "Ask the kids what they think of the boy" while Elvis "says little or nothing. He leans heavily on the advice of the Colonel, and to date he has had little reason to doubt the wisdom of this sage advice. For it was this same Colonel Parker who built Eddy Arnold into a musical legend. He listens as the Colonel talks–talks contract terms to the recording company and the motion picture producers–guarantees to the promoters of Presley's in-person appearances, and listens as reporters seek new angles to a story which really has no new angles."

Weiser concluded that "After surveying a number of teens in various parts of the country, the consensus boils down to the fact that there is no middle of the Presley road—either he is considered great or he is nothing. 'We love the beat of Rock'n'Roll,' say those who are not Presley fans, 'but there are a lot of singers who are much better than he is–and who don't bring criticism on the teens because of his actions on and off stage.'"[41]

On May 31, Elvis went home to Memphis after finishing his six weeks of basic training. He had two weeks of Army leave before he had to report back and needed to spend some of that time recording songs to be released while he was away on Army duty.

Elvis did not have fond memories of recording in Nashville—Chet Atkins did not hire the Jordanaires like he requested and the studio was not good acoustically—so he avoided recording there for two years, until June 10, 1958, when he was on leave from the Army and did not have time to go to New York or Los Angeles to record. In the meantime, RCA Victor had established a new studio in Nashville at the corner of Seventeenth Avenue South and Hawkins Street (today the streets are known as Music Square West and Roy Acuff Place).

The studio building is 65 feet by 150 feet and cost $39,515 to build. It was built by the J.B. Regen Company for Dan Maddox, who actually owned the building and lot and leased it to RCA. RCA Victor's chief engineer, William Miltenburg, oversaw the design and building. Inside were offices for Chet Atkins, then the head of RCA's Nashville division, and Ed Hines, manager of RCA's custom service.[42]

The building was started in July, 1957 and on November 7, the first session was held there with The Statesmen, a quartet that Elvis loved. On December 3, Don Gibson recorded "Oh, Lonesome Me" and "I Can't Stop Loving You." "Oh Lonesome Me" became the first Number One country hit recorded at the studio, and it crossed over to the pop charts.

Tennessean reporter George Barker went to the Elvis session and wrote "The army's million buck Private Elvis Presley limousined back to Nashville last night for his first record-cutting date since he was drafted last March. 'The army only changes men who want to be changed,' Elvis said. 'I was satisfied with my self when I went into service. I hope things will be the same when I get out.'"

Elvis arrived around 7 p.m. driving a nine-passenger black Cadillac limousine. In the car were the Jordanaires, Colonel Tom Parker, puffing on a cigar, and some of Elvis' Memphis buddies—but not a girlfriend. Elvis wore an Army uniform and did not have his trademark sideburns. "I can't say I miss 'em much," Elvis told the reporter. "At any rate, they're gone now. And they won't grow back until March 24, 1960—my gettin' out date."

Barker stated that Elvis had lost 15 pounds during basic training at Fort Hood and "as he sang—even though there was no audience to watch—you could see the old trick left knee jumping to the beat." With Elvis was his boyhood friend, Red West, who was a private in the Marine Corps. "Elvis and I grew up together and went to Humes High School," West told the reporter. "He was a good guy then and he still is. He'd give you the shirt off his back if you needed it. And he'll fight for you if you need that, too. He's got a lot of guts. I think he'll be a good soldier."

Barker noted that, after the session ended in the early morning, Elvis would head back to his home in Memphis and then leave for Fort Hood where he'd start advanced training in tanks and then head to Germany in September as part of the Second Armored Division.

Elvis told the reporter that his life as a soldier is much like that of other men in his outfit. "I miss certain things," he said. "I miss having a car to drive when I want it. A tank is only a tank—three or four cars is a way of life."

Elvis related that "Some of the guys asked me to sing in the barracks one night [and] I gave 'em 'Hound Dog,' I think. They haven't asked me again since that time. I hope they're just being polite."[43]

Nashville *Banner* reporter Red O'Donnell was also at the session and referred to Elvis as "the Army buck private of many bucks." In his article O'Donnell stated that Elvis "pooh-poohed reports of any serious romance and appears, conversationally-wise at least, to be taking his military career in stride...'Marriage? Ha,' he shrugged without trace of smile. 'Good gosh, no. I haven't given it a thought. There are more important things on my mind' (he didn't elaborate on the latter statement). ...'I take a girl to a movie or invite her over for a swim—and bingo, she's lovely, she's engaged.'"

Elvis told O'Donnell that "I've been in service less than three months, so I don't think I'm qualified to discuss military life too much. I don't mind the discipline. After all for the past several years I've been doing what I am told to do. I learned to take orders; it doesn't go against my grain. The fellows I went through basic training with were okay. Believe me, I had no trouble with them, whatsoever."

When asked how many songs he intended to cut that evening Elvis said, "I really don't know. I was notified to come up here and here I am."

O'Donnell reported that after Elvis completed advanced training at Fort Hood and became a tank commander he would receive a pay raise from $78 to $82 a month. "I didn't request the Armored Divison (tanks)," Elvis told O'Donnell. "Fact is, I didn't ask for anything. I wouldn't mind it a bit if they put me in Special Services—and assigned me to entertain the troops. I have two years to soldier and I am going to do the best I can."

Producer Steve Sholes stated that "Elvis has made 16 records—and each one has sold more than a million dollars" and Colonel Parker added that "Elvis picks all of his tunes. He's a once-in-a-lifetime entertainer."

O'Donnell also noted that Elvis' latest movie, *King Creole* would open in Nashville on July 2 at the Paramount Theater.[44]

The session was instigated by Steve Sholes, who insisted that RCA needed singles before Elvis left for Germany in September. Songwriters were contacted by Freddy Bienstock in the New York office of Hill and Range with an emphasis on hit singles. Clyde Otis and Ivory Joe Hunter were in Louisiana, duck hunting, when they received word from Hill and Range asking if they had any songs for an upcoming Elvis session. "We said, 'yes,'" remembered Otis, "But really we didn't have anything. So we sat down and wrote that song, and rushed it off to them." The song they wrote was "Ain't That Lovin' You Baby."[45]

Playing guitar on the session was Hank "Sugarfoot" Garland, one of the most talented guitarists to ever record in Nashville. Garland had a recording career of his own and had performed with Elvis in the fall of 1957 after Scotty and Bill resigned. The bass player was Bob Moore, Floyd Cramer—who played piano for Elvis during the Louisiana Hayride era—was on the session along with Murray "Buddy" Harman, who joined Elvis' regular drummer D.J. Fontana on drums and percussion. The Jordanaires sang back-up.

With the exception of Fontana, these were all Nashville A Team Musicians, the group which gave Nashville an identifying sound as well as a reputation for musical excellence combined with efficiency. These musicians were used to quickly learning a song, running it down once or twice and then recording it with an air of professionalism.

There was a new member of the Jordanaires for this session; bass singer Ray Walker had replaced Hugh Jarrett.

Ray Walker had sung with the Jordanaires several times before he became an "official" member of the Jordanaires. A graduate of David Lipscomb University in Nashville, he was teaching at a high school and called the main office at David Lipscomb early one morning to leave a message for a teacher there. Buddy Arnold answered the phone and told Walker that he had spoken with Gordon Stoker, who called looking for a bass singer. Since it was about six weeks before the school year ended, Walker said he didn't think he could do it but Arnold replied "You said a couple of years ago that if you went into professional singing you'd do it with a quartet and the Jordanaires were the only ones you felt comfortable with." Walker then relented and told Arnold to give Stoker his name and number.

Walker was offered a job singing on a USO tour during his sophomore year in college for $500 a week but turned it down. When Stoker called, Ray said that he wanted to make a change on May 31 but Stoker pressed him to accompany the Jordanaires to Los Angeles earlier because they had a recording session scheduled there. Walker went and sang on four songs and then the group backed up four songs by Ricky Nelson and four songs by Tommy Sands before they came back to Nashville.

The day after they came back Stoker called and asked Walker if he could go with the Jordanaires to do a Dick Clark show. Walker replied, "No, I've been away from my students for two weeks and they've had a substitute and I've got to get them ready for their SATs." Stoker then told him, "Well, what if I told you that if you can't go on this trip then we'll have to take our next choice as a singer?" Walker replied, "That's just something you'll have to do because if I break this contract and go with you then later I'll break a contract to go with somebody else and I don't break contracts."

Stoker then replied, "Well, when can you start coming to the Opry?" Walker replied that he could do that and began singing with the group on the Grand Ole Opry. School ended on May 30 so on June 1, 1958 Ray Walker became an "official" member of the Jordanaires. The very first session he did with the group was on June 10 when they recorded with Elvis at the RCA Studio.[46]

Ray Walker was standing in the studio when Stoker said, "Here comes Elvis." "I just turned around and he had his hand out and said, 'I'm Elvis Presley,'" remembered Walker. "I shook his hand and said 'I know who you are. I'm Ray Walker' and he said, 'And I know who you are.'"

"He'd done some checking on me," said Walker. "When I looked at him I saw the best listener I've ever seen in my life. From the expression on his face I could see that all his fame was gone—it just left—and he was a human being from the bottom of his feet to the top of his head."

Elvis and Walker quickly hit it off; Ray and Elvis shared a mike as Ray doubled several words and lines on the first song, "I Need Your Love Tonight," which came from the Hill and Range offices in New York. Elvis insisted on 18 takes of the song before he was satisfied. The next song was "A Big Hunk O'Love," which was blusier than the first.

Then they recorded "Ain't That Loving You Baby" but the song didn't seem to have the same energy as the first two. Finally, Chet Atkins came out of the control booth, picked up a guitar (as Elvis said "Boogie, Chet") and played a walking bass figure on guitar which helped with the rhythm. Still, the song didn't feel like it was falling into place, so the musicians, after 11 takes and two different versions—one with a faster tempo than the other—moved on to "(Now And Then There's) A Fool Such As I." This song had originally been a hit for Hank Snow in 1953 during the time when Colonel Parker managed him—and before he met Elvis. Tom Diskin felt strongly about the song and encouraged Elvis to record it. Chet Atkins played rhythm guitar on the song.

Since Hill and Range did not have the publishing on that song, Tom Diskin approached the publisher—Bob Miller—and requested a deal. It was made and, without that deal, that song would probably never have become a single. Between takes, Elvis used some Army jargon, saying "At ease."[47]

On "I Got Stung" Elvis was in a groove, although Parker felt the band was too loud and therefore could not fully showcase Elvis' singing. As the session continued, the musicians began to feel tired and Elvis himself continued making mistakes, saying "Man, you better hurry up, my brain's getting weaker every minute." Finally, Elvis altered the melody, Hank Garland carried the solo, the Jordanaires worked out their part and, with Elvis announcing "Ready on the left, ready on the right, ready on the firing line," they did take 24, which was the keeper.[48]

Early in the morning of Wednesday, June 11—sometime around 6 a.m.—Elvis walked out of his first session at the RCA Studio in Nashville and headed back to Memphis. When he left the studio he left a group he had bonded with and who would record with him later. In the studio, Elvis was a huge star but a "regular guy," someone who served in the Army and who was down to earth and friendly with the other musicians, one of them. Elvis endeared himself to the Nashville musicians during that recording session.

Elvis returned to Fort Hood on Saturday, the fourteenth. In July the EPs "King Creole Vol. 1" and "King Creole Vol. 2" were released and the movie *King Creole* opened nationally.

Tragedy struck the Presley family on August 9 when Elvis' mother, Gladys, was taken to Methodist Hospital in Memphis. That same day Elvis completed advanced tank training.

Gladys and Vernon had returned earlier from Fort Hood, where they visited their son. Concerned about his mother's health—she had been feeling ill, lost her appetite and had a deepening depression—Elvis put her and Vernon on a train to Memphis so she could see her regular physician, Dr. Charles Clarke. On Saturday, an ambulance took Gladys to Methodist Hospital where her condition was listed as "grave" from a liver ailment. Elvis received a seven-day emergency leave from the Army to visit his mother in the hospital and arrived on Tuesday, August 12.

On the morning of August 14, readers of the Nashville *Tennessean* saw an article which said "The homecoming of Pvt. Elvis Presley has apparently had the desired effect on his seriously ill mother. The drafted rock'n'roll singer spent the day at her hospital bedside. Mrs. Vernon Presley was reportedly in better spirits yesterday after her famous son made a flying trip to Memphis from his Fort Hood, Texas army base to be with her." The newspaper stated that "her condition is still serious" and that "Elvis says he plans to follow the same routine for the remainder of his leave. Such a flood of flowers from well wishers across the country have been sent to the hospital that Presley said he would probably have to take some of them home."[49]

Gladys had died at 3:15 that morning—after the *Tennessean* had been printed. In the Nashville *Banner* the following day Elvis told a reporter, "I told my ma I'd be in early to take the flowers out to the house" as tears streamed down his cheeks. The newspaper reported that "Elvis cried without shame. He and his father sat on the steps of the big house, stared into space and embraced each other. Looking down the big driveway leading to the iron gates where the curious assembled, Elvis said, "When ma was feeling bad we used to walk with her up and down the driveway to help her feel better. Now it's over."[50]

That same day the *Banner* printed a story stating, "Private Elvis Presley moved his mothers' body to the family's mansion here yesterday and opened the doors of his $100,000 home to friends for a last look at his 'best girl friend.'" The article noted that "Elvis' 42-year-old mother, Mrs. Vernon Presley, took a sudden turn for the worse before dawn yesterday, gasped for breath in her hospital room and succumbed to an apparent heart attack. The plump Mrs. Presley, who seldom was quoted in the news but followed her son from coast to coast, was devoted to her son. 'She's all we lived for,' Elvis sobbed when he reached the hospital room shortly after 3 a.m., a few minutes after her death."

The article continued, "Elvis' father, a former Mississippi cotton sharecropper, was asleep on a cot in Mrs. Presley's room when he heard his wife 'suffering for breath.' The husband summoned a doctor, but the soft-spoken Mrs. Presley, who had been hospitalized here last Saturday with a liver ailment, died within minutes. Elvis, asleep at the Graceland mansion was awakened by telephone. 'I knew what it was before I answered the telephone,' Elvis said.'"[51]

On Friday, August 15, her funeral was held, with arrangements made by Colonel Tom Parker.

An Associated Press story stated that "Elvis Presley remained at his $100,000 mansion today, recovering from the torrent of grief that seized him when they buried his mother. The famed rock'n'roll singer was near hysteria at the funeral Friday. He and his father, Vernon Presley, 43, wept throughout the services...[and he] nearly collapsed at the graveside. 'Goodbye, Darling,' he cried. 'Goodbye, goodbye...we loved you'...Elvis, 23, had to be helped to the big black limousine that carried him from the cemetery. His father strode ahead, eyes streaming. 'She's gone,' he said. 'She's not coming back'...About 500 persons accompanied the Presleys to the grave ...Police held much of the crowd back ... Police also were on hand at the funeral home, overflowing with relatives, friends and fans ...The sanctuary and every wall of the chapel were banked with flowers. Nearly 600 people crowded the seats and stood in the aisles. Several hundred more were outside...[the] 300 seat chapel."

Rev. James E. Hamill of the First Assembly of God Church delivered the sermon, saying, "'Women can succeed in most any field these days, but the most important of all is being a good wife and a good mother. Mrs. Presley was such a woman.' A Gospel quartet, out of sight in the organ room behind the sanctuary, sang hymns ...Along the route of the funeral procession police officers were stationed at strategic intersections. Nearly every corner had a small crowd to watch the line of cars move by."[52]

An article in the Nashville *Banner*, datelined August 14, 1958, opined that "Private Elvis Presley's heart 'broke' today with the death of his

42-year-old mother he had always described as 'my best girl.'"[53]

Elvis returned to Fort Hood on Sunday, August 24; on September 19 he left Fort Hood for New York and then boarded a troop ship for Germany, where he arrived on Wednesday, October 1.

In September the album *King Creole* shipped; three days later the EP "Christmas With Elvis" shipped with tracks from his 1957 Christmas album and RCA shipped the single "One Night" b/w "I Got Stung."

Although Elvis remained in Germany with the Army throughout 1959 and early 1960, Colonel Tom Parker continued to promote him and RCA continued to release product. In February, 1959, the album *For LP Fans Only* was shipped; in March the single "A Fool Such As I" b/w "I Need Your Love Tonight" shipped and in April the EP "A Touch of Gold Vol. 1" was released; this sold about 130,000 units although it did not chart.

A rather odd story, headlined "Elvis' Songs Keep Seagulls Away from London Airport" appeared in the Nashville *Tennessean*. The article stated, "Elvis Presley's rock'n'roll singing...has proved a new secret weapon in scaring off seagulls which have become a flying hazard at Staines, near the London airport ... sent one of its men to Holland to record the cry of a gull in distress...The official took a tape recorder, which had been used to record a children's Christmas party at his home where one of Presley's recordings was played. In the first tryout, the gull distress call failed to rustle a feather. But when Presley's voice unexpectedly boomed out of the loudspeaker: "Rock! Roll!" the gulls took off in a hurry."[54]

In June, the single "A Big Hunk O' Love" b/w "My Wish Came True" was shipped. This was the last single RCA released while Elvis was in Germany. In July the album *A Date With Elvis* was shipped, which contained five cuts from his Sun recordings, four movie songs and a final song that had only been released on an EP.

During the time Elvis was in the Army, RCA released four two sided singles, which produced eight songs on the *Billboard* Hot 100 chart: "Hard Headed Woman," "Don't Ask Me Why," "One Night," "I Got Stung," "(Now and Then There's) A Fool Such As I," "I Need Your Love Tonight," "A Big Hunk O' Love" and "My Wish Came True." Two reached number one on the charts—"Hard Headed Woman" and "A Big Hunk O' Love," while "(Now and Then There's) A Fool Such as I" was number two, "I Need Your Love Tonight" and "One Night" both peaked at number four and "I Got Stung" reached number eight on *Billboard's* Hot 100 chart.[55]

In September, the EP "A Touch of Gold Vol. 2" was released and in November the album *Elvis' Gold Records Vol. 2* was shipped. On the cover of this album was a picture of Elvis in his gold lame suit.

In December an article by David Halberstam in the Nashville *Tennessean* informed readers that although Elvis was in Bad Nauheim, Germany, he and the Colonel had sent out 1.3 million Christmas cards. "Elvis has a lot of friends," stated Colonel Parker in the article, which described him as "the singer's guiding light, close friend and instrumentor."

On the card were two pictures of Elvis—one with a dog and the other with a horse—and one picture of Parker dressed as Santa Claus. The article noted that "The card itself was a massive project requiring the talents of about 50 people for a week, plus approximately $20,000. It will go to RCA distributors, from there to record dealers, and from there to fans.... Fifty-thousand of them will be mailed and addressed directly to higher level Presleyites (such as presidents of fan clubs, newspaper columnists, disc jockeys and other celebrities)."

"It's a job you know," the Colonel said, "but we like to keep his name alive." Parker added that his office had already shipped 18,000 cards from fans to Elvis in Germany and that last year Elvis received about 400,000 cards from fans. The Colonel then reminded the reporter that, although Elvis would not be discharged until March, he "has a full schedule waiting him: a TV show with Frank Sinatra, and then right off the bat, three movies."[56]

On Christmas Day, 1959, an article appeared in the Nashville *Banner* by Henry Gris that asked "When Elvis Presley comes home from the Army, presumably next March, what girl will he call for a date?" The article continued, "Most of Presley's former girlfriends have replaced the image of their blue-eyed, hip-swinging Adonis with that of some other man—somebody closer to home. At least two are married. Some admit their romancing with Presley was all for the sake of publicity in the first place."

The article quoted Debra Paget, Elvis' co-star in *Love Me Tender* and "object of his first studio-tailored romance," who said, "I was told the publicity would do me a lot of good. The truth of the matter is that I didn't date him at all. He wasn't really my cup of tea. Too much backwoods, if you know what I mean."

Anita Wood, Elvis' girlfriend in Memphis who was a disc jockey on a Memphis radio station told the reporter, "Elvis called me a few times from Germany. Not in recent months, though. Mostly in the beginning. Would I go out with him again? I'd be happy to. But I would never marry him because Elvis shouldn't marry anyone. Not at this stage of his career, at least."

Anne Neyland, who was in the movie *Jailhouse Rock*, was married but said, "He's a joke, and anyone who associates with him is also considered a joke in this town. He is just a small town boy, animalistic and honest but small-town. I want nothing more to do with what he stands for." Dotty Harmony, a Las Vegas showgirl who Elvis had dated while in Vegas, said "Elvis has called me and written since he went to Germany. He has written me about the girls he dates there and I write him about the fellows I go out with here. Would I date him again? Yes, I would. But I could never marry him because we can't pick up where we left off. Too much water has gone under the bridge,"

Finally, Ziva Rodann, who appeared with Elvis in *King Creole* told the reporter "Elvis was irked because I refused to go out with him. We had nothing in common. He wore the most atrocious clothes—I would have felt embarrassed to be seen with him."[57]

Chapter 7: January - March, 1960

During the late 1950s it felt like a dark cloud hovered over the Nashville music business. The dark mood came from a prevailing belief that rock and roll was killing country music, a sentiment echoed over and over again by those in the country music community.

In 1954 there were number one hits on the country charts by Jim Reeves ("Bimbo"), Webb Pierce ("Slowly," "Even Tho" and "More and More"), Eddy Arnold ("I Really Don't Want to Know"), Kitty Wells and Red Foley ("One By One") and Hank Snow ("I Don't Hurt Anymore"). In 1955 there were number one country singles by Webb Pierce ("In the Jailhouse Now," "I Don't Care" and "Love, Love, Love"), Eddy Arnold ("The Cattle Call" and "That Do Make It Nice"), Carl Smith ("Loose Talk"), Hank Snow ("Let Me Go, Lover!") Porter Wagoner ("A Satisfied Mind") and Faron Young ("Live Fast, Love Hard, Die Young").

Then came 1956 and there were five number ones by Elvis Presley: "I Forgot To Remember To Forget," "Heartbreak Hotel," "I Want You, I Need You, I Love You," "Don't Be Cruel," and "Hound Dog." Marty Robbins had a number one hit with "Singing the Blues," Johnny Cash had "I Walk the Line" and Carl Perkins had "Blue Suede Shoes." Except for the Louvin Brothers, "I Don't Believe You've Met My Baby" and Ray Price's "Crazy Arms," the country hits didn't sound *country*. The young rock and rollers had unseated the reigning king of country music, Webb Pierce, and they didn't wear rhinestone outfits like Webb, either. The charts were labeled "Country and Western" but none of the rock and rollers wore cowboys hats or boots.

In 1957 there were three number one country hits by Elvis: "All Shook Up," "Teddy Bear" and "Jailhouse Rock." Also hitting number one that year were "Young Love" by Sonny James, "Gone" by Ferlin Husky, "A White Sport Coat (And a Pink Carnation)" by Marty Robbins, "Whole Lot of Shakin' Going On" by Jerry Lee Lewis, "My Special Angel" by Bobby Helms and two by the Everly Brothers: "Bye Bye Love" and "Wake Up Little Susie."

For those yearning to hear steel guitars and twin fiddles there was only Ray Price with "My Shoes Keep Walking Back to You," "Fraulein" by Bobby Helms and "Honky Tonk Song" by Webb Pierce. The smooth sound of Jim Reeves singing "Four Walls" clashed with the sounds of Elvis, Jerry Lee Lewis and the Everly Brothers.

In 1958 there were no Elvis records on the country chart; however, Jerry Lee Lewis had "Great Balls of Fire," The Everly Brothers had "All I Have to Do Is Dream" and "Bird Dog," Marty Robbins had "The Story of My Life" and "Just Married," Johnny Cash had "Ballad of a Teenage Queen" and "Guess Things Happen that Way."

The "sound" of traditional country music, a sound rooted in post World War II honky tonks sung by artists who claimed an allegiance to country music, returned in 1959 with songs like "El Paso" by Marty Robbins, "The Battle of New Orleans" and "When It's Springtime in Alaska (It's Forty Below)" by Johnny Horton, "Billy Bayou" by Jim Reeves, "The Three Bells" by the Browns and "The Same Old Me" by Ray Price. Gone from the country charts were artists like Elvis, Jerry Lee Lewis, Carl Perkins and the Everly Brothers.

The jukeboxes were the major buyers of country records and many of those country records disappeared during the late 1950s, replaced by rock and roll records. There wasn't much country music on the radio; most of the Saturday night "barn dances," or live shows featuring country performers had been cancelled. There were a few disc jockeys playing country records a few hours a day but, after television came in and radio lost its national sponsors and national shows, the radio station owners switched over to disc jockeys playing rock and roll. The record labels felt a loss of income from sales while the performers lost income from a lack of demand previously created from exposure via radio. According to Ralph Emery, Patsy Cline only had one date where she made over $1,000; most of the country performers had their income slashed; "stars" were playing on the road for $500-700 a night.[58]

It's easy to see why members of the country music community in Nashville felt that rock and roll was killing country music. They responded by forming a trade organization, The Country Music Association in 1958;

they concentrated their initial efforts on convincing advertisers to buy time on country stations.

On the other hand, there were some substantial benefits that Nashville felt from rock and roll. Because Elvis sold so many records, RCA built a studio in Nashville and established a permanent office there. Chet Atkins was named head of that label's Nashville branch and had his office in that studio. Owen Bradley opened his Quonset Hut for business in 1955; a number of rock and roll artists recorded in that studio.

Country music had to depend on "Crossovers" or records that landed on both the country and pop charts, in order to achieve major sales. Artists such as Marty Robbins, Eddy Arnold, Johnny Cash, Jim Reeves and Johnny Horton all managed to have crossover hits. A number of rock and roll songs were published by Nashville publishers; Tree had "Heartbreak Hotel," Acuff-Rose writers Felice and Boudeleaux Bryant wrote "Wake Up Little Susie," "Bye, Bye Love" and a number of other Everly Brothers hits.

Still, for those who yearned for the sound of country music from the late 1940s and early 1950s, it felt like "real" country music was dead, replaced by the loud, raucous offensive sound of rock and roll that murdered the country music of story songs, weeping steel guitars and lonesome fiddles.

On March 2, 1960, Elvis left Germany for the United States. The Nashville *Tennessean* sent a reporter to cover Elvis' discharge and trip home; the reporter was joined by a number of other reporters, including those from the wire services whose articles often appeared in the *Tennessean* and *Banner*.

On March 4 the *Tennessean* published an article, datelined from snowy Fort Dix, New Jersey, which informed readers that Sgt. Elvis Presley "was not giving up rock'n'roll" or his "gaudy attire" or his "hip-swinging style." Asked what he would do if rock'n'roll died, Elvis quipped, "I, and a lot of other people, will have to find something else to do." Although he insisted he would continue to do what he had always done, he stated that he would not grow back his side-burns and would "keep his Army haircut." During the brief interview with newsmen, Elvis revealed that "his real ambition was to become a serious actor."

Colonel Tom Parker informed the newsmen that Elvis' first public appearance would be as a guest on a television special hosted by Frank Sinatra on May 12, for which the singer would receive $125,000, and that Elvis would film three movies that year for $725,000 and a percentage of the take with the first titled *The G.I. Blues*. When Army officials announced that Elvis would draw his final sergeant's pay of $125.24 a month the next morning, Parker informed the newsmen that Elvis had grossed $1,600,000 the previous year to supplement his Army pay.[59]

On March 5, 1960, Elvis was discharged from the Army.

In that morning's *Tennessean*, Nashville readers learned that Elvis spent his final day in the Army going through paperwork, stripped his sergeant's chevrons off so they could be used again, and drew his final Army paycheck which, according to an Army spokesman, was $1,099.54. Colonel Parker informed readers that Elvis' income bracket meant the government received 91 percent of his income, so only $9.86 of that check was Elvis' to keep. Plans called for Elvis to leave Fort Dix for Memphis.[60]

Two days later, under the headline "Will Elvis Still Rule the Roost?" the Nashville *Tennessean* surveyed some Nashville residents about their thoughts on Elvis and noted "seven of the 10 persons questioned during a survey downtown last week...say he may wiggle his way into an even brighter spot. Three persons...point out that his future may be ill-starred because 'somebody else has taken his place' or 'a comeback is tough' or 'Americans are tired of Presley.'"

The article asked "Will Elvis have lost his punch after 18 months as a soldier in Friedberg, Germany? Or do Americans long to hear him again?" and collected responses. Mrs. Nina Hendrick said "He loved his mother and that means more than anything. He's a fine boy" while 11-year-old Sandra Deans said "Presley will probably go down. He's been gone and other people have come in to take his place. People like Frankie Avalon." Eighteen-year-old Pfc Raymond Ritter said "The army might help his appeal with the women some" while Mrs. Delmer Holland stated "The army has made a better man out of him."[61]

An article in the Nashville *Banner* on the afternoon of March 7 informed readers that when the Southern Railway train stopped in Knoxville for about 20 minutes, Elvis walked out on the rear platform and smiled and waved but did not speak to the approximately 500 teenagers cheering and yelling "We want Elvis." Police hauled down one girl who tried to climb in the car while another sobbed "I saw Elvis."

Elvis arrived in Memphis in a private car on the train and, according to the article, "There were almost as many newsmen as early morning fans to greet the rock and roll idol." It snowed the night before and there was drizzling rain when Elvis arrived. Fans chanted "We want Elvis" and that Elvis put his hand through an iron gate to reach some waiting girls. The head of "The Tankers," an Elvis Presley Fan Club, was Gary Pepper, who stood with a sign that said "Welcome Home Elvis. The Tankers."

Asked about his plans, Elvis said "I'm just going home" before entering a waiting police car for the drive to Graceland.

There were reports that Elvis' father, Vernon, had returned to Graceland a few days earlier with a thin mustache and escorted a "mysterious blonde" woman named "Dee" as they shopped for a $12,000 car. Elvis was asked about "Dee" and replied, "My father has been seeing her quite a bit. 'Dee' is all I know. My father doesn't discuss his private life with me unless I ask." Vernon denied that he had remarried, saying that if he did "I'll announce it all at once."[62]

In 1959 the sales of records were down; the sales of singles were dropping while albums–by rock'n'rollers–had not developed a market big enough to compensate for the decline in single sales. The top album sellers were Broadway cast recordings like *West Side Story, The King and I* and *My Fair Lady*." Rock'n'roll was still a singles market but it was a market in transition as consumers began to purchase more albums with stereo sound.

The sales of Elvis' singles–while still over the million mark–were less than the pre-"Jailhouse Rock" days. Further, neither Elvis' Christmas album nor his *Golden Hits* album had achieved the sales of the *Loving You* album.

RCA released "Elvis Sails," an EP of Elvis' press conference before he left for Germany, which sold about 100,000 units, which showed his sales were declining, although still strong. "A Fool Such As I" b/w "I

Need Your Love Tonight" was released in March, 1959 and the two-sided hit reached numbers two and four, respectively on the *Billboard* Hot 100 chart. "A Big Hunk O'Love" b/w "My Wish Came True" was released on July and "A Big Hunk O'Love" was number one for two weeks while "My Wish Came True" reached number 12 on the Hot 100.

There was a transition going on in the market. Rock'n'roll had been a singles business; the radio played hit singles, jukeboxes held hit singles and consumers purchased hit singles. Some record executives balked at putting a hit single on an album because this created a dilemma with consumers; if the consumer bought both the single and the album they paid twice for the hit song. On the other hand, if there was no hit single on the album, the album had less appeal for fans. Colonel Parker and RCA juggled Elvis' limited number of recordings and repackaged a number of Elvis' songs until they had saturated the market with recordings while limiting exposure to new product. There might be a song on a hit single that would be packaged on an EP and then again on an album. Or perhaps a song on an EP would be released as a single.

During Christmas, 1959, RCA released "Santa Claus Is Back in Town" as a single after it had already been on an EP and LP. However, since "Santa Claus Is Back in Town" was already on a previously released EP, RCA packaged an EP of four other Christmas songs to release that season.

Elvis' ambition was to become a movie star and, since there was greater prestige in being a movie star than a recording star, Colonel Parker set his sights on the movie industry and secured a commitment for Elvis to do three films in 1960. Still, music was the foundation on which Elvis had built his career and it was his first love. Further, it was where he was a genuine star. He had a long-term contract with RCA Victor and the label needed recordings to release.

Colonel Parker believed in limiting the exposure of a hot act. He wanted to avoid "overexposure" while RCA Victor, knowing that Elvis records sold well, wanted as many records into the market as they could get in order to increase their profits. This was the essential conflict between Parker and Steve Sholes. Sholes' job depended on Elvis selling a lot of records; Parker's job was to advance the career of Elvis, whether that meant recordings or movies.

The RCA contract required Elvis to release four singles and one album per year. Since Elvis accounted for about 40 percent of the total sales of RCA's records, there was a lot on the line.

When Elvis returned from Germany in March, 1960, RCA had seven unreleased masters from him: "Tomorrow Night" (which was recorded at Sun), "Tell Me Why" (the label feared there would be copyright problems because the song sounded so similar to "Just a Closer Walk With Thee"), "One Night," "Your Cheatin' Heart," "Ain't That Loving You Baby," and "When It Rains, It Really Pours." Since Elvis had to approve any recording released–and since he had proven quite adept at picking hits–the label did not want to release any of those without Elvis' okay, and Elvis, at that time, did not feel any of those met his expectations.[63]

Steve Sholes wanted Elvis to record 22 songs after his release from the Army; this would give him five singles and an album. Since there was demand for a new single, Sholes and the Colonel felt that "One Night" would be a good choice, but Elvis objected. The decision hinged on a publishing agreement whereby Hill and Range made a deal to receive part of the publishing royalties but only if the song was released as a single before October 31, 1958. That is why that song was coupled with "I Got Stung" from the first RCA Studio session in Nashville after he left for Germany.

Freddy Bienstock, who worked with Hill and Range as the liaison who brought songs to Elvis, met with Elvis in Paris while the singer was on leave. Bienstock brought some demos and played them for Elvis, then returned home with a list of songs Elvis was interested in recording. The RCA executives and Parker debated about where to record Elvis after he returned from the Army. After considering New York, they finally settled on Nashville because (1) Nashville was close to Memphis; (2) the June, 1958 sessions turned out well; (3) Elvis liked recording at the RCA Studio in Nashville and (4) Bill Porter, the engineer at the RCA Studio had engineered several million sellers.

Nashville had long been known as a songwriter and publisher town, ever since Patti Page's big hit "Tennessee Waltz" written by Pee Wee King and Redd Stewart and published by Nashville-based Acuff-Rose became a number one song in 1950-1951. A number of Hank Williams' songs had been recorded by Tony Bennett, Jo Stafford and Rosemary Clooney and Elvis' first big hit, "Heartbreak Hotel" was published by Tree. But Elvis would not look to Nashville songwriters and publishers for his songs; they came from a New York-based publisher, Hill and Range, because Colonel Tom Parker had engineered an agreement with the firm's owners, Julian and Jean Aberbach, when Elvis was signed with RCA Victor. Colonel Tom Parker established two publishing companies, Elvis Presley Music (BMI) and Gladys Music (ASCAP) which published the songs Elvis recorded. Elvis (and the Colonel) received half the publishing income for these recordings while Hill and Range received the other half.

Hill and Range was headquartered on the eighth floor of the Brill Building at 1650 Broadway in New York. Hill and Range's stated mission was to "celebrate America's folk music." It was formed by Jean and Julian Aberbach, two Jewish Austrians from Vienna who fled Europe before World War II. They pioneered the practice of signing artists to songwriting contracts; when the artist wrote a song the publisher shared the royalties. During this time, most publishers paid songwriters a salary and kept all the royalties. If the artist found a song that was not published, then Hill and Range published it and the artist received part of the publishing royalties. Under these arrangements, Hill and Range signed country artists Eddy Arnold, Ernest Tubb, Bill Monroe and Bob Wills.

The Aberbach's were not particularly well-liked in publishing circles. They spoke with heavy German accents and disliked the publicity-seeking, socializing manner of the songwriting and publishing industry in New York. Publishers generally loved to hang out, to be available to anyone who had a song. Most publishers came from the street; their language and manners tended to be coarse. The Aberbachs were elegant, cultured, aloof and sophisticated–especially compared to other rank and file publishers—and they collected modern art. There was also the issue of envy; the Aberbachs were successful music publishers, especially with country music, which their competitors dismissed and denigrated. Rivals called the Hill and Range office "Auschwitz West."

The head of the Hill and Range office in New York was Freddy Bienstock, who was a younger cousin of the Aberbachs and whose tastes and personal style mirrored his older cousins. The day-to-day song plugger for Hill and Range was Paul Case, a Jew from Iowa who has been described as "warm, paternal, and unpretentious...liked equally by the songwriters he nurtured and the record company A&R men with whom he placed their songs. He smoked a pipe, dressed in the slouchy tweed suits of a stylish police detective, doted on a menagerie of plants he kept in his office's every cranny, hosted high-stakes poker games out of the same office on Friday afternoons, and trailed the reassuring, fatherly scene of 'Canoe' men's cologne. Unsurpassed as a song doctor, Case could pinpoint a weak line, write a bridge, and pair a song or a songwriter with a singer."[64]

The unpublished songs Elvis recorded were placed in his two publishing companies. Parker originally demanded that Elvis' name be listed as co-writer on songs he recorded; however, when Elvis discovered his name on songs he did not write he stopped that practice. For all other songs in the Hill and Range catalog that Elvis recorded he received a percentage of the publishing income; in addition, Parker demanded that each songwriter give up 30 percent of their songwriting royalties to Elvis if the singer recorded their song.

Elvis knew of these arrangements and approved them. Colonel Tom Parker kept Elvis informed of the money he could make just recording Hill and Range songs. Parker also assured Hill and Range that Elvis would record songs they published except for those that Elvis had a special fondness for. Elvis informed Hill and Range, through Parker, of songs he intended to record during an upcoming session and Hill and Range contacted those publishers to obtain an agreement whereby the other publisher sent part of the publishing and songwriting income to Hill and Range for that company and Elvis. If a publisher did not agree to this arrangement it was unlikely that Elvis would record their song, although if Elvis was adamant about a song he could record whatever he wanted to.

What emerged was an in-house arrangement whereby Hill and Range informed their songwriters when an Elvis session was scheduled. The writers competed with each other writing songs. The best songs were selected by Paul Case and Freddy Bienstock; Bienstock then took a stack of demos, recorded on acetates, to Elvis who listened and decided which he wanted to record. Sometimes the demos were sent to Elvis' home but most often they were brought into the studio by Bienstock where Elvis listened on a small, portable phonograph.

In the studio, Bienstock pulled certain ones out for Elvis to listen to, or Elvis went through the stack, setting some in a "discard" pile, another in a "maybe" pile and, if he liked a song, might say, "let's do this one." A lot of the demos had singers who sounded like Elvis so the session musicians basically copied the demo most of the time.

RCA needed to keep the March, 1960 session a secret so prying fans and reporters would not know about it. The musicians booked on the session were told that the date was for Jim Reeves. Musicians on the session were guitarists Hank Garland and Scotty Moore, bass player Bob Moore, pianist Floyd Cramer, Buddy Harman and D.J. Fontana on drums, and backup vocals by the Jordanaires: Gordon Stoker, Neal Matthews, Jr., Hoyt Hawkins and Ray Walker.

Scotty Moore and D.J. Fontana, from Elvis' old band, were on the session because loyalty was important to Elvis. During the time when Elvis was in the Army, Scotty formed the Fernwood label and had some success. Bass player Bill Black formed The Bill Black Combo that was successful; he was not interested in becoming a sideman again, even for Elvis. The rest of the musicians were members of Nashville's "A Team" of studio players.

On Sunday, March 20, 1960, a chartered bus brought Elvis and his entourage from Memphis to Nashville. Engineer Bill Porter remembered that he was the only engineer working on that Sunday night session that was scheduled to start at 7 p.m. Porter arrived at five, set up the studio and the musicians all arrived by seven. Porter had been an engineer at RCA's Nashville studio for about a year but this was his first time to work with Elvis. Porter had engineered several hit records, including "The Three Bells" by the Browns "and I was feeling pretty good about myself," he said.[65]

Elvis showed up at 8:30 and when he walked in the back door, every eye immediately focused on him. At the studio were RCA executives Steve

Sholes, Chet Atkins and Bill Bullock, Colonel Parker and his assistant, Tom Diskin and Hill and Range publisher's representative Freddy Bienstock. There was a great deal of tension in the air; the executives were especially nervous because there were pre-orders of 1.4 million copies of Elvis' first single—no matter what it was. RCA already had the color sleeves pre-printed which announced, "Elvis' 1st New Recording For His 50,000,000 Fans All Over the World." Since nobody knew what the song would be, there was no song title listed on the sleeve.

Elvis was hungry when he arrived so Lamar Fike, a member of Elvis' "Memphis Mafia" entourage, was sent to Krystal's for some hamburgers, sweet milk and fries as Elvis talked about being in Germany, the Army tank maneuvers he went on and other small talk. Bass player Bob Moore and Elvis demonstrated some karate—both enjoyed it and had taken lessons–before they began the first song, "Make Me Know It." The group did 19 takes of the song before they moved on to "Soldier Boy," which took 15 takes. "Stuck On You" was the third song, which ran smoothly, then "Fame and Fortune," which caused some problems because Elvis was putting too much air into the microphone when he sang the "f's." Engineer Porter had to remind him several times to back away from the mike. The final song on that session, recorded as daylight was breaking, was "It Feels So Right."

Although Chet Atkins and Steve Sholes were in the control booth "producing" the session, it was obvious that Elvis called the shots. He picked which songs to do, worked them up with the musicians and kept doing takes until he was satisfied.[66]

Porter noted that Elvis did not come into the control room to talk with the engineer or producer. "He would talk to the band sometimes if he didn't like something," said Porter. "He would stop and do a tune over again. Or the producer, which was either Chet or Steve Sholes, would say 'The tempo's wrong,' or 'change the chord structure here.' Stuff like that. And Elvis would pick out the songs. Freddie Bienstock, who was [with] Hill and Range Music, used to bring a stack of records in–most of 'em were 78s–I'm talking about a foot high. Freddie would go down through the stack and pick one out and put it on the turntable, 'Here, Elvis. Listen to this.'"[67]

Nashville *Tennessean* reporter Pat Anderson was at the studio and reported in the next day's paper that Elvis "can still belt out a rock-and-roll tune with the best of them." Standing outside the studio with about a dozen teenagers, the reporter stated that the first song was "an old-style Presley R&R tune called 'Make Me Love'" which, "according to the teenagers 'it was the greatest.'"

Actually, the song was "Make Me Know It," written by Otis Blackwell.

The reporter saw Elvis, who wore a pork-pie hat with tight black pants and a black jacket with a white shirt and saluted; Elvis returned the salute. An Elvis session generally went all night long and this was no exception; the next day Elvis was scheduled to travel to Miami for the Frank Sinatra television special.[68]

When the session ended, *Tennessean* reporter Pat Anderson talked with Elvis who, according to Anderson, "wants to keep pleasing the teenagers—even at risk of life and limb. 'They don't mean to hurt you,' said Elvis of the countless mob scenes his appearances has sparked since 1955, 'but when you get five or six hundred kids pulling at you, somebody's bound to miss and get some flesh.'" Elvis added "I wouldn't have it any different. It shows they care about you and there's no entertainer who don't eat that up, no matter what they say."

Commenting on his 11 hour recording session, Elvis said, "After two years, it was sorta strange at first. But after singing a couple of hours it all came natural again." Plans were to release two songs on a double sided single and put the others in an album.

After the session, Elvis was taken to Union Station and spent the day sleeping in a chartered Pullman that was parked underneath the Broad Street bridge. Elvis' location that day was a secret so fans had to guess his whereabouts; however, two fans were allowed to see him. Catherine Newcomb, 15 and Joyce Cook, 14, were both patients at the Junior League home for Crippled Children. Catherine had curvature of the spine and was confined to a stretcher while Joy had cerebral palsy; Elvis chatted with them for about 15 minutes.

Elvis, wearing black pants, black shirt, white shoes, a white scarf, a black and silver cummerbund, a black and silver sweater, a gold bracelet and gold watch, talked with reporters before his train left at 6:30 p.m. "It's not what you'd call a flashy outfit," Elvis said of his attire. "There's not any loud clothes." Addressing the question of criticism of him before he left for the Army, Elvis said, "Some of it bothered me, but there wasn't anything I could do about it. I just tried to be myself. I don't read much of what they say." Talking about his fanatical fans, Elvis said, "After five years you get used to it. If an entertainer says he wishes they'd leave him alone, I tell him to go get another job. It's the greatest compliment they can give you."

About his time in the Army, he said, "I guess it matured me in some ways, but I don't feel much different. I wasn't a complete nut before I went in."

"When I was getting started I'd beg them to let me sing for nothing," said Elvis. "It gave me a thrill. I never thought I'd get rich. It's still the same today—if I don't please the audience the money don't mean nothing. I played in Las Vegas one time and I was getting good money but I wasn't getting across to the audience. After that first night I went outside and just walked around in the dark. It was awful." He said about his singing that "It has to be natural. The audience can tell if it's faked. If I didn't feel it, I wouldn't do it."[69]

As soon as the recording session was finished, a tape of "Stuck On You" and "Fame and Fortune" was rushed to the pressing plant and RCA pressed 1.4 million copies of the single and, within 48 hours after Elvis walked out the studio's door, copies of the single were shipped to radio stations and retailers.

Colonel Parker and the RCA executives finalized the arrangements for the next session, scheduled for after the Miami trip, which would finish the album, *Elvis is Back*, scheduled to be released in mid-April, before Elvis left for Hollywood to film *G.I. Blues*.

On the train to Miami with Elvis were Joe Esposito, Lamar Fike, Gene Smith and Cliff Gleaves. The TV taping saw Elvis and Sinatra swap songs; Sinatra did "Love Me Tender" while Elvis did "Witchcraft."

In April, an article by Joe McDavid in the Nashville *Banner* appeared under the headline, "Elvis' Star on Downgrade, Or Is It Now?" In the article, the writer asks, "Is the sleepy-eyed pied piper of Rock'n'Roll a has-been? Or is he about to skyrocket to new entertainment heights?" The writer stated "the Presley magic seemed to have worn thin" because "only 35 faithful followers turned out at the train station to welcome Elvis home. Throngs no longer ringed his $100,000 'Graceland' Mansion, hoping to catch a glimpse of their hero."

The article continued: "From several quarters came predictions that 'Elvis is all washed up' or that 'he'll never be as big again as he used to be.' They said the drop in popularity of Rock'n'Roll had doomed Presley, that he'd never be able to make the grade if he switched to another style of singing."[70]

Chapter 8: April, 1960

After the TV taping for the Sinatra special, Elvis returned to Nashville, where he received a letter from Colonel Parker cautioning that "all that he had to deliver in order to fulfill his contractual obligation to RCA were eight additional tracks...he should record no more." The Colonel was always concerned that RCA not gain any leverage in future contract negotiations and the best way to do that was to limit the number of recordings that RCA held, thus putting Elvis and the Colonel in a strong position when bargaining about new releases. Parker also informed Elvis that Bienstock had cleared "Fever" at a royalty rate and requested he record "Are You Lonesome Tonight," a hit in 1927 for both Vaughn Deleath and Henry Burr which had been part of Gene Austin's performances; Austin was the first act that Parker had managed. Also, "Are You Lonesome Tonight" was a favorite song of Parker's wife, Marie. This was the only time Parker ever requested Elvis to record a song. Bienstock cleared the publishing on "Are You Lonesome Tonight" as well as "Girl Next Door Went A'Walkin,'" a song that Scotty Moore published and had agreed to the publishing stipulations of Hill and Range.[71]

RCA needed enough material to release an album so their goal for the session was to record ten songs. The album cover for *Elvis Is Back* had already been drawn up; the photographs were taken in Germany and there was a blank space for the list of songs. They had a deadline of April 5 for the album master to be completed so there was no time to waste.

On Sunday, April 3, 1960, Elvis and his buddies again rode to Nashville in a chartered bus for another recording session at the RCA Studio. At the studio were the musicians from the earlier session: Scotty Moore and Hank Garland on guitars, Bob Moore on bass, D.J. Fontana and Buddy Harman on drums, Floyd Cramer on piano and the Jordanaires on background vocals with one new addition: saxophonist Boots Randolph. Elvis played guitar on the session.

The session began at 7:30 in the evening and the first song recorded was "Fever," written by Otis Blackwell (under the pseudonym "John

Davenport") and Ed Cooley. The song was originally a R&B hit for Little Willie John, then covered by Peggy Lee, who had a top ten pop hit in 1958. Elvis' version of the song closely mirrored Peggy Lee's version; the only instrumental accompaniment on the song was the bass of Bob Moore and Buddy Harman's congas.

"Like a Baby" was the second song on the session. It was written by Jesse Stone, who wrote a number of songs for the Clovers, one of Elvis' favorite groups. Stone also wrote "Shake, Rattle and Roll" (under the pseudonym Charles Calhoun) for Big Joe Turner, who had an R&B hit with the song in 1954 (three weeks at number one) before Bill Haley and the Comets covered it that same year and had a top ten pop hit prior to their "Rock Around the Clock" hit in 1955.

The next song on the session was "It's Now or Never," which was the melody of "O Sole Mio" with new lyrics by Aaron Schroeder. Elvis told Freddy Bienstock how much he loved the Tony Martin hit "There's No Tomorrow" from 1949 and that his mother had owned a 78 of "O Sole Mio" by Caruso. Elvis recorded "O Sole Mio" on the home tape recorder he had in Germany and loved the vocal challenge the song presented. Since the melody was in the public domain, Bienstock assigned Aaron Schroeder and Wally Gold to write new lyrics for the song.[72]

As Elvis rehearsed the song with the studio musicians he struggled a bit; the song ends with a full-voiced operatic ending and Elvis had trouble with that ending. "He definitely was going to do the song all the way through," said engineer Bill Porter. "Elvis was basically a baritone singer [but] he was getting into the tenor range on that. And we had done maybe seven or eight takes on that song. I recall specifically pushing the talk-back button. I said, 'E.P., we can just do the ending; I can splice it on; save yourself the trouble." He said, 'Bill, we're gonna do it all the way through or I'm not gonna do it." So he finally did it all the way through. He liked what he did."

"There was an overdub [second generation master] on that tune, by the way," added Porter. "Floyd Cramer played the little castanets...Floyd had the idea. I took the tape off, put it on another machine and ran it back through the console, got a level on his [castanets] with the microphone.

He put headsets on, and we did it in about fifteen minutes."[73]

By the time they finished "It's Now or Never" it was midnight and they had done three masters. They took a break for some Krystal burgers and at 12:45 a.m. started the next group of songs.

"The Girl of My Best Friend" was completed in ten takes and they moved on to "Dirty, Dirty Feeling," a song written by Jerry Leiber and Mike Stoller and originally intended for the *King Creole* soundtrack; however, the song was not recorded for the soundtrack and conflicts with the Colonel kept songs by Leiber and Stoller off other Elvis sessions.[74]

"Thrill of Your Love" was written by Stan Kesler, the Memphis musician who had written "I Forgot To Remember To Forget" and "You're Right, I'm Left, She's Gone" for Elvis during his Sun sessions and also wrote "Playing For Keeps," which Elvis recorded for RCA. The song came to Elvis through Jack Clement, formerly an engineer at Sun who now worked for Chet Atkins. Elvis recorded it in three takes. "I Gotta Know" came from Freddy Bienstock. The song had recently been recorded in England by British superstar Cliff Richard. Elvis finished the song in about ten minutes. Those four songs took about three hours to record and the group then took a break.

The final group of recordings began with "Such a Night," which had been originally recorded by the Drifters. It was around four in the morning when Elvis started "Are You Lonesome Tonight?" Playing on the song were Bob Moore on bass, Buddy Harman on drums and Hank Garland on acoustic guitar. Elvis requested the lights be turned down and then "chased everybody out of the studio, all the guests and everything" so it was nearly dark when he sang the song.[75]

Engineer Bill Porter was editing "Such a Night," preparing it for the master reel while the group ran down the song, a fairly standard practice so that at the end of the session all the master takes were on one tape reel. According to Porter, "I had a lot of echo set up on the console. When I looked out in the studio, the lights were off. Steve Sholes was sitting there at the A&R position. I said, 'Mr. Sholes, I'm ready to listen.' He said 'Roll the tape, Bill.' 'But I haven't heard the song.' 'Roll the tape!' 'Yes, sir.' So I roll the tape, and I still can't see anything out there. After a few bars, I realize we don't have a lot of people playing. There's no piano, and there's no electric guitar, there's just acoustic guitar and bass and the Jordanaires. I'm turning a few mikes off to isolate things as much as I possibly can, and all of a sudden Elvis starts talking. I thought, 'Uh-oh, all this echo. That ain't too good, 'cause it sounds like he's back in a cavern somewhere. Okay, next take I know when it comes. I'll turn it down.' We do the take all the way through. The Jordanaires had made a mistake on the end–wrong chord. Started the second take, got maybe one, two lines into it, and Elvis said, 'Hold it!' and they stopped. Lights are still off in the studio. He said, 'Mr Sholes, I can't do this song justice. Throw it out.' Steve looked at me and he said, 'Don't you dare, Bill. That's a hit and I know it.' He pushed the talk-back button and he said, 'E.P., I'd like to get one good cut all the way through if you don't mind so we'll have it. Let's just do the ending, 'cause the Jordanaires made a mistake.' 'Okay.'"

"So they did just the ending, a couple of chords back, you know," said Porter. "Steve looked at me and said, 'I took it as far as I could,'" remembered Porter, "and 'to' is one side of the splice, and 'night' is on the other. 'To-night!'" Sholes told Porter, "Now, you splice that after I'm gone and send it to me tomorrow. I want you to use the original as far as you possibly can and just put the ending on it."

"If you listen to that recording on a high-quality playback system, you'll hear somebody bumping a microphone stand," said Porter. "It was Elvis because he couldn't see."[76]

After "Are You Lonesome Tonight," Elvis recorded "Girl Next Door Went A'Walking," the song he did as a favor for Scotty Moore; he finished the song in four takes then "Freddy Bienstock watched unhappily as Elvis ditched stacks of new songs he'd worked hard to get...the singer was building the session repertoire out of his own record collection."[77]

Elvis met Charlie Hodge on the ship going over to Germany; Hodge had also been drafted. Hodge was a singer; he had sung with the Foggy River Boys, a gospel group, as well as behind acts such as Red Foley and Gene Autry. Hodge owned an album by the Golden Gate Quartet, the most popular and influential of the early Jubilee quartets, that he played for Elvis. Elvis loved the group. On that album was "I Will Be Home Again" and Elvis and Hodge had sung the song as a duet back at Graceland in Memphis. Now Elvis recorded the song as a duet with Hodge.

They needed ten songs for this session and had recorded eleven. Dawn was breaking and the session musicians were tired; most had a full day's schedule of recording ahead: sessions were scheduled 10 a.m. to 1 p.m.; 2 to 5 p.m. and 6 to 10 p.m. and, since the musicians were on the Nashville "A Team," their schedules stayed pretty booked. Elvis was still ready to sing and began strumming on his Gibson J-200 and singing "Reconsider Baby," a song by Lowell Fulson that the singer had first released in 1954. Fulson was a legendary rhythm and blues performer who wrote and recorded "Come Back Baby," "Three O'Clock Blues" and "Every Day I Have The Blues," which were all recorded by B.B. King. (The last song became King's theme song.)

Elvis tried the song when he was recording at the Sun Studio but never recorded a version. Now, taking the lead with his own rhythm guitar, the rest of the musicians fell in with the piano, guitar and saxophone all taking a turn at lead. When Boots Randolph took a sax solo, this became the first sax solo on any Elvis Presley recording.[78]

At the end of the session, Porter had all the songs they recorded on one reel and Elvis "always wanted to hear 'em back before he left. They didn't make tape copies or disc copies back then; he did not take anything with him. (That changed down the road.) But 'It's Now or Never'–he had me play that at least a half dozen times, and the so-called Memphis Mafia (that's the term the media hung on 'em), which were guys like Joe Esposito, Lamar Fike, people like that, they all came in. When recording sessions were going on, these guys would be up front playing cards. They weren't back in the back watching sessions; they could care less. So when they'd hear a tune played back, they'd all run in the studio: 'Yeah, man! This is fantastic!' When Elvis asked to hear 'It's Now or Never' over and over again, they were just going crazy in the studio. They were climbing the wall and running up and down the halls and just going crazy because he liked it."[79]

The album *Elvis Is Back* contained "Make Me Know It," "Fever," "Girl Of My Best Friend," "I Will Be Home Again," "Dirty, Dirty Feeling" and "Thrill of Your Love" on side one; on side two were "Soldier Boy," "Such a Night," "It Feels So Right," "Girl Next Door Went A'Walking," "Like a Baby" and "Reconsider Baby." Four days after the session was completed, RCA shipped the album to distributors and retailers. Since no one knew which titles would be on the album, the songs were listed on a sticker placed over a blank spot on the back. Although the album was much anticipated, it did not go "Gold," selling instead 300,000 copies.

On Monday, April 18, Elvis and his entourage (Army buddies Joe Esposito and Charlie Hodge, Lamar Fike, Sonny West and Elvis' cousin Gene Smith along with Colonel Parker and his staff) caught the Southern Pacific Sunset Limited train to Hollywood, where Elvis was scheduled to film his first post-Army movie, *G.I. Blues*. Elvis began recording the movie soundtrack in Los Angeles at the RCA Studio at 6363 Sunset Boulevard but finished at Radio Recorders on Santa Monica Boulevard.

In July, RCA shipped "It's Now or Never" b/w "A Mess of Blues." The single had been delayed because Elvis did not like the mix on "It's Now or Never" after it had been mastered and insisted that RCA re-master the single. In August, Elvis began filming *Flaming Star* and recorded the soundtrack in L.A.; by the end of October the film was complete. Also in October, the album *G.I. Blues* was released and went "Gold"—selling 700,000 copies.

Elvis was still in Germany on February 1, 1960 when the first sit-in occurred at the Woolworth's lunch counter in Greensboro, North Carolina. African-American students in Nashville held their first sit-in on Saturday, February 13 at three five-and-dime stores on Fifth Avenue. The students purchased items from the stores then sat down at the lunch counters but the lunch counters were closed by the store owners; on Thursday, February 18, the students were back. On Saturday, students sat at lunch counters and one week later there were 400 African-American students sitting at lunch counters, waiting to be served. Demonstrators were arrested and bail was $5 but the students refused to pay and remained in jail.

In March, Africa-American protestors at the Greyhound Bus Station were served but badly beaten afterward. Racial unrest dominated Nashville during the Spring of 1960 when Elvis came to the RCA Studio to record, but the newspapers, for the most part, downplayed the civic unrest. On Friday, March 25, CBS reporters and camera crews came to Nashville to film the sit-ins.

On April 19, the day after Elvis left for Hollywood to film *G.I. Blues*, the home of a prominent civil rights leader, Z. Alexander Looby, was bombed. During that afternoon, 3,000 protesters marched from Fisk University to the Nashville courthouse in complete silence. On the steps of the courthouse, Mayor Ben West met the protesters and when Diane Nash, a young student, asked the Mayor, "Do you recommend that the lunch counters be desegregated?" the Mayor answered "Yes."

After this meeting, the students marched back to Fisk. The next day's *Tennessean* newspaper had a front page headline, "INTEGRATE COUNTERS-MAYOR" which was a turning point in the civil rights struggle in Nashville.

By this time, the radio airwaves were fully integrated with Chuck Berry and Fats Domino played next to Elvis and Johnny Cash. Elvis did not join in any civil rights protests and, because the studio is like an island, he was not confronted with the civil rights issues in Nashville. Elvis began his recording career at Sun 49 days after the Brown vs. Board of Education decision by the Supreme Court that declared schools would be integrated and his recording of a number of songs by African-American songwriters and artists played a role in the changing attitudes of southerners towards civil rights.

Although he was not active in Civil Rights, Elvis Presley stood at the center of the South changing its treatment of African-Americans. White southerners called early rock and roll "nigger music" and taunted early rock performers as "white niggers" but Elvis stood above that; he was never afraid to acknowledge his debt to African-American performers or his love of blues and rhythm and blues.

Chapter 9: October - December, 1960

On a Saturday afternoon in late October 29, Freddy Bienstock went to Graceland to go over songs for the gospel session scheduled the next day in Nashville. There would only be one session—which would start at 6:30 and go all night—and Bienstock wanted to make sure Hill and Range controlled the publishing on all the songs Elvis recorded. Since Elvis knew so many gospel songs, he was confident of what he wanted to record.

Bienstock had compiled a list, which included "I'll Meet You in the Morning," "If We Never Meet Again," "When You Travel All Alone," "His Hand in Mine," "Only Believe," "Mansion On the Hilltop," "Room At the Cross," "Angels In The Sky," "Milky White Way" and "Over The Moon."[80]

In addition to the gospel material, Bienstock brought "Surrender," a song by Doc Pomus and Mort Shuman that Bienstock commissioned the duo to write from a Neopolitan ballad "Torna a Surriento," which was in the Public Domain. Because "It's Now or Never" had been successful and because Elvis was headed in a new musical direction, confounding his critics who considered him "only" a rock'n'roll singer, Elvis wanted another song which allowed him to stretch artistically.[81]

On Sunday, October 30, Elvis and his buddies again rode from Memphis to Nashville in a chartered bus. Scotty Moore, D.J. Fontana and Freddy Bienstock were also in the bus when it arrived at the RCA Studio. Elvis wore "black pants, a shiny silk shirt, and a sailor's cap he fancied at the time." His left hand was bandaged because he had broken his finger during a touch football game.[82]

The musicians on the session were the same as the previous session: Hank Garland, Scotty Moore and Elvis all played guitar; Bob Moore played bass; Buddy Harman and D.J. Fontana were on drums; Floyd Cramer played piano; Boots Randolph was on saxophone; the Jordanaires—Gordon Stoker, Hoyt Hawkins, Neal Matthews and Ray Walker–were there in addition to a new addition to the Nashville sessions, Millie Kirkham, who had worked with Elvis in Los Angeles during the recording of his first Christmas album.

The first song recorded was "Milky White Way," a public domain song where Elvis is listed as "arranger," thereby guaranteeing him songwriting income from the song. Unfortunately, Elvis never received any income directly from BMI, the performance licensing organization, because Parker never allowed Elvis to sign a contract with BMI. Over the span of his career, this lack of a signature cost the singer millions of dollars. The Colonel may have objected to the fact that BMI paid songwriters directly, so the money would not go through him and therefore he could not collect a commission.

"Milky White Way" came from the black gospel tradition and Elvis' version was inspired by the Trumpeteers recording in 1947. According to Ernest Jorgensen, Elvis' "awareness of the black gospel tradition was nearly as extensive as his knowledge of the white. He always prided himself on his gospel repertoire."[83]

The next song, "His Hand in Mine" was written by Mosie Lister and originally recorded by the Statesmen, a favorite gospel group of Elvis and one of the most exciting southern gospel groups during the 1940s and 1950s. The leader of the Statesmen was Hovie Lister, who was a disc jockey who started a quartet in 1948. Lister heard that Major Howell, Chairman of the Board of the newspaper the *Atlanta Constitution* planned to start a radio station in Atlanta and requested airtime for his quartet. He received the airtime and in October 1948 the Statesmen Quartet debuted on WCON with Mosie Lister singing lead, Bobby Strickland on tenor, Bervin Kendricks on baritone and Gordon Hill on bass with Hovie playing piano. When Mosie Lister left the quartet he was replaced by Jake Hess and the group signed with Capitol Records.

Hovie Lister was drafted in the Army during the Korean conflict; at the end of his tour, he returned to the group which coalesced around a line-up of Jake Hess on lead, James "Big Chief" Wetherington on bass, Cat Freeman on tenor, and Doy Ott on baritone. The "Big Chief" was known to move his leg freely while singing and many gospel fans insist that Elvis learned his stage moves from Wetherington. For "His Hand in Mine," Charlie Hodge sang harmony with Elvis, like they had done back at Graceland.

Elvis had a number of 78s of the Statesmen and "His Hand in Mine" was on one of those old records. On the other side of that record was "I Believe in the Man in the Sky" with Jake Hess as lead singer; that was the next song he did on that session. After this the group took a short break.

Although Elvis had compiled a list of songs for Freddy Bienstock to clear for publishing and songwriting rights, once he began recording Elvis changed his mind. He had informed Bienstock that he wanted to record "When You Travel All Alone," written by Mosie Lister, but in the studio he changed his mind and decided to record "He Knows Just What I Need." Fortunately, Lister also wrote that song, so clearing the publishing was no problem. The only problem came when Charlie Hodge could not reach the highest register, so Millie Kirkham sang those notes.

The next song was a break from the gospel material. Elvis and the musicians ran down "Surrender" a couple of times but Elvis had problems with the ending, where his voice had to soar. After several blown takes, Ray Walker, the Jordanaires bass singer, "noticed he was looking kind of quizzical. So he said, 'Let's take a break guys,' and that was rare. He rarely took a break. So he came by me and said, 'Uhh, Ray, you teach voice don't you?' I said, 'Well, sometimes. What do you need?' He said, 'Well, I want to go up real high on the word 'tonight' and I know I'm not going to be able to hit it.' And I said, 'Oh, that's the hardest thing to hit if you're going to go up into that register.'"

Ray and Elvis went into the bathroom, closed the door, and Ray asked "Can you throw up?" Elvis said, "What?" Ray repeated, "Can you vomit? Can you act like you're going to vomit?" Elvis laughed and said, "What do you mean?" and Ray replied "like HUA!" Elvis said "hu" and Ray said, "No, you've got to HUA, HUA HUA like that." Elvis "tried it a couple of times but he broke up," remembered Walker. "I said, 'Look, bend over, put your hands on your knees and let's run the vowels. So we sing 'A E I O U.' When he would do it, he would get to o and go hu. I said, 'No, you've got to keep it right in your stomach.' So he did it one more time A A E E I I O O U U and I said 'put a Y U and I said, 'that's it.!'"

The session players and singers came back to the studio and "he came in and did the song, all except the ending. He did about nine or ten where he's singing 'Tuoo, toa, toua-night!' Well, he finally got the one that hit and said, 'that's it" and winked at me. So that closed it down but he said, later, 'I'll get you back for wanting me to vomit!'"[84]

Elvis wasn't the only one spending time in the bathroom during this session; engineer Bill Porter had an upset stomach, a result of food poisoning, and spent a considerable amount of time vomiting in between takes.[85]

After completing "Surrender," Elvis recorded "Mansion Over the Hilltop," a song recorded by the Blackwood Brothers and written by Ira Stamphill, which was released in 1954. The Blackwoods and the Statesmen had toured together since 1952 and in 1954 the Blackwoods won the top prize on "Ted Mack's Amateur Hour" with "Have You Talked to the Man Upstairs." A little over two weeks after the Blackwoods won on the Ted Mack Show, a plane crash took two of their members. At the memorial service at Ellis Auditorium in Memphis, Elvis, his girlfriend Dixie Locke and his parents sat at the service, just a few days before Elvis' first recording session for Sun Records.

The studio group took a break, then Elvis recorded "In My Father's House," another song recorded by the Blackwoods. The next two came from the Golden Gate Quartet, who Elvis had seen perform when he visited Paris on leave with the Army; he sang "Swing Down Sweet Chariot" with them backstage. "Joshua Fit the Battle" and "Swing Down Sweet Chariot" were both from the Jubilee tradition and were in the Public Domain so the publishing rights were no problem.

The Jordanaires had recorded "I'm Gonna Walk Dem Golden Stairs" in 1949; the song was written by Cully Holt, who was their bass singer at the time. Elvis and the group recorded the song in one take and Freddy Bienstock assumed the song was P.D. and did not ask questions about the songwriter or publishing. When Gordon Stoker called Holt to inform him that Elvis had recorded the song he told Holt to "keep quiet until the record was released to escape the co-publishing pressure from Hill & Range."[86]

After another break, the musicians and singers started the final four songs around 5 a.m. By this point, Chet Atkins had been long gone and was home asleep. The musicians were tired—and knew they had to face a full day of recording sessions—and Bill Porter was "violently ill." "Around five in the morning I said, 'Mr. Sholes, I've got to quit. I can't keep this up,'" said Porter. "'One more song, Bill, one more song. Just hang in there.' I heard that about four times."[87]

Elvis began the final group with an Albert Brumley number, "If We Never Meet Again." Brumley was one of the greatest songwriters in southern gospel; he wrote "I'll Fly Away," "Turn Your Radio On" and "I'll Meet You in the Morning"—all standards in the southern gospel tradition. "Known Only To Him" was written by Stuart Hamblen, the West Coast radio star and songwriter who also wrote "It Is No Secret (What God Can Do)" and "This Old House."

"Crying in the Chapel" was written by Artie Glenn and first recorded in 1953 by his son, Darrell Glenn. The song reached number four on the country charts and was covered by the Orioles whose version, also released in 1953, was number one on the R&B charts for five straight weeks but did not cross over to the pop charts because, at this point, black rhythm and blues groups did not receive significant radio airplay from pop stations. The Statesmen also recorded a version of the song on a custom pressing. Elvis and the group began "Crying in the Chapel" as the sun was breaking over the horizon.

It was light outside but Elvis wanted to continue so Gordon Stoker suggested "Working On The Building," a song from the black gospel tradition that the Jordanaires sang during their performances and which was one of their most popular numbers. On this song, Elvis became a member of a quartet, blending his voice in the group performance.[88]

The recording session ended at eight in the morning; during that 13 and a half hour session Elvis recorded 14 songs. The 13 gospel numbers were enough for an album.

Of the songs that Elvis had originally picked to do, he did not get around to recording "I'll Meet You in the Morning," "When You Travel All Alone" "Only Believe," "Room At the Cross," "Angels In The Sky," "Over The Moon," "You'll Never Walk Alone," "I Believe In The Man In The Sky," "Jezebel," "Jesus Is The One," "God's Gonna Cut You Down" and "Who At My Door Is Standing."[89]

The recording session was finished on Halloween morning—October 31—and RCA rushed out the album, *His Hand in Mine,* for Christmas release. The album contained 12 songs; "Crying in the Chapel" was not on the album because Elvis was not satisfied with his version.

In November, 1960, "Are You Lonesome Tonight" b/w "I Gotta Know" was released. The test pressing was rejected by Elvis, who was angry because "the New York engineers, with their usual taste for equalization and compression, had lifted his voice at the expense of the Jordanaires' and he insisted that the single be re-mastered to correct the imbalance."[90] "Are You Lonesome Tonight" reached the number one position on the *Billboard* Hot 100 chart and remained there for six consecutive weeks. "I Gotta Know" reached number 20 and the single sold two million copies in the United States.

In November, Elvis began filming *Wild In the Country*, based on the novel *The Lost Country* by J.R. Salamanca and recorded the soundtrack in Hollywood. That month, the film *G.I. Blues* opened nationally and reached number two on *Variety's* National Box Office Survey in its second week and became the fourteenth most successful film of the year based on gross revenues. In December an article appeared in the Nashville *Tennessean* titled "Movie Making With Elvis Can Be Fun." In the article reporter Pat Anderson interviewed the Jordanaires about their trip to Hollywood to work on *G.I. Blues* with Elvis.

The article noted that the group spent almost a month in Hollywood for the film but only a week in front of the camera; the rest of the time they worked on the soundtrack. The Jordanaires are on the screen, pictured in a train compartment, singing "Frankfurt Special" with Elvis. Stoker stated that "Most of the time they're not shooting Elvis likes to play around if he's in a good mood. We'll sing spirituals or maybe he'll show us some karate (a sort of thinking man's judo) he learned in Germany."

Regarding his acting, Stoker stated that "Elvis is left pretty much to his own devices. If anything, they're too complimentary. He's the biggest thing in show business, so everybody figures 'who am I to tell the guy how to act?' And after they get to know him they like him so much they don't want to hurt his feelings."

Elvis enjoyed having the Jordanaires with him on the movie set and the singer was "usually pretty cheerful unless somebody's cut him," said

Stoker. "It's funny. Some people will pull a million strings to get to meet him. They delight in trying to put him down. It bugs him."[91]

Chapter 10: 1961

On January 4, 1961 readers of the Nashville *Tennessean* saw an article that asked "if the post-war Presley would pull the record-buyers as he had in his civilian heyday." The article went on to say that every record Elvis had released since his discharge had sold over a million copies and that, because of Elvis, sales of singles "shot up 33% in 1960 over 1959."

In the article, Chet Atkins credited Elvis' success to "two things–talent and promotion. He's way above average as a singer. And even more important, he's got the smartest manager in the business–Tom Parker. If it wasn't for Col. Tom, he would have cooled down a long time ago from over-exposure." The article noted that Parker himself credits Presley, with Tom Diskin, Parker's associate, stating "Elvis makes all the decisions on records for himself. He senses what the kids want. He goes home and listens to records for hours. We don't advise him. He just gets sold on something and sings it and it sells."[92]

Elvis wasn't the only Nashville act who did well in 1960; Brenda Lee had hits with "I'm Sorry" and "I Want to be Wanted," the Everly Brothers had a hit with "Cathy's Clown," Jim Reeves hit with "He'll Have To Go" and Marty Robbins' "El Paso" was a huge crossover hit. The Nashville music community benefited from Elvis' success, too; the "A Team" of musicians played and the Jordanaires sang on his recordings that were cut in the RCA Studio at 17th and Hawkins.

Elvis was scheduled to return to Memphis for the "Memphis Charity Show" in February, after he finished filming *Wild in the Country*. For the Memphis show, held at Ellis Auditorium, Elvis had Scotty Moore, D.J. Fontana, bassist Bob Moore, drummer Buddy Harman and the Jordanaires perform with him.

That month RCA released the single "Surrender" b/w "Lonely Man" and the EP "Elvis By Request–Flaming Star" that consisted of two songs from the movie, "Flaming Star" and "Summer Kisses, Winter Tears" as well as two that had been hit singles, "It's Now or Never" and "Are You Lonesome Tonight."

Readers of the Nashville *Banner* were informed that Elvis would appear before the State Legislature at 11 a.m. on Wednesday, March 8.[93] That day Elvis drove his Rolls Royce to Nashville, accompanied by Joe Esposito, Alan Fortas and Sonny West. For the occasion, he wore a black silk suit–with a blue and black Karate pin–with a white silk shirt, black sox and black shoes.

The Governor's staff was seated around a conference table, waiting for Elvis to arrive, when the door opened and "this entity was standing in the doorway [with] this black suit on, and every hair immaculately combed. There was absolutely dead silence in the room. It was just like somebody had sucked all the air out of it." Elvis and Governor Ellington shook hands, Elvis sat at the table and chatted a few minutes, then it was time to go before the legislature. In the room was Ann Ellington, daughter of the Governor who attended Middle Tennessee State University, about 30 miles south of Nashville; she had skipped classes that day.

Elvis asked Ann, "You're going, aren't you?" and she answered that she was not scheduled to be part of the event but Elvis insisted "I need for you to go" as he took her hand and led her to the legislative chamber.[94]

In the *Banner*, Red O'Donnell noted that Elvis entered the House with pretty blonde Ann Ellington on his arm. Earlier, in the Governor's office when asked what he was doing at the State Capitol, he answered with a smile at Ann: "I came up to see the Governor's daughter" and the Governor reportedly replied, "Sis, you'd better let that Hound Dog alone!"[95]

The Nashville *Tennessean* article noted that Elvis "drew the biggest crowd that has engulfed the legislative corridors and chambers in the last 35 years" and, at a pre-appearance press conference in the Governor's office, quipped, "I'm thinking about running for the legislature, and the first bill I'll propose is to lower taxes," while grinning at Governor Buford Ellington.[96]

There were screams as Elvis entered the House chamber with women crying, squealing and trying to touch him. There were no empty seats; people were lined against the walls and the galleries were packed. He did not speak long; his opening remark drew laughter when he addressed the audience, "Governor Buford Ellington, members of the legislature–and those who skipped school. I'm not allowed to sing and not as funny as

Tennessee Ernie Ford (who had appeared and sang before the Joint Assembly the previous week), except with sideburns. I was funny with sideburns. I thought it was exciting when I got my first gold record, and it was exciting. I was making money. But this is one of the nicest things that's ever happened to me. God bless all of you as He has blessed and guided me through my career." Elvis assured the audience that Tennessee would always be his home. "People frequently want to know if I plan to settle down eventually in Hollywood," he said. "Now, I like to go out there to play (laughs) er, er, work, but my home is in Memphis, Tennessee and that's where it's going to be."[97]

Governor Ellington made Elvis an honorary Colonel and announced, "Colonel Tom Parker is no longer the number one Tennessee Colonel, from now on, it's Colonel Presley" as he handed Elvis his colonel's certificate.

House-Senate Joint Resolution No. 52 praised Elvis for his record sales of 75 million and his Army service. Reporters noted that Elvis sat in the Governor's chair, banged the gavel, and observed that he had a gold telephone similar to Ellington's. He had his arm around Ann as he stated he wanted to be a serious dramatic actor and said of his Rolls Royce that he'd had for six months, "It's smooth, no rattles or bumps. They don't tell you the horsepower. Just guarantee it for three years and tell you to enjoy it. So I am." Ann—wearing a "fur-collared white leather coat over a bright citron yellow sweater and skirt"–and his three buddies drove to the Governor's mansion where Elvis sat in the Governor's private office and checked out the music room.[98]

It was noted that Colonel Tom was in Hawaii attending to details for Presley's next movie and for a charity show he would give there. It was also announced that the Jordanaires would appear at the State Legislature the next week.[99]

On his way back to Memphis from Nashville, Elvis stopped at the Tennessee State Prison where he met with Johnny Bragg, a member of The Prisonaires, inmates at the Tennessee State Prison who formed a singing group and recorded their hit, "Just Walking in the Rain" at Sam Phillip's studio. Bragg wrote "Just Walking in the Rain" and Elvis may have dropped by the studio during one of their recording sessions.

There had been a lockdown because of a recent near-riot so Bragg was in his cell when a guard informed him the warden wanted to see him. In the courtyard, with the warden and another state official was Elvis with three members of his entourage, some state policemen and some prison guards.

When Bragg saw Elvis he said, "Presley! What are you doin' in these parts?"

Elvis responded, "Heard you had some trouble. Thought I'd drop by, kinda check up on you."

Moving over to a wall, about fifty feet away from the others, Elvis reportedly told Bragg he wanted to get him an attorney but Bragg said he already had a lawyer—though he appreciated the gesture. Apparently, Elvis told him, "I know you're a proud man, Johnny, but I'll bet my lawyers can help shorten your time."

Bragg replied, "Only God and the Governor could do that." Elvis then said, "Well, let me do something for you, Johnny. Do you need any money?"

"No, everythin' is fine right now," said Bragg, who told Elvis that the Governor "is helpin' me and his daddy's gonna help me."

Elvis then told Bragg, "Well, you know, I'm planning on recording 'Just Walkin' in the Rain.' That'll help some more royalties come in." Bragg replied, "Presley, you don't have to do that. Me and you's good friends, we go way back to when you were a kid in Memphis. I'm fine. You look after Presley. Hell, I sing as much as you and spend a lot less."[100]

Finally, the two shook hands and Elvis left.

Elvis really did love "Just Walkin' In The Rain" and his friends remember him singing it at home or when he was relaxed; however, Elvis never recorded the song.

On Saturday evening, March 11—three days after his appearance before the Tennessee Legislature—Elvis came back into Nashville and visited Ann Ellington at the Governor's mansion. The two talked during the evening in the downstairs living room then, around 2 a.m., the police sergeant on duty knocked on the door and said, "Miss Ann, the Governor's just called down and says he thinks it's time for the gentleman to go." Elvis invited her to his session the following evening, then left. After he was gone, the patrolman admitted that her father had actually said, "It's time for the Hound Dog to go."[101]

At six on Sunday evening in the RCA studio, with musicians Hank Garland and Scotty Moore on guitars; Bob Moore on bass; Buddy Harman and D.J. Fontana on drums; Floyd Cramer on piano, Boots Randolph on sax and the Jordanaires (Gordon Stoker, Hoyt Hawkins, Neal Matthews and Ray Walker) with Millie Kirkham supplying background vocals the session began. Steve Sholes and Chet Atkins oversaw the recording with Sholes the producer and Bill Porter the engineer.

The session started with "I'm Comin' Home," a record released on Sun by Carl Mann which was produced by Sam Phillips; it was written by Charlie Rich. Chet Atkins never liked the all night sessions with Elvis because he had to be at work early in the morning and regularly produced sessions during the "normal" times of 10 a.m. to 1 p.m. and 2 to 5 p.m. so, after the session was up and running, he left.

"Gently" came from England; the British office of Hill and Range had submitted it. "In Your Arms," by Aaron Schroeder and Wally Gold, was done in two takes and "Give Me the Right," by Fred Wise and Norman Blagman, was also done in two takes.

Starting at 9:30, after a thirty minute break, they recorded four songs: "I Feel So Bad," which had been a hit by Chuck Willis in 1954, then "It's a Sin," an Eddy Arnold hit from 1947 that held the number one position on the country charts for five weeks. Elvis saw Arnold perform that song with the Jordanaires at Ellis Auditorium in 1954 when he first met Arnold and the group and told the Jordanaires he wanted them to back him on records.

"I Want You With Me" was a Woody Harris rocker that Elvis, who met Bobby Darin in Las Vegas, learned from Darin's album, *For Teenagers Only*.[102]

The group began the final four songs at 1:45 in the morning after a forty-five minute break. "Sentimental Me" was a cover of an Ames Brothers hit from 1949. "Judy" was a cover of a recording by Teddy Redell on Atco in 1960 and Elvis played acoustic guitar on this song. "There's Always Me" was written by Don Robertson, who had written "I'm Counting On You" for Elvis' first RCA session in January, 1956. Robertson had fallen out of favor with producer Steve Sholes when he submitted a song for Elvis' second session but then withdrew it, saving it for his own recording career. However, in the ensuing years Robertson had written

"Please Help Me I'm Falling," a hit for Hank Locklin on RCA, as well as other hits.

When he got to "There's Always Me," Elvis announced, "This is my song."[103]

The final song of the evening was "Put the Blame On Me." This was a fast session for Elvis; he completed a master almost every hour and the songs were mixed well with covers of rock'n'roll songs along with original ballads.

During the evening, he played "Can't Help Falling In Love" for Ann Ellington; he planned to record it the next week in Los Angeles for the *Blue Hawaii* soundtrack.

During the time that Elvis was in the studio, he had four hubcaps stolen from his 1961 Cadillac, which was parked near the RCA Studio while he was inside singing. Two witnesses told police they saw some people get out of a car and remove the hubcaps. The next day two of the four missing hubcaps were discovered hanging on a teen-age girl's bedroom wall. According to police, the girl's boyfriend reported he obtained the hubcaps from "some other boys." Elvis did not want to prosecute the two and police said they would mail the hubcaps to him in Memphis.[104]

Eight days later, Elvis began work on *Blue Hawaii* in Los Angeles. After recording songs for the soundtrack that week, Elvis flew to Honolulu on the evening of Saturday, the twenty-fifth, with Nashville musicians Hank Garland, Bob Moore, Floyd Cramer, Boots Randolph and the Jordanaires joining long time band mates Scotty Moore and D.J. Fontana and performed a show that raised money to build a memorial over the U.S.S. Arizona, lying on the bottom of Pearl Harbor with sailors entombed. Also accompanying him on the trip was Grand Ole Opry comedienne Minnie Pearl.

On April 20 the film crew returned to Hollywood to complete the filming of *Blue Hawaii* and in May the single "I Feel So Bad" b/w "Wild in the Country" was shipped. In June, the movie *Wild in the Country* opened nationally and that same month the album *Something for Everybody* was released.

On Sunday, June 25, 1961, Elvis arrived in Nashville at the RCA Studio for an all night recording session. The first song on that session was "Kiss Me Quick," written by Doc Pomus and Mort Shuman. The song had a Latin feel with the mandolin part replicated by Scotty Moore on guitar. The second song was "That's Someone You Never Forget," a song that Red West wrote after Elvis gave him the title.[105]

Red West had never been successful at getting Hill and Range interested in his songs or himself as a songwriter. Elvis had never recorded one of his songs, but he had managed to have several other singers, including Pat Boone and Johnny Burnett, record his songs and had released some singles on his own label.[106] The title, "That's Someone You Never Forget" came from Elvis and biographer Peter Guralnick notes that "Elvis might be singing of his mother, an ambiguity that Red encouraged by the lack of specificity in his writing."[107]

At one in the morning, after a short break, Elvis recorded "I'm Yours" by Don Robertson, a song that had been rejected for the *Blue Hawaii* soundtrack. The song was good—Elvis sang harmony with himself on the recording—and Colonel Parker wanted to hold it for another movie but Elvis decided not to wait. On piano for this song was Gordon Stoker of the Jordanaires, who began his professional career as a piano player for a gospel quartet; Floyd Cramer played organ.

The next two songs came from Hill and Range's staff songwriters Doc Pomus and Mort Shuman. They were hot songwriters so Snuff Garrett, head of A&R for Liberty Records flew them to Hollywood to write songs for his artists on Liberty Records. The duo stayed at the Roosevelt Hotel on Hollywood Boulevard and wrote two songs in their hotel room: "(Marie's the Name) His Latest Flame" and "Little Sister." Garrett was disappointed when he heard Pomus and Shuman play them; they didn't seem to fit any of his artists. Pomus and Shuman played the songs for Bobby Vee who turned them down; finally, they arranged for Bobby Darin to record them. Darin recorded several takes of each of the songs before giving up; he couldn't capture either song on record. The Darin recordings were the demos that Pomus and Shuman brought back to New York. Bienstock included the two songs in a stack of acetates he brought to the RCA Studio for Elvis to listen to. Elvis listened and was immediately attracted to the songs and began working them up with the session musicians. For "Little Sister," Elvis slowed down the tempo from the demo and made it an all-out rocker.

According to Mort Shuman, "When I wrote 'Little Sister,' I played it in a totally different way. It had a different rhythm. Elvis cut the tempo in half and slowed it down."[108] During the session Elvis called Shuman and asked how he had gotten the piano sound. Elvis also called Pomus but "thinking it was a prank, Doc grumbled some bleary-eyed answers into the receiver, not realizing who the caller had been until the following morning."[109] Doc Pomus and Mort Shuman never met Elvis; the only time they spoke to the singer was during that middle-of-the-night phone call.

"(Marie's The Name) His Latest Flame" "was like a party. 'It's a good song, I like it,' Elvis ventured, 'even if it takes us thirty-two hours.'"

Hank Garland had an agreement with Gibson to play only Gibson guitars; however, he needed a different sound on "Marie's the Name" so he borrowed Harold Bradley's Fender Jazz Master guitar for the electric lead. The fourth take was the master but "Elvis and the group were all so excited they played the song over and over until 7:30 in the morning."[110]

On July 1, 1961, Red West married Pat Boyd, Elvis' blond 19-year-old secretary. Elvis was supposed to be best man at the wedding but was late, so Joe Esposito served in that role. The next day, Elvis was back in Nashville for more sessions, this time for the movie soundtrack for a picture tentatively titled *Pioneer Go Home*, which was later changed to *Follow That Dream*. The producer on the session was Hans Salter while Bill Porter was the engineer.

The first four songs recorded that evening were for the movie soundtrack: "Angel," the title song "Follow That Dream" (written by Fred Wise and Ben Weisman), "What A Wonderful Life" and "I'm Not the Marrying Kind." Those four songs, along with "A Whistling Tune" and "Sound Advice" were all recorded in the three hour stretch between seven and ten p.m. The last two songs were not included on the soundtrack because Elvis did not like "Sound Advice" and the producers dropped "A Whistling Tune."

After the session, which ended at 10 p.m.—early for an Elvis recording session–he checked into the Anchor Motel on West End Avenue before he returned to Memphis.

Between July 11 and August 11, filming was done for *Follow That Dream* in Florida. The film crew then went to Hollywood to finish the picture. In August, RCA Victor released "(Marie's the Name) His Latest Flame" b/w "Little Sister." The songs were both strong so airplay was split; "Little Sister" entered the *Billboard* Hot 100 chart on August 21 and reached number five while "Marie's the Name" entered the *Billboard* Hot 100 chart a week later and reached number four. Those songs stayed on the charts for three months. If they had been released as separate singles, each would undoubtedly have reached number one.

In September, Elvis spent time in Las Vegas, then returned to Memphis before going to Nashville on Sunday, October 15 for a recording session at the RCA Studio. Because of the filming schedules for his movies, it was difficult for Elvis to get into the studio to record singles for RCA Victor. The session was scheduled so Elvis could meet his contractual obligations with the label.

Freddy Bienstock had to come up with songs so he turned to proven hit makers Doc Pomus and Mort Shuman. Mort Shuman was aware that Elvis was drawn to first person songs, which led to the idea of "Night Rider." Freddy sent it to Elvis with four other songs: "Just For Old Time Sake," "For the Millionth and the Last Time," "Ecstasy" and "You Never Talked to Me."[111]

Hank Garland had been seriously injured in a car accident in September; he spent a week in a coma and never regained his career. Replacing him on guitar was Jerry Kennedy, who admitted "I was nervous" as he sat in the studio, waiting for Elvis, "but he made me feel comfortable when he came in."[112] Kennedy and Scotty Moore played guitars on that session.

For the first song on the session, "For The Millionth And the Last Time," Gordon Stoker played accordion. This was followed by "Good Luck Charm" and "Anything That's Part of You," then the musicians took a break and finished with "I Met Her Today" and "Night Rider." After the session, Elvis returned to Memphis then, on Saturday left for Los Angeles, driving out with his entourage in several cars. On Monday Elvis reported to the film studio to begin filming *Kid Galahad* and recorded songs for the soundtrack.

That same month—October—the album *Blue Hawaii* was released; it became his most commercially successful album. On Wednesday, October 22, the film opened nationally and reached number two on *Variety's* "National Box Office Survey." This was the most commercially successful film Elvis ever did and became one of the top grossing movies in both 1961 and 1962. In November the single "Can't Help Falling In Love" b/w "Rock-A-Hula Baby" from the *Blue Hawaii* soundtrack was shipped to retailers by RCA Victor.

Elvis was in Las Vegas from the end of December, 1961 until the end of January, primarily because he was uncomfortable living at Graceland with his father and step-mother; however, at the end of 1961, Vernon and Dee Presley, with her three sons, moved to a nearby home.

Chapter 11: 1962 - 1963

From January 30 until Sunday, March 17, 1962 Elvis was in Memphis; during that period the single "Good Luck Charm" b/w "Anything That's Part of You" was released by RCA Victor. On Sunday, March 18, Elvis arrived in Nashville at the RCA Studio for an all night recording session. The Hill and Range publishing group faced a major challenge because of the volume of recording activity for the movies as well as singles and albums. RCA needed ten more songs for their singles and album releases, as well as songs for 13 scenes in the *Girls! Girls! Girls!* movie.

The musicians for Elvis' Nashville sessions tended to remain a small group, although on this session guitarists Grady Martin and Harold Bradley replaced Jerry Kennedy.

The session began with "Something Blue," then "Gonna Get Back Home," "(Such An) Easy Question," "Fountain of Love," "Just For Old Time Sake" and another version of "Night Rider," which no one was satisfied with from the previous session; unfortunately, this second shot at "Night Rider" did not come off either.

Because of the problem with finding songs where Hill and Range could obtain publishing, Elvis, Charlie Hodge and Red West began listening to public domain songs. The trio decided to use the melody to Cole Porter's "Begin the Beguine" and write new lyrics; that song became "You'll Be Gone." The song had developed during informal jam sessions over a year. Bienstock quickly found out that Porter was not willing to make deals with his publishing so it looked like the song would be discarded until Charlie Hodge substituted some chords which created an entirely new melody which could be copyrighted under their names. According to Ernest Jorgensen, this was "the only song in which Elvis was ever seriously involved as a writer." "You'll Be Gone" was recorded in the early morning hours, then Elvis checked into the Anchor Motel on West End Avenue to rest before returning the next evening.

The session the next evening began with "I Feel That I've Known You Forever" then a Leiber-Stoller song, "Just Tell Her Jim Said Hello."

That song had been recorded previously but had never been a hit; the musicians attempted it with a number of different tempos before settling on the sixth take.[113]

When they cut "Suspicion" everyone agreed that it sounded like a hit. "She's Not You" showed Elvis with an incredibly honey sweet smooth voice. That made ten songs Elvis recorded that evening, which meant he had recorded exactly half of what his RCA contract required him to record in 1962. It was becoming increasingly difficult to schedule these non-soundtrack recordings in a schedule that was dominated with making films and doing soundtracks, which were more lucrative than the RCA sides. Elvis and the Colonel, through their arrangement with Hill and Range, were guaranteed publishing on all of the soundtrack songs. Because of this business arrangement, "The Colonel increasingly saw these non-soundtrack sessions as a waste of time, a diversion from their principal business of making movies," according to author Peter Guralnick.[114] The publicity generated by the movies meant the soundtrack albums sold and the money guarantees from the films meant there was no reason to record anything other than songs for the soundtrack albums, according to the Colonel's logic.

The RCA recording sessions had gone from being a thrill to a chore. RCA executives Steve Sholes and Bob Bullock spent their time trying to arrange and cajole Elvis and the Colonel into doing the sessions; Freddie Bienstock was immersed in making sure all the songs recorded had publishing deals so the Hill and Range group could collect royalties and Elvis' buddies, with the exception of Red, Charlie and Lamar Fike, found the time spent in the studio a bore with nothing to do until Elvis finished.

"Sometimes studio players sensed what they took to be almost a soul weariness on Elvis' part, an acceptance of things as they were which, while it never compromised his professionalism, led to a numbing sense of defeat," observed Peter Guralnick. He quoted Gordon Stoker, who stated "He always tried to make the best out of any situation. Sometimes he'd walk over to us [at the sound track session] and say, 'Man, what do we do with a piece of shit like this?' Sometimes he'd back up so far from the microphone that they would say, 'Elvis, you've just got to get closer to the mike'; they'd put a soundboard around him just to try to pick him up. But most of the time he would console himself with the idea of, 'Well, regardless of what I say, [they're] going to demand that I do this song, so I'll just do the best I can.'"[115]

At the end of the evening, there were dubs made of "Just Tell Her Jim Said Hello" and "You'll Be Gone" for Elvis, the Colonel and Freddy Bienstock, who felt that would be the next single.

On Tuesday, March 20, Elvis and his group left Memphis for Los Angeles in his new Dodge motor home. On the following Monday he reported to the movie studio to begin work on his new picture, *Girls! Girls! Girls!* and recorded the soundtrack in Los Angeles. In addition to the L.A. studio musicians, Scotty Moore, D.J. Fontana, Boots Randolph and The Jordanaires came from Nashville for the sessions

In April, the EP "Follow That Dream" was released; in May the movie *Follow That Dream* opened nationally and in June, after filming for *Girls! Girls! Girls!* was complete, the album *Pot Luck* shipped. In July, the single "She's Not You" b/w "Just Tell Her Jim Said Hello" shipped and in August the EP "Kid Galahad" was released, followed by the movie's national release the next day. At the end of August, Elvis began work on *It Happened At the World's Fair,*" with location shooting in Seattle in September and sessions for the soundtrack held at Radio Recorders in Los Angeles.

In October, the single "Return to Sender" b/w "Where Do You Come From" was released and in November Elvis finished work on *It Happened At the World's Fair*; that same day the album *Girls! Girls! Girls!* was released followed by the film, *Girls! Girls! Girls!"* which opened nationally.

In January, 1963, Elvis began work on his next picture, *Fun in Acapulco* and did the soundtrack recording in Los Angeles at Radio Recorders. The single "One Broken Heart For Sale" b/w "They Remind Me Too Much of You" was released and in March Elvis finished his work on *Fun in Acapulco*.

On Wednesday, April 10, *It Happened at the World's Fair* opened nationally and later that month the album *It Happened at the World's Fair* soundtrack was released, priced at $4.98 for the monaural version and $5.98 for stereo.

On March 13 one of Elvis' employees, Richard Davis, backed out of Elvis' driveway in the Bel Air section of Los Angeles and ran over the gardener, Harvey Henslin; in May, Henslin's widow, Leona Henslin, sued Elvis for $501,400 in damages in Santa Monica Superior Court.[116]

By this time, a young teenager had moved into Graceland. Elvis met Priscilla Beaulieu while he was stationed in Germany; Priscilla's father, an Army officer, allowed Priscilla to visit Elvis in Los Angeles for two weeks in June, 1961. Priscilla then returned to her family in Germany but Elvis convinced the Beaulieu family to allow Priscilla to live in Memphis at Graceland during her senior year in high school. Priscilla arrived at Graceland in March, 1963.

On May 26 Elvis returned to Nashville and the RCA Studio for a full night of recording that lasted from 6:30 that evening until 5:30 the following morning. Scotty Moore, Harold Bradley and Grady Martin all played on that first night and the majority of songs came from the demos Freddy Bienstock brought in from Hill and Range.

The first song was "Echoes of Love" for the *Kissin' Cousins* soundtrack, then "Please Don't Drag that String Around," which was written by Otis Blackwell and sounded a lot like two other songs he wrote that Elvis recorded: "Return to Sender" and "One Broken Heart For Sale." Next came "(You're the) Devil in Disguise" with Grady Martin on lead electric guitar.

Those were followed by "Never Ending," "What Now, What Next, Where To," and "Witchcraft," which was written by Dave Bartholomew, the songwriter and producer behind Fats Domino, with co-writer P. King. This song had been an R&B hit by the Spiders in 1966. The session finished with Elvis recording "Finders Keepers, Losers Weepers" and "Love Me Tonight."

The next evening, guitarists Scotty Moore and Harold Bradley were joined by Jerry Kennedy, who replaced Grady Martin at 10 p.m. The session began with a Chuck Berry song that Elvis loved, "Memphis," followed by "(It's a) Long Lonely Highway," "Ask Me" and "Western Union," which was a re-write of "Return to Sender."

In Los Angeles the core group of studio musicians were known as

"The Wrecking Crew." Members of that group—guitarists James Burton, Tommy Tedesco and Glen Campbell, bassist Carol Kaye, pianist Leon Russell and drummer Hal Blaine—played behind singer P.J. Proby on the demo for "Slowly But Surely," which Elvis recorded as Jerry Kennedy played fuzz tone guitar. The final song on the session was "Blue River," but Elvis never finished the song.

Elvis chose his own singles and picked "You're The Devil in Disguise" b/w "Please Don't Drag That String Around," which was released by RCA in June.

In early July, Elvis went to Hollywood and began production for *Viva Las Vegas*, co-starring Ann Margaret and recorded the soundtrack at Radio Recorders with Nashville musicians Scotty Moore on guitar, Bob Moore on bass, D.J. Fontana on drums, Floyd Cramer on piano, Boots Randolph on sax and The Jordanaires joining the L.A. musicians. In August, RCA Victor released the album *Elvis Golden Records Vol. 3.*

The soundtracks for Elvis' movies were usually recorded in Los Angeles; however, the soundtrack recordings for *Kissin' Cousins* were recorded in Nashville at the RCA Studio because both the film and soundtrack sessions for *Viva Las Vegas* ran over budget, which reduced the amount of money for Elvis and The Colonel. This led Colonel Parker to decide that *Kissin' Cousins* would be a low-budget film—the first that Elvis did—and filming took only four weeks.

The Nashville sessions were set for September 29 and 30 with Gene Nelson and Fred Karger, the musical directors for MGM, serving as producers while RCA engineer Bill Porter manned the board.

On the session were Scotty Moore, Grady Martin, Jerry Kennedy and Harold Bradley on guitars; Bob Moore on bass; D.J. Fontana and Buddy Harman on drums; Boots Randolph and Bill Justis on sax; Cecil Brower on fiddle with the vocal background provided by the Jordanaires along with Millie Kirkham, Winnie Brest and Dolores Edgin.

Elvis had a cold so the musicians only laid down the tracks to the songs; Elvis recorded his vocals later in Los Angeles. Elvis played a double role in the movie so the title song had to be recorded as a duet with himself. On the first evening, the musicians recorded "There's Gold

In the Mountains," "One Boy, Two Little Girls," "Once Is Enough," "Tender Feeling" and "Kissin' Cousins No. 2." During the second night the musicians recorded "Smokey Mountain Boy," "Catchin' On Fast," "Barefoot Ballad," "Anyone (Could Fall In Love With You)" and "Kissin' Cousins." Interestingly, Boots Randolph played "jug" and Harold Bradley played banjo on "Barefoot Ballad" while Jerry Kennedy played banjo on "Smokey Mountain Boy."

On October 19 Elvis recorded his vocals for the soundtrack in Los Angeles; filming for *Kissin' Cousins* began on October 14 and finished on November 14. In October, the single "Bossa Nova Baby" b/w "Witchcraft" was shipped. "Memphis, Tennessee" was intended to be the "B" side but Elvis was not satisfied with his recording, so the song was held back. In November, the album and film, *Fun in Acapulco* was released.

In December, readers of the Nashville *Banner* saw the headline "Cuban Elvises Get Army Duty" and discovered that Army head Raul Castro "warned Cuban students that if they begin emulating the long-haired, hip-twitching crooner, they would be inducted into the army immediately." Cuba had just instituted is first peacetime draft for men 17 to 44.[117]

Elvis spent Christmas, 1963 at Graceland.

Chapter 12: 1964 - 1965

On Sunday, January 12, 1964 Elvis rode his motorcycle from Memphis to Nashville, arriving at the RCA Studio around 6:30 and immediately ordered food to be brought in. For the next three hours, Elvis and the musicians ate and chatted, then at 9:30 they began recording.

Elvis wanted to re-record two songs: "Memphis, Tennessee" and "Ask Me" because he felt he could do a better job. He recorded those two songs as well as the ballad "It Hurts Me," then left the studio at midnight. There was little talking, clowning around or long breaks—it was an all-business session. Producing the session was Chet Atkins; this was the last session where Chet sat in the producer's chair for Elvis. The two never really got along, dating back to their first session when Elvis requested The Jordanaires and Chet hired one Jordanaire—Gordon Stoker–and two members of the Speer Family for the back-up group. Chet disliked the all night sessions that Elvis did; Chet was head of the Nashville office of RCA and had to be at work the next morning. Elvis sensed that Chet had no enthusiasm for working with him. Each was great at what he did, but there was no chemistry when they worked together.

Elvis did not know this at the time, but he would not return to Nashville's RCA Studio for a recording session for two years and four months.

During 1963 Music Row grew; manager, booking agent and publisher Hubert Long built an office for Capitol Records at 806 16th Avenue South, next door to the Quonset Hut and Columbia Records, which had purchased the house and Quonset Hut from Owen Bradley in 1962, established their headquarters at that building under the leadership of Don Law. In 1963 Columbia spent $650,000 on additions and re-modeling of the building and studio.

After the Nashville session, Elvis spent time in Las Vegas, relaxing and catching shows. In February the single, "Kissin' Cousins" b/w "It Hurts Me" was released.

In early March, Elvis began work on the soundtrack and film, *Roustabout* and *Kissin' Cousins* opened nationally, followed by the soundtrack, which was released in April. Singer Terry Stafford had covered "Suspicion" from Elvis' *Pot Luck* album and his single entered the *Billboard* Hot 100 chart, which led RCA to release Elvis' version of "Suspicion" b/w "Kiss Me Quick." Two weeks later RCA released "What'd I Say" b/w "Viva Las Vegas." With four singles competing for radio airplay, "Kiss Me Quick" only got to number 34, "Suspicion" did not chart, "What'd I Say" reached number 21 and "Viva Las Vegas" peaked at number 29 on the *Billboard* Hot 100 Chart. Terry Stafford's version of "Suspicion" reached the number two position on *Billboard's* Hot 100 Chart.

By mid-May, Elvis had finished work on *Roustabout* and in early June began work on *Girl Happy*, with soundtrack recording again done at Radio Recorders. On Wednesday, June 17, *Viva Las Vegas* opened nationally.

The beginning of the British Invasion came in 1964, led by the Beatles, who appeared on "The Ed Sullivan Show" in February and then dominated the singles charts. In theaters *Viva Las Vegas* did better than the Beatles' first movie, *A Hard Day's Night* at the box office; *Viva Las Vegas* peaked at number 14 in *Variety's* National Box Office Survey and became Elvis' highest grossing film with $5.5 million in revenues.

In July, the single "Such a Night" b/w "Never Ending" shipped; "Such a Night" was originally released on the 1960 album *Elvis is Back*, his first album after his discharge from the Army. In September, RCA shipped the single "Ask Me" b/w "Ain't That Loving You Baby" after Elvis' plan to release "Memphis, Tennessee" as a single was thwarted when Johnny Rivers released his version of "Memphis," which he originally heard as a guest at Graceland. The "B" side, "Ain't That Loving You, Baby," had been recorded in 1958 but had never been released.

In October, the album *Roustabout* was released; the album reached number one on the *Billboard* album chart, replacing *The Beach Boys In Concert* album, but then dropped out of that slot as the *Beatles '65* album hit number one.

In early October, Elvis began work on the movie *Tickle Me*, which was originally titled *Isle of Paradise*. In November, RCA Victor released "Blue Christmas" b/w "Wooden Heart"; "Blue Christmas" came from Elvis' 1957 Christmas album while "Wooden Heart" came from the soundtrack to *G.I. Blues.* Joe Dowell had covered "Wooden Heart," which he recorded in Nashville in 1961 and had a number one single on the country chart. On Wednesday, November 11 the film *Roustabout*" opened nationally; at the end of November, Elvis finished work on *Tickle Me* and drove back to Memphis, where he spent Christmas and New Years.

During 1964, RCA built and moved into a new, much larger office building located next to their small studio. The new building had a much larger studio, which became known as "Studio A" and the smaller studio, where Elvis recorded, became known as "Studio B." Many of the RCA artists preferred to record in the new, larger studio, but Elvis remained loyal to "B," where he was most comfortable.

That year, Roger Miller was the hottest country act out of Nashville with his hits "Dang Me" and "Chug-A-Lug" but the hottest act in country music was Buck Owens out of Bakersfield, California. Nashville-based Johnny Cash, Marty Robbins, Stonewall Jackson, Jim Reeves and Connie Smith all recorded hits in Nashville studios—either the Quonset Hut or RCA Studio B.

Both RCA Victor and Columbia built new studios in Nashville during the 1960s, a city with a population of about 200,000 in the city proper. The performance rights organization BMI, which collects money for songwriters and publishers, moved into their newly constructed building about a block north of the Quonset Hut. There were ten recording studios, 26 record companies, 700 songwriters, 265 music publishers, and a thousand musicians in the local union. Nashville was the third busiest recording center, behind New York and Los Angeles and ahead of Chicago.[118]

The popularity of country music was credited to the "Nashville Sound," which used violins instead of fiddles for a smoother, more pop-oriented sound that evolved in contrast to the whining steel guitars and traditional honky tonk sound that dominated earlier country music and was still prominent on the records by Buck Owens coming out of Bakersfield.

Chet Atkins, head of RCA's office in Nashville and Owen Bradley, head of Decca's country division were credited as the architects and producers of the "Nashville Sound."

On the pop charts, Roy Orbison's "Oh, Pretty Woman" came out of a Nashville studio but the British and Motown sounds dominated the pop world in 1964.

Elvis turned 30 on January 8, 1965 and celebrated quietly at Graceland. Elvis' next movie was *Harum Scarum* and, at the last minute, it was decided to record the soundtrack at the RCA Studio in Nashville. Because many of the musicians who regularly recorded with Elvis were booked, some new faces were in the studio when Elvis arrived on February 24.

Producers for the session were Fred Karger and Gene Nelson from MGM. On guitar was Scotty Moore, joined by Grady Martin and Charlie McCoy—who had never played on an Elvis session. Two other newcomers were Henry Strzelecki on bass and Kenny Buttrey on drums. D.J. Fontana also played drums while Floyd Cramer was on piano and the Jordanaires provided background vocals. Jordanaire Hoyt Hawkins added tambourine and, because the soundtrack needed a "Middle Eastern" feel, Rufus Long played flute, Ralph Strobel played oboe and Gene Nelson played congas.

Elvis worked on the first song, "Shake That Tambourine" for four hours—until 3:30 in the morning—before calling it quits. The next day's session yielded five songs: "So Close, Yet So Far (From Paradise)," "My Desert Serenade," "Wisdom of the Ages," "Kismet" and "Hey Little Girl." On the third session, held on February 26, there were five songs recorded: "Golden Coins," "Animal Instinct," "Harem Holiday," "Go East, Young Man" and "Mirage."

The single "Do the Clam" b/w "You'll Be Gone" was shipped in February; "Do The Clam" came from the movie *Girl Happy*. In March, the album *Girl Happy* was released and Elvis began work on *Harum Scarum* while *Girl Happy* opened nationally on April 7. The day before, the single "Crying in the Chapel" b/w "I Believe In the Man in the Sky" was released–scheduled just before Easter. "Crying in the Chapel had been recorded in 1960 during the gospel sessions that produced the *His Hand in Mine* album but had never been released.

In mid-May, Elvis began work on the film and soundtrack for *Frankie and Johnny*, which was a re-make of the 1938 film starring Helen Morgan. The single "(Such An) Easy Question" b/w "It Feels So Right" was shipped. "(Such An) Easy Question" was originally recorded for the *Pot*

Luck album while "It Feels So Right" came from the *Elvis is Back* album.

In June, the EP "Tickle Me" was released, which contained five cuts; it did not chart. On July 7, *Tickle Me* opened nationally and the next month Elvis began work on the soundtrack and film *Paradise Hawaiian Style;* on Thursday, August 5, Elvis, his entourage and the film crew flew to Hawaii for location shooting; he returned to California two weeks later.

In August, the single "I'm Yours" b/w "(It's a) Long Lonely Highway" was shipped; the album *Elvis For Everyone* was also shipped that month. On Friday, August 27, the Beatles visited Elvis at his home on Perugia Way in Las Angeles. There were no cameras or recorders to document the event and it was the only meeting of these two giant acts of rock'n'roll. The musicians reportedly chatted and jammed a bit during their visit and John Lennon encouraged Elvis to record more rock records.

In September, 1965 readers of the Nashville *Banner* saw an article by Bob Battle which informed the world that no longer would clippings from the singer's hair be sent to fans. Elvis' personal hair stylist, Larry Geller, had clipped Elvis' hair every week, then sent 100 of these "hairs" to the Colonel, who sold them to fans for 25 cents a strand. However, the Colonel refused to send drops of Elvis' blood to fans who requested them. Geller continued to clip Elvis' hair then "sweeps up the cuttings and throws them out."[119]

In early October, filming for *Paradise Hawaiian Style* was completed and Elvis returned to Memphis. That month the single "Puppet on a String" b/w "Wooden Heart" was released–five years after the *G.I. Blues* soundtrack had been released that contained those songs. "Wooden Heart" had already appeared on the "B" side of another single a year previously. Another single, "Santa Claus is Back in Town" b/w "Blue Christmas" shipped in October; both of those recordings were on the 1957 album *Elvis' Christmas Album* and "Blue Christmas" had been released on the "A" side of a single the previous Christmas.

In November, *Harum Scarum* opened nationally and the soundtrack– without a single–was also released. In December, the single "Tell Me Why" b/w "Blue River" was shipped; "Tell Me Why" had been recorded eight years before but had never been released. This made seven singles, one EP and three albums released in 1965.

Elvis spent Christmas and New Year's in Memphis. Early the next year, on January 19, 1966 reporter Bob Battle informed readers of the Nashville *Banner* that Elvis, "one of the richest young men in the world," had received a race car set from Priscilla Beaulieu, who lived at Graceland, for Christmas. The set, which cost $100, had a circular race track and several electrical cars. The reporter noted that Elvis did not hit the night clubs or circulate amongst the Hollywood social set; instead, he went to L.A. to do his films, then headed back to Memphis when they were finished. According to the reporter, Elvis enjoyed small dinner parties and his "eating habits are simple. I prefer steak, vegetables and fresh fruits."

The article stated that Elvis neither smoked nor drank, reads "a lot" and "listens to the recordings of all popular stars, some of whom are among his friends." Colonel Parker noted that "more than 100,000,000 copies of Presley records have been sold throughout the world" and that "he's still selling 'em by the millions for RCA." The Colonel pointed out that Elvis gave $100,000 to charities during Christmas, including "a $5,000 check to the United Service Organizations for use at the four USO clubs for American soldiers in Saigon." Parker was quoted saying "That boy has devoted the past 10 years to one course–setting an example for other young people to follow. There can be no question about it. In this, he has been as successful as in his entertainment endeavors."[120]

Nashville's Music Row continued to grow. During 1965 there was an addition of 14,250 square feet to the building at 806 16th Avenue South that housed Capitol Records; the new addition, which housed 21 suites, was occupied by Hubert Long's company. Next door, Columbia Records added onto their structure so that, when both were finished, they sat within inches of each other. The Country Music Association, whose offices were at 801 16th Avenue South, announced plans to raise $300,000 to build offices, a museum and a Country Music Hall of Fame.

Chapter 13: January - May, 1966

In February, RCA Victor released two singles on Elvis: "Joshua Fit the Battle" b/w "Known Only to Him" and "Milky White Way" b/w "Swing Down Sweet Chariot." Unfortunately, neither single charted.

Elvis began work on *Spinout* in February, with soundtrack work in Los Angeles at Radio Recorders, and Scotty Moore, Bob Moore, D.J. Fontana, Buddy Harman, Floyd Cramer, Boots Randolph and the Jordanaires continued to travel to Hollywood for the sessions. The single, "Frankie and Johnny" b/w "Please Don't Stop Loving Me" was released in March and the soundtrack and film *Frankie and Johnny* was also released that month.

Elvis and his "Memphis Mafia" left Los Angeles for Memphis on the weekend of April 16 and arrived at Graceland the following Saturday. The RCA contract required that Elvis record a new album, two singles of new songs and a Christmas single. Since "Crying In The Chapel" had been a big hit—it reached number three on the *Billboard* Hot 100 in the midst of the British Invasion and was also a major hit in England—RCA wanted a gospel album to capitalize on this. During their time in California, Elvis, Charlie Hodge and Red West had gathered material. Red and Charlie recorded songs on tape—both religious and non-religious–for Elvis to listen to.

Elvis had grown fascinated with Peter, Paul and Mary and listened to their albums, *Peter, Paul and Mary in Concert* and *See What Tomorrow Brings* as well as *Odetta Sings Dylan*. Elvis enjoyed singing Dylan's "Blowin' In The Wind" around the house, although he disliked Dylan's voice and politics. At home, Elvis often quipped, "My mouth feels like Bob Dylan's been sleeping in it."[121]

As they drove from Los Angeles to Memphis, Elvis, Charlie and Red sang and listened to tapes of songs that Charlie and Red had compiled. Elvis spent most of April and May in Memphis and reconnected with music, ready to record again. He let Tom Diskin and Freddy Bienstock know that he wanted to cut "Down in the Alley," an old hit by the Clovers, and "I'll Remember You" by Hawaiian songwriter Kui Lee. Elvis liked the soul ballad, "My Special Prayer," so Bienstock worked on securing a publishing deal.[122]

Elvis knew a lot of gospel songs and made a long list of those he was interested in recording, which included "Lord, I Need You Again Today" by the Statesmen, "Room At The Cross" by the Blackwood Brothers, "Wasted Years" by Stuart Hamblen, "He" by Roy Hamilton, "Don't Knock" by the Staple Singers, and "You Better Run" and "Run On" by the Golden Gate Quartet. The gospel list continued to grow: "How Great Thou Art," "Walk That Lonesome Valley," "Where No One Stands Alone," "By and By," and Thomas A. Dorsey's "I'll Tell It Where I Go." Red West had written two songs, "He Lifted Me" and "If Every Day Was Like Christmas" that were on the list, and Lamar Fike, who worked in the Nashville office of Hill and Range, sent "Indescribably Blue," written by Darrell Glenn, whose father, Artie Glenn, wrote "Crying In The Chapel" but Elvis dismissed the songs that Freddy Bienstock sent from the staff writers in New York.

There were other songs that Elvis liked: "Fools Rush In," which had been a hit for Brook Benton, Etta James and Rick Nelson; "I Will Be True"; "Love Is A Many Splendored Thing," which was a hit in 1955 for the Four Aces; and the 1963 hit by Sunny & The Sunliners that Jackie Wilson often performed, "Rags to Riches."[123]

The decision was made to book three nights of sessions—May 25, 26 and 27—at the RCA Studio in Nashville, in case Elvis felt inspired to record more. Parker's assistant, Tom Diskin, made the arrangements but ran into some complications. The Nashville "A Team" members stayed busy and booked, so The Jordanaires and Floyd Cramer had to miss the first three hours on the second night and no one was able to locate gospel bass singer Jimmy Jones, who Elvis had requested for the sessions.

As it turned out, the same line-up of musicians was not available for three nights in a row. Initially booked were Scotty Moore, Grady Martin, and Chip Young on guitars, Bob Moore on bass, Charlie McCoy on guitar, bass and harmonica, Buddy Harman and D.J. Fontana on drums, Floyd Cramer on piano, Henry Slaughter on piano and organ, Pete Drake on steel guitar, Boots Randolph and Rufus Long on saxophone. However, Bob Moore was not available on the third night, so Henry Strzelecki played bass that evening. Guitarist Jerry Kennedy joined on the second night when Charlie McCoy had to miss and Henry Slaughter could not be there on the twenty-eighth. On the second night, David Briggs played piano and organ while Ray Stevens played trumpet on the third night.

There was even a problem with engineers; Jim Malloy engineered the first two nights, then Al Pachucki manned the board on the third night.

Elvis wanted a big choir sound so, in addition to the Jordanaires, Millie Kirkham, June Page and Dolores Edgin were hired. There were even changes within the Jordanaires; Joe Babcock had replaced Hoyt Hawkins. Since the Jordanaires could not be there on the third night, he needed another gospel group. RCA had built a new, large office building with a studio on 17th Avenue South, next to their small studio, and the Imperials had offices in that building; Chet's secretary Mary Lynch knew them and booked them for the third night. Elvis certainly knew of the Imperials—one of his musical heroes, Jake Hess, founded the group and was their lead singer.

Felton Jarvis had been hired as a staff producer for RCA after he carved a career cutting pop and R&B hits. Felton had served in the Marines and, after his discharge, recorded "Don't Knock Elvis," an Elvis imitation record, then wrote songs for Bill Lowery's companies in Atlanta, which nurtured the talents of Joe South, Ray Stevens, Jerry Reed, Mac Davis and Freddy Weller. In 1961 he produced a hit on Gladys Knight and the Pips, which led to an A&R position at ABC Records where he produced the pop hit "Sheila" on Tommy Roe. In 1963 Felton moved to Nashville to open ABC's office. In 1965 Chet Atkins hired him as a staff A&R man for RCA and Felton produced Willie Nelson, Mickey Newbury, Jim Ed Brown, Floyd Cramer and Cortelia Clark.

With the Elvis sessions only a few days away, Chet Atkins came into Felton's office and told Felton he thought he would make a good producer for Elvis. Chet "just said, 'I'm going to carry you over, and maybe you all will hit it off.' And so we did," said Felton.[124]

On Wednesday morning, May 25, Elvis and his entourage left Graceland in a chartered Greyhound bus for the RCA Studio in Nashville; he had not been in that studio in almost two and a half years. When Elvis arrived at the studio around eight that evening, he was introduced to Felton Jarvis and the two began to talk. It was obvious that Elvis "was taken with the hopped-up, almost hyperactive enthusiasm of this skinny young producer—it was a hell of a relief after Chet's damned indifference... Elvis couldn't get enough of hearing about Felton's experiences with Fats Domino, and Lamar, who hung out with Felton and his friends on a semi-regular basis, goaded Felton to reveal more of himself."[125]

Biographer Peter Guralnick wrote that the two discussed "the sound of the records that Elvis had been putting out lately...Felton was well aware that 'for a while before I started working with him, what they were doing was turning the band way down and Elvis way up, and it sounded like–it was just bad...What Elvis wanted, he explained to Felton, was the kind of sound the Beatles and some of the other English bands were getting; it was a hotter sound; it jumped out at you, you got the sense that something was really happening...it became clear almost immediately that they would become not only friends but musical allies...Chet recognized just as quickly that the two of them had hit it off and went home before a note was struck."[126]

After gathering around the piano and singing gospel songs with the assembled singers for awhile, telling stories, and laughing until about ten that evening, Elvis finally got down to recording the first song, "Run On," which had been made famous by the Golden Gate Quartet. The next song was "How Great Thou Art," which had become a standard through the performances by George Beverly Shea on the Billy Graham Crusades. Elvis did not learn the song from the Shea performances or recordings; Charlie Hodge made a copy of the Sons of the Pioneers version on the song. Tim Spencer, a founding member of the Sons of the Pioneers, was the American publisher of the song, which had originally come from Sweden and was translated into English by a missionary, Stuart K. Hine before George Beverly Shea received a copy of the sheet music in London when Billy Graham was conducting a Crusade there. Elvis was also aware of the song because the Statesmen had recorded it.

Elvis learned the song with Charlie and Red and instructed the singers on how he wanted their parts to go. The musicians did not rehearse the song much before they recorded it and Elvis gave a dramatic rendering. Jake Hess observed that "Elvis was one of those individuals, when he sang a song, he just seemed to live every word of it...he had that certain something that everyone searches for all during their lifetime. You know, he sang a lot with his eyes closed, and I think the reason for that was because he [wanted] to have a picture in his mind at all times; if something was distracting him to where he couldn't put his heart into what he was doing, he would close his eyes, so he could get that picture of what he was talking about. That's the reason he communicated with the audience so well."[127]

This was the first session that Jerry Shilling, a new member of the 'Memphis Mafia' saw and he observed that "by the time of the "How Great Thou Art" sessions, most of the other guys had sat through dozens of recording sessions, and some of the mystique of Elvis in the studio had worn off for them. As on the movie sets, a lot of the guys that came with Elvis would spend some time watching and listening, but also spent a fair amount of time playing cards. Red and Charlie, though, were often very active participants in the studio sessions. They could speak the language of the Memphis guys as well as the language of the session players, and they worked as a pair of very critical bridges between the groups. Elvis made the final calls musically, but Red and Charlie were both talented and comfortable enough to offer musical input as well as moral support."[128]

When he sang "How Great Thou Art" that evening, Shilling stated that he "watched as Elvis delivered a transcendent performance while belting out the track...All the showmanship of his stage performances just dropped away—it was just voice and microphone—but you could see in the intensity of his expressions that this one was coming straight from the soul. When he got to the dramatic finish of the song, there was a strange hush in the room–nobody wanted to break the spell....I've never seen a performer undergo the kind of physical transition he did during that recording. He got to the end of the take and he was as white as a ghost, thoroughly exhausted, and in a kind of trance. He was on, and everybody in the studio knew it."

When the song was finished, "Elvis was hunched over, almost down on his knees. He seemed shaken—like he'd been touched by a little of what he had been searching for in his spiritual readings. He happened to look up...and a beautiful smile spread across his face."[129]

The next song, "Stand By Me," came from the black gospel tradition and Elvis requested the lights be dimmed in the studio, then found he could not read the lyrics in the dark and started to leave the song but Felton Jarvis encouraged him to keep working on it and they finished the song in eleven takes. This cut was followed by "Where No One Stands Alone," which had been recorded by the Statesmen and the Ink Spots.

At four in the morning, they recorded an old Clovers' hit, "Down In The Alley," written by Jesse Stone; they recorded it in nine takes. After this song, the Imperials left and Elvis tackled the Bob Dylan song, "Tomorrow Is a Long Time" that he had heard on the *Odetta Sings Dylan* album. Scotty Moore, Chip Young and Charlie McCoy all played acoustic guitars on this song while Bob Moore moved from upright to electric bass. A tambourine was the only other instrument on this five minute track they recorded in three takes.[130]

After the session ended, Elvis and Felton sat and talked about the all-night gospel sings both had attended. They talked until the business day began and the secretaries started coming in; at that point, Felton drove Elvis back to his motel.[131]

The next evening, Floyd Cramer had another session from 6 to 10 p.m. so David Briggs, a 23-year old piano player who had been in Nashville a year, was called to sub for Floyd. Since Elvis rarely started recording before 10 p.m., Briggs thought he'd just sit around and wait until Floyd arrived; Cramer was booked on a Bill Anderson session at Bradley's Barn. However, Elvis was ready to roll soon after he arrived and wanted to start the session with "Love Letters," a former pop hit for Big Band singer Dick Haymes and a song that needed a strong piano. Briggs stated "I was scared to death. I mean, I had done a Beatles tour with Tommy Roe, but Elvis was something else. And then he wants the piano pulled up in front of him. He had all the lights turned out, put candles on the piano so he could see the lyrics, and he made everybody lay out except the bass player and D.J. on drums and Buddy Harman on tympani, I think. He had the piano moved up so he could be right on top of it—there was just that six-foot piano between us; man, it was a pretty tense situation."

They ran the song down and just as they were ready to turn on the tape to record, Floyd Cramer came in. David got up from the piano to give Floyd his seat and, as Floyd ran through the song, Elvis requested Briggs to return to the piano because "he had gotten used to the way I was doing the song. That's just the way Elvis was. If he got used to something, and if he liked you, then you were just better than the next guy, even though you might not be a tenth as good. So—now talk about pressure. Not only was it Elvis, it was Floyd, who was probably the number-one keyboard player in town, sitting behind me on organ and laughing because he didn't give a shit; he'd been working all day and was sick of it...I probably had knots coming out of the back of my neck."

After nine takes, the song was done.[132]

Now it was past midnight but Elvis wanted to get back to gospel so the next song was "So High," a song that had been recorded by the Harmonizing Four with bass singer Jimmy Jones. Elvis was disappointed that no one in his organization had been able for find Jones but he used Jones' arrangement of the song. "Farther Along" was an old gospel standard that had also been recorded by the Harmonizing Four and once again Elvis used Jones' arrangements. Elvis continued with the Jubilee sound with "By and By" with Pete Drake playing a fuzz-tone steel guitar.

It only took one take for Elvis to record "In The Garden," a song all the musicians knew well and Elvis had sung his entire life.

At the completion of "In the Garden" it was six in the morning but Elvis, Red and Charlie gathered to harmonize on "Beyond the Reef," a song they had often sung together. Elvis played piano on this number while Bob Moore played bass and Pete Drake played steel guitar. Bing Crosby had made the Hawaiian song popular in 1950 and it was on the "B" side of one of his records. That completed their second evening of recording and it had proven quite productive; they had gotten 12 masters on tape.

On the third night of recording, Elvis started with "Somebody Bigger Than You and I," a song that had been done by a number of gospel groups but Elvis favored the version by Jimmy Jones and the Harmonizing Four.

Their first run throughs of the song were in a key that was a little too low for Elvis—it was the key Jimmy Jones sang it—so they had to raise it a notch. It took 16 takes before Elvis was satisfied with his performance.

"His music meant everything to him, and when it came to creating something he really cared about, he put himself into it completely," observed Jerry Shilling. "He picked the material. He worked out the arrangements. He went through all kinds of back and forth with the session players to work out all the subtleties of their parts. He brain stormed with his new producer, Felton Jarvis, over the general sound and setup for each track…[and] when he sang he was at his most open and exposed. His singing was at the core of who he was, and to perform as well as he wanted to, he had to feel some creative spark and a degree of inspiration. That spark couldn't always be tightly scheduled. I learned that studio hang-out time was crucial to Elvis' getting into the right frame of mind. The studio was always part social club and part sanctuary for him, and whenever he was there, that's exactly where he wanted to be. He loved spending time with the musicians, and enjoyed talking shop with them. There'd be laughing and talking and story telling between Elvis and his players–his way of taking the pressure out of the situation."[133]

When Elvis recorded in the studio, one song led to another and he often left the playlist that had been compiled and sang whatever struck his fancy or, in some cases, searched for a song that was compatible with his mood. After "Somebody Bigger Than You and I," Elvis searched for a song that appealed to him but none of those on his planned list—or any of the demos Freddy brought—fit the bill. The group sang the Hank Williams song "I Saw the Light" as they tried out different songs and then Elvis asked those around him for suggestions. A relatively new song, "Without Him," written by Mylon LeFevre and recorded by the Statesmen, was suggested and Elvis liked the idea but did not know the lyrics, so Jake Hess walked over to the Imperials office in the next building and got the sheet music. In 14 takes it was done.

Henry Slaughter, the piano player for the Imperials, had written "If The Lord Wasn't Walking By My Side" and they recorded that next, with Jake Hess' vocal prominent in the mix. It was four in the morning but

Elvis was on a roll. Next came "Where Could I Go But To The Lord," a song recorded by the Statesmen and Jimmy Jones' group that Elvis often sang with his father. It was recorded in a bluesy, soulful tempo. It was done in two takes.

At five in the morning, "My Special Prayer" was next on the list but Elvis was tired and elected to call it a night. That ended the third day of recording and gave them 22 songs, but RCA wanted songs to release as pop singles as well as a Christmas single. And so a fourth night of recording was scheduled, which caused problems with the musicians, who had scheduled other sessions.

The Imperials could not be at the studio on the fourth night; they were booked on a Canadian tour, engineer Jim Malloy had to leave and was replaced by Al Pachucki, Bob Moore had to leave so Henry Strzelecki took over on bass, and Ray Stevens, Felton's brother in law, joined the group on trumpet.

The first song that evening was "Come What May," which was paired with "Love Letters" for a single. "Come What May" had been an R&B release for Clyde McPhatter in 1958 and Jerry Lee Lewis recorded the song in the Sun Studio. On the eighth take, they had the song on tape. Next up was the Drifter's hit, "Fools Fall in Love" and, after that, Charlie McCoy and Boots Randolph left for previous commitments. Ray Edenton came in to play rhythm guitar and Sandy Posey replaced one of the female singers as Elvis prepared to record a Christmas song but, before they gave the Christmas song a try, Elvis announced he was tired and that another session would have to be scheduled. Elvis thought that "Love Letters" and "Come What May" could be a single so he asked the engineer to make a dub of those two songs on lacquer.

Less than two weeks later—on June 10—Elvis was back in Nashville but, instead of driving in, Elvis and his entourage flew in.

"Elvis decided he wanted to start flying, right before we went to Nashville," said Marty Lacker, who quoted Elvis as saying 'I don't want to take a bus. I want to fly up there, and I want to fly up there real quick."

Lacker was "surprised because up until then, he was really afraid to fly. And he got airsick, too. Even the few times we'd fly to L.A. he'd throw up. He always had to have two barf bags in his seat." Lacker told Elvis "we don't have any reservations, and we don't know the flights" but Elvis instructed him to "see if you can get Kemmons Wilson's Lear jet." Wilson, the Chairman of Holiday Inn, had founded the chain which was headquartered in Memphis. Lacker called and got the Holiday Inn jet "and from Memphis to Nashville, all a Lear jet does is go straight up and come straight down," said Lacker, who told Elvis "I'm not going on a Lear jet" because he'd never been on a private plane.

Elvis got to Nashville but he did not come to the studio. He sent word that he had a "bad cold" but, according to insiders, that wasn't the whole story. According to Marty Lacker, "Elvis was in a pissy mood. So he faked one of his illnesses. Said his voice was hurting. But nothing was really wrong."

Elvis told Lacker the he wanted him and Red "to handle the session," instructing them to "be sure they do what I wanted them to do because we talked about how he wanted the songs laid out. He liked the high part that Millie Kirkham, the background singer, did on this particular song, and it really did give the song a fantastic effect." Lacker noted that Red "could almost sound like Elvis."

Marty Lacker and Red West went to the studio to record the tracks and Lacker noted that "at first, the musicians were a little ticked that Elvis wasn't there. But Red did a really great job of putting this together."[134]

Meanwhile, Elvis stayed at the Albert Pick, a rather run-down motel and Jerry Shilling kept him company. Shilling noted that "it could sometimes be considered hazardous duty to be sitting up with a moody Elvis." Shilling described his room as nothing special but "as usual, tin foil was up on the windows to keep it dark, and Elvis had the air-conditioning turned up so high it felt like a meat locker. His mood was about as dark and cold as the surroundings. I did what I could to keep him distracted and comfortable, and between ordering some food and watching some TV, I tried to keep the conversation light and minimal."[135]

The session began at 10 a.m. with Red singing "Indescribably Blue," then the Hawaiian song "I'll Remember You" and, finally, the Christmas song that Red wrote, "If Every Day Was Like Christmas." Red remembered that it may have been "a bad throat, an excess of pills or even surreptitious advice from the Colonel" that caused Elvis to avoid the studio. "I was a nervous wreck," remembered Red, "and I'm in there singing 'Indescribably Blue,' 'I'll Remember You,' and [my song] 'If Every Day Was Like Christmas.' And he's calling every hour and half, two hours, and saying 'How's it going? How's it going?' And after we finished the third, he said, 'Come on, bring what you got, that's it.' We were going to do a lot more, but we did those three, and that was the end of it.'"[136]

According to Jerry Shilling, a tape of the songs was made and Red and Charlie Hodge (Shilling did not mention Lacker) took it back to the hotel. Shilling remembered that "there was a knock at the motel door, and I let in Red, who was carrying a small tape machine. He asked if Elvis wanted to hear the results of the evening's work there, and Elvis gave him a not very enthusiastic O.K. Red played the tape of the three tracks, with and without his scratch vocals…[and] for the first time that night, I saw Elvis' expression warm, and he let himself relax. He sat cross-legged on his bed, nodding along with the rhythm, mouthing the words and getting lost in the music."

After the tape finished, Elvis said, "That's it, man, that's it," and then "he wanted to make some music." Red "hooked up the machine's dinky little microphone and flipped a few switches so that Elvis could hear one channel while recording into the other, said Shilling. "Elvis plumped up the pillows behind him on the bed, got himself settled against the back-board, pulled the little tape machine close, and set the mike out in front of him. Then he started playing the backing track. And he started singing."

"Sitting there in his pajamas at the Albert Pick Motel, with a battery-powered tape player in front of him, Elvis nailed it," remembered Shilling. "But his vocal performance was almost the polar opposite of what I'd heard him do in the studio. This time, the music came out of him so easily, as naturally as breath. I sat there on the foot of the bed as Elvis moved from the song's almost whispered, confessional opening to its heartbroken crescendo, and then back down to its trembling finale. With his eyes shut, singing out of that little plastic mike with calm and tenderness, he casually, quietly packed everything he loved about singing into the two and a half minutes of 'Indescribably Blue.' I think, for him, the Albert Pick Motel just disappeared. He didn't know where he was, and he didn't care. He let himself get lost in that song."[137]

According to Marty Lacker, whose version of that evening is a bit different, there were acetates cut at the studio, which he and Red took back to the motel where Elvis "had a stereo set up in his room so he could listen to them." Lacker and West left the acetates with Elvis and that afternoon, when Elvis got up, "we went in his room, and he was playing the dubs, and he said, 'Boy that sounds good. I'll probably go to the studio tonight.' However, in talking with Elvis, Lacker "mentioned that the studio guys weren't too happy about Red and me coming over and telling them what he wanted done."

Elvis then flew into a rage and said, "What do you mean you told them? Who the fuck do you think you are telling those guys how to do it?," adding "you've got a lot of nerve doing that" and "I don't want anybody going with me tonight except Red. The rest of you guys just stay back here at the motel!"[138]

Still, Elvis did not come to the studio on the second night either and, although Felton Jarvis wanted to record some more songs with Elvis, he had to wait until the third night when Elvis came in and, in about thirty minutes, recorded the vocals for "Indescribably Blue," "I'll Remember You" and "If Every Day Was Like Christmas," then left for Memphis with acetates of the three songs.

According to Marty Lacker, when Elvis arrived back at the motel he "was all peaches and cream. He came in and said, 'What's going on?' We said, 'Nothing. We've been playing cards.'" Elvis told Lacker "I want you on that Lear jet in the morning" so the next day, Elvis and Lacker sat across the aisle from each other and Elvis "just smiled and smiled." Elvis was "thrilled to be on that jet. And when we landed, Priscilla and the wives were there, and Elvis spent another hour taking people for rides. He was fascinated by it. That's when he got in his mind that he wanted his own plane."[139]

It was rare for Elvis to write letters or notes but, after he returned to Memphis, he sent Felton a note that read, "Dear Felton, Please convey how much I deeply appreciate the cooperation and consideration shown to me and my associates during my last two trips to Nashville. I would like to thank you, the engineers, musicians, singers and everyone connected with the sessions. Please see that every one of them know my feelings. And as General McArthur once said, 'I shall return.'"[140]

Chapter 14: June - December, 1966

In June, 1966, the single "Love Letters" b/w "Come What May" and the album *Paradise Hawaiian Style* were shipped to retailers. On Sunday, June 26, Elvis went back to Los Angeles and began work on his next movie, *Double Trouble*. The soundtrack recording was done at Radio Recorders with Nashville musicians Scotty Moore, Charlie McCoy, Bob Moore, D.J. Fontana, Buddy Harman, Floyd Cramer, Pete Drake, Boots Randolph, and The Jordanaires.

In July, Elvis' movie *Paradise Hawaiian Style* opened nationally and in early September, Elvis finished work on *Double Trouble* and a week later the single "Spinout" b/w "All That I Am" was shipped. The album *Spinout* was released in October while the movie opened in November. At the end of September, Elvis began work on his next movie, *Easy Come, Easy Go* where he played a Navy frogman; he finished his work on that film in mid-October.

In October, readers of the Nashville *Banner* were treated to three long stories on Elvis by reporter Bob Battle. Battle was in Hollywood because Paramount Pictures ran a contest for newsmen to obtain a small cameo role in the movie *Teacher's Pet*, which starred Clark Gable, Doris Day, Gig Young, Mamie Van Doren, and Nick Adams; Bob Battle won that role.

Battle contacted Colonel Parker to see if he could obtain an interview with Elvis and one day at lunch in the commissary, Battle sat with Elvis, Colonel Parker and Clark Gable and chatted. Also in the commissary eating near by were Doris Day and Mamie Van Doren. That chat at lunch resulted in the three part series published in the *Banner*.[141]

Battle reported that Elvis "has never changed," adding that if the studio required Elvis to be on the lot at 8 a.m. Elvis and "his boys" would drive through the East Gate at MGM at 7:30.

Battle observed that "surrounding Elvis as friends and employees are former classmates, childhood friends and Army buddies, many now married with their own families but still loyal to the entertainer. His fairness, respect for the skills of others and his rapport with people have prompted this nucleus of old friends to stand by Elvis through good times and bad. They have enjoyed his success as much as Elvis' real family."

Battle stated that "Elvis prefers to eat in his dressing-room on the set. This gives him time to rest and prepare for the afternoon scenes. He is notable for being well prepared, another indication of the sense of responsibility instilled in him as a child."

Battle quoted Shelly Fabares, his leading lady on *Spinout*, who stated that Elvis "is so pleasant and well-mannered that his attitude spreads to everyone. It makes a lot of difference." "He awes us all," continued Shelley. "He's always the perfect gentleman and so thoughtful of every little thing."

Actress Deborah Walley, who also appeared in *Spinout*, said, "Actors work under real tensions, but when Elvis relaxes, he's so amusing he relaxes everyone else. We all love to gather around and listen to him talk. He has a wonderful, spontaneous sense of humor."

Actress Diane McBain added, "I've never seen anyone work so hard. He is constantly striving for perfection and so constantly that we feel guilty if we don't match his efforts. Everyone prepares a little harder just to keep up with him."

The reporter compared Elvis to Clark Gable, stating both had an "open door" policy on the movie set. Between takes, Battle noted that Elvis sat with friends and fellow workers who all "know him as a pleasant, likable young man who is a perfectionist in every sense of the world."

Norman Taurog, director of *Spinout*, stated that "Not many realize that Elvis selects every song he records. He works actively at his career. He senses what is best for him and feels he owes his fans the best he can deliver." Battle added that "Not only does Elvis select all his own material, but he is in full control at recording sessions and the musicians know it. They've worked with him long enough to realize his creativity. He improves all he touches. He communicates with the various members of the orchestra and can in an instant, in a glance, transfer his thoughts on a certain passage."

Taurog continued, "To a God-given gift he adds hours of hard work. He is constantly striving to improve himself. His reading covers a wide range of subjects, books on music theory, medical research, psychology, mechanics, good fiction, you name it." During the filming, said Taurog, "Sometimes he'll make suggestions on the set, or say he'd be more comfortable doing something another way. Most of the time he's right, but he never insists. He has a respect for other people's judgment and experience. If he's wrong, I just tell him and that's that. But most important, he is the nicest guy you'll ever meet, a real gentleman. We're the best of friends, yet, on the set I am always 'Sir'. His parents raised him well and he is, most certainly, a picture of the Southern gentleman."

Taurog concluded, "I sincerely feel that Elvis has yet to realize his great potential as an artist. He has surprised us all with his amazing talent and with what he has accomplished. I predict he has even more surprises in store."

"He has an astounding core of inner-strength," reported Battle. "He's got what all women love in a man. He's gentle, yet strong. Behind the glamorous show figure, however, is an Elvis that only his close friends really know." Battle added that Elvis "doesn't drink or smoke" and "shuns gourmet dishes in favor of the simple foods he's preferred since childhood." Battle reported that Elvis "works our regularly by playing hectic football with his Memphis clan" and "his buddies know the man capable of concentrating 100 per cent on the immediate challenge, whether sports or music."

Battle noted that Elvis has an "easy going" relationship with the film crew and is an "inveterate TV watcher and reader." As for dating, Battle stated that Elvis does not make his dates "public events" and that his dates are often with "unknowns" and quoted Elvis saying that what he did on a date with a girl was "not really anything different than I'd do if not on a date. I'd sooner go out and get a hamburger or go to a movie than go into a nightclub."

When asked about marriage, Elvis stated the girl "would have to like Memphis."

"Elvis is a man who shares his success, not only with family and friends but also with people he has never met," wrote Battle. "His mammoth contributions to charity are well-known despite attempts to keep such activities personal and unpublicized. He has contributed more than generously to such funds as the Motion Picture Relief and the Motion Picture Home. In

1961 he made a benefit appearance in Memphis which raised $50,000 for 49 Memphis charities and one charity in Tupelo." He had not appeared at a benefit since but annually makes the same contribution to these charities.

"In the final analysis," reported Battle, "Elvis likes people as much as they like him. Presley is admittedly grateful for the magnanimous way life has treated him and he has but one unfulfilled ambition. As a child he wanted to become a doctor and to this day he reads and collects books on medicine."

The reporter stated that Elvis was a "Master Showman" who had ten "unexcelled years of motion pictures and looks forward to a future every bit as bright," adding that during the next two years Elvis is contracted to do eight more films and had just signed a new, long-term contract with RCA.

Elvis received over 15,000 letters a week, according to Battle, and "in a newspaper poll conducted in London querying readers about whom in the world they would most like to meet, Queen Elizabeth and Prince Phillip ranked first and second, and Elvis Presley third!"

Battle concluded his article saying "While other stars flicker out, Elvis shines on brighter than ever, stronger with every picture and every recording. Elvis' type of electricity is fused to a talent that recharges itself with each performance. Long may he perform."[142]

In his next article in the *Banner*, Battle recounted Elvis' career in movies, stating "Each of Presley's pictures have been resounding hits at the box-office, an individual star record unequalled in the annals of film-making." Battle noted that there were 44 gold records hanging on the walls at Graceland and that Elvis "is the highest paid artist in the history of show business and those who should know, namely RCA Records, declare he has one of the most heard voices in the history of mankind."

Although these were impressive achievements, Battle stated that "the most remarkable element in the Presley story is Elvis himself, a boy from humble beginnings who became famous before he reached the age of 30 and through all of the adulation and sudden stardom has managed to remain strictly himself. He dresses well, lives handsomely but otherwise has retained the sincerity, polite manner and almost shy public demeanor he exhibited when first arriving on the Hollywood scene. He has always possessed a fine balance between artistic sensitivity and athletic zest."

Battle then told the story of Elvis' birth and growing up in Tupelo, where his mother, Gladys, "a devout Christian woman, who encouraged Elvis to join the church choir and who, on Sunday mornings, would sit in the family pew hearing her son's voice above all the others" as she demonstrated the "great devotion that existed between parents and son."

Battle talked about the entry into the talent contest in Tupelo, his first guitar and then the family's move to Memphis, where Elvis entered Humes High School and "quickly became a favorite and took to entertaining his chums with the guitar during the lunch hour. He also won praise for his singing at school assemblies and a senior variety program."

Battle concluded his article by noting Elvis' jobs at Loew's theater and recording his first record as "a birthday gift for his mother" at Sun Studio where he came to the attention of Sam and Judd Phillips.[143]

The following day, the Nashville *Banner* published Battle's third and final article about Elvis. The article began with an overview of Elvis' early Hollywood movies, his success as a recording artist but noted that "From the beginning, Elvis considered the most wonderful part of his success was the things it made possible for him to do for his father and mother, to make up in some measure, for those years in which they had so little."

The article stated that for Gladys Presley, the success of Elvis created problems. "Accustomed to a quiet life she found it trying to accept the new excitement, the lack of privacy, fans at the doorway, strangers invading their home," wrote Battle, who stated "Things were better when the family moved to Graceland."

Battle reported that when Elvis was drafted into the Army he "gave a firm no to Special Service" and instead reported to regular boot camp where "his native charm, good manners and hard work quickly won him the admiration and respect of fellow GIs."

The death of Gladys Presley was covered and Battle stated that a week before her death Elvis told a reporter "I enjoy having my family around. I don't look at it as a 'must' duty, something I ought to do. I love them, I like them and I enjoy having them with me. They can't be replaced. They are all I really have in the world."

"Presley's two year absence from show business could have been a body blow to his career," observed Battle, but in Europe "his magnetic personality won him new and enthusiastic fans and in America there was no lag in either his popularity or his record sales."

Battle concluded his third article by noting Elvis' success in movies, personal appearances and recordings after the Army.[144]

In November, the single "If Every Day Was Like Christmas" b/w "How Would You Like To Be" was shipped; however, those songs never charted.

Elvis spent Christmas at Graceland where, on Christmas Eve, he proposed to Priscilla Beaulieu, who had been living there for several years.

Chapter 15: 1967 - 1969

On January 10, 1967, the single "Indescribably Blue" b/w "Fools Fall in Love" was shipped, the third single to come out of the Nashville sessions from the previous year.

In December and January, Elvis fell in love with horses and bought a number of them for riding. He also bought a 160-acre "ranch" near Walls, Mississippi, about ten miles south of Graceland, where he kept his horses. Named "Twinkletown Farm," Elvis changed the name to the "Circle G" (for Graceland).

Elvis did not want to report to Hollywood for his next movie, *Clambake*, and delayed his departure as long as he could, remaining at his ranch in Mississippi. Finally, with time running out, the decision was made to record the soundtrack in Nashville at the RCA Studio. Elvis rented a Learjet and flew to Nashville for the session.

On February 21, MGM's Jeff Alexander and RCA's Felton Jarvis were both in the control room with engineer Jim Malloy. Musicians on the session were Scotty Moore and Chip Young on guitars, Charlie McCoy on guitar and harmonica, Bob Moore on bass, Buddy Harman and D.J. Fontana on drums, Floyd Cramer and Hoyt Hawkins on piano, Pete Drake on steel guitar, Norm Ray on sax, with vocal background provided by The Jordanaires with Millie Kirkham.

Ray Walker remembered that "the happiest we ever saw Elvis was when he first bought that ranch. He had some horses down there, and he was exercising and he looked great and felt great. As I remember, he even let his hair go back to its natural color for a while. He walked in one day, and he had a tan, and we couldn't get over how good he looked. We just stood there and stared at him. Finally, he broke into a smile and said, 'Shall we dance?'"[145]

The first song he did that evening was "The Girl I Never Loved," followed by "How Can You Lose What You Never Had," both for the *Clambake* movie. He then recorded the country classic "You Don't Know Me" written by Eddy Arnold and Cindy Walker. This seemed to be the only song on the session that appealed to Elvis; he did 21 takes and was still not satisfied with his performance. He finished this recording session at 6 a.m. with another song for the *Clambake* movie, "A House That Has Everything."

The next day, Elvis remained in his hotel room while the musicians recorded tracks for four songs for the *Clambake* movie: "Who Needs Money?" "Confidence," "Hey, Hey, Hey," and "Clambake." On "Who Needs Money?" Ray Walker did a duet while four female singers, June Page, Priscilla Hubbard, Dolores Edgin and Millie Kirkham sang background on "Confidence."

On the last day of recording, Elvis recorded "Clambake" (reprise), and then provided the vocals on the previous day's instrumental tracks. He was obviously anxious to get back to his ranch; he came to the studio for these last overdubs dressed in a full cowboy outfit, complete with chaps.

In February the album *How Great Thou Art* was released. Although sales were a bit disappointing—about 200,0000 were sold initially—it became Elvis' first Grammy-winning album (for "Best Sacred Performance").

In early March Elvis was in Hollywood to begin work on *Clambake*. Also in March the six song EP "Easy Come, Easy Go" was released but never charted. This was Elvis' last EP release; the EP format was phased out. On March 22 the movie *Easy Come, Easy Go* was released but had disappointing results as fewer and fewer people went to theaters to see Elvis' latest film release.

Double Trouble opened nationally–less than two weeks after *Easy Come, Easy Go*–and also had disappointing box office sales. In April, Elvis finished work on *Clambake* and the next day the single "Long Legged Girl (With the Short Dress On)" b/w "That's Someone You Never Forget" was shipped. The single's A side came from the *Double Trouble* soundtrack.

Meanwhile, Elvis headed to Las Vegas, where he married Priscilla on Monday, May 1, 1967 at the Alladin Hotel. The couple spent two days in Palm Springs then headed back to the Mississippi ranch.

In June, Elvis reported to the MGM Studio to begin work on his next movie, *Speedway*, which co-starred Nancy Sinatra. He recorded the soundtrack at the MGM studio in Culver City, with Nashville musicians Chip Young, Bob Moore, Buddy Harman, D.J. Fontana, Pete Drake, Boots Randolph, Charlie McCoy and The Jordanaires on the session. That month the album *Double Trouble* was released and in mid-August, Elvis' work on *Speedway* was finished.

In August, the single "There's Always Me" b/w "Judy" was released; those songs came from the album *Something for Everybody*, which was released in 1961.

Elvis was scheduled to record more non-soundtrack material for RCA at RCA's Hollywood studio but the session was cancelled and re-scheduled for the RCA Studio in Nashville. On Sunday, September 10, Elvis came to the studio with producer Felton Jarvis in the control room and engineer Jim Malloy at the board. Musicians on the session were Scotty Moore, Harold Bradley and Chip Young on guitars; Bob Moore on bass, D.J. Fontana and Buddy Harman on drums, Floyd Cramer on piano, Charlie McCoy on guitar, organ and harmonica, Boots Randolph on saxophone, Pete Drake on steel guitar, Ray Stevens on trumpet, and backup vocals by Millie Kirkland and the Jordanaires.

The session began with "Guitar Man," a song written and recorded by Jerry Reed which was a country hit for him. Elvis heard the song on the radio and wanted to do it. They began the session by running down "Guitar Man" but it became obvious that only Jerry Reed could play the guitar like Elvis had heard it. After some scrambling, Mary Lynch, Chet Atkins assistant, got Reed on the phone and he came to the studio with about a week's worth of whiskers wearing old, funky clothes. When Elvis saw Reed he said, "Lord, have mercy, what is that?!"[146]

Jerry Reed sat down, plugged in his guitar and started to work on his guitar part—but kept blowing it. Elvis was standing "about a foot or so away" while Reed was working on his part. Finally, Reed looked up at Elvis and said, "God, you're handsome!"[147]

Reed finally got his guitar part down and they recorded the song. The next song, "Big Boss Man" was an R&B hit for Jimmy Reed (no relation to Jerry) in 1961. Jerry Reed also provided the blues based guitar on this song.

They took a break and Freddy Bienstock approached Jerry Reed, who owned the publishing on his song, about a deal where the Hill and Range group would get a cut of his publishing and Reed would take less as a songwriter. This turned into a confrontation and resulted in Reed refusing to give up his publishing and leaving the session.

"One element of the session that had kept him hopeful was the upbeat energy supplied by guitarist Jerry Reed," said Jerry Shilling, who was at the session. "He knocked out a killer version of 'Guitar Man,' but then the whole deal was almost squelched when Hill and Range came down hard on Reed, pressuring him to give up a huge chunk of his publishing rights...Jerry Reed was in no mood to give up his song, though, and he was tough enough and smart enough to say 'screw you,' to Hill and Range, who consequently couldn't quite figure out a way to tell Elvis that they wouldn't go forward with a song he had gotten so excited about because it wasn't cheap enough."[148]

After a short break, the next three songs were recorded between one and 5:30 in the morning: "Mine" (with Jordanaire Hoyt Hawkins on organ) and "Singing Tree," both from the Hill and Range offices in the Brill Building. The final song recorded early that morning was "Just Call Me Lonesome" (with Hoyt Hawkins again playing organ) which had been a country hit for Eddy Arnold in 1955. Hoyt Hawkins played organ on this song.

The next evening, the sessions began with "Hi-Heel Sneakers," an R&B hit for Tommy Tucker in 1964. Jerry Lee Lewis had released the song that year but it barely made the pop charts. The following year it was a hit by Stevie Wonder.

"Hi-Heel Sneakers" came at the suggestion of guitarist Harold Bradley. Elvis had recorded "Big Boss Man" the day before and when he came to the studio Harold asked, "Do you want to do another song like 'Big Boss Man?'" Elvis replied, "I don't know, what have you got?" and Harold said, "Hi-Heel Sneakers." Bradley said that Elvis "didn't say anything" but went over to the stack of demos and started going through them. Finally, Elvis "slammed one down and came over and said, 'you got the words to that?'" Bradley replied, "Nah, I don't publish no words, but

Charlie McCoy and Boots Randolph sing it in the night clubs" so Elvis got the words to the song from them "and we did it." After they recorded the song, "I was going in the control room, because I never liked to hear the play back out in the studio," said Bradley, "and I met Felton Jarvis, right in the door jam and he said, 'Don't ever do that again!' I said, 'Do what again?' He said, 'Suggest a song. Freddy Bienstock went nuts so I told him Elvis suggested it!'" According to Bradley, he then said "Okay. I didn't know we were playing games; I though we were making records."[149]

Harold Bradley observed that Elvis would listen to a stack of demos while the musicians sat around and waited until he found one he wanted to record and "the amazing thing about him is that once he found a song he liked, he pretty well had the song down and knew the style he wanted to do it in by the time he walked back to his microphone. He learned a song faster than anybody I knew."[150]

For the next song, Elvis took another stab at "You Don't Know Me," then did "We Call On Him." Elvis sat at the piano in the studio and played while he sang "You'll Never Walk Alone," written by Broadway composers Richard Rodgers and Oscar Hammerstein for the musical *Carousel*. The song was a hit for Roy Hamilton in 1954 and also charted for Patti LaBelle in 1964 and Gerry & The Pacemakers in 1965.

After a short break, at one in the morning Elvis re-cut "Singing Tree." The Hill and Range songs were "bonus tracks" to fill out the album soundtrack for *Clambake*.

Elvis returned to RCA Studio B on Sunday, October 1 to record songs for the soundtrack of his next movie, *Stay Away, Joe*. Jeff Alexander and Felton Jarvis were both in the control room with engineer Al Pachucki. In the studio were Scotty Moore and Chip Young on guitars, Bob Moore on bass, Buddy Harman and D.J. Fontana on drums, Floyd Cramer on piano, Charlie McCoy on harmonica, Gordon Terry on fiddle and The Jordanaires provided background singing.

Elvis recorded three songs, all from the Hill and Range catalog: "Stay Away, Joe," "All I Needed Was the Rain," and "Dominick." The songs were required for the movie and Elvis was less than enthused with the selections; "Dominick" was sung by Elvis to a bull in the movie and

Elvis made Felton Jarvis promise the recording would never be released.

In October the soundtrack album *Clambake* was released.

Elvis spent a few days in Las Vegas before going to Sedona, Arizona, for location shooting for *Stay Away, Joe*. On November 22, *Clambake* opened nationally about the same time he finished work on *Stay Away, Joe*. At this point, Elvis had fulfilled his film contracts. He was no longer a top box office draw and his films had become increasingly commercial disappointments; so were his soundtrack albums.

Elvis spent Christmas and New Year's Day in Memphis.

On Monday, January 15, 1969 Elvis flew to Nashville to record two songs for the movie *Stay Away, Joe* as well as some material for RCA. There would be two days of sessions, overseen by Felton Jarvis; Al Pachucki was engineer the first day while Bill Vandevort engineered on the second day. The musicians were the familiar line-up of Scotty Moore, Jerry Reed and Chip Young on guitars, Bob Moore on bass; Buddy Harman and D.J. Fontana on drums; Floyd Cramer on piano; Pete Drake on steel guitar; Charlie McCoy on harmonica with The Jordanaires on background vocals.

The first song they put down was a Chuck Berry song, "Too Much Monkey Business" followed by "Goin' Home," which Elvis worked on for several hours and 30 takes before giving up. He then left the studio in a rented Lincoln and spent the next day sleeping at the Jack Spence Motor Hotel on Murfreesboro Road.

Work resumed the next evening at 10 p.m. with "Stay Away," a song whose melody is a variation of the old British song "Greensleeves" (also known as "What Child is This?"). For the second song, Elvis had rejected all the demos that Freddy Bienstock offered, cutting short one attempt at a song from Bienstock and yelled, "Doesn't anyone have some goddamn material worth recording?" Jerry Reed brought out "a little reluctantly" his song, "U.S. Male" and "handed Elvis a demo, which Elvis took back to the studio's listening room," remembered Jerry Shilling. "Felton Jarvis, Freddy Bienstock, Joe Esposito, Lamar, Charlie, Red and I were there, listening along with Elvis. He had to hear only about twenty seconds of the song before his energy shot right back up. 'Let's cut it,' he said. He was finally hearing something he could grab a hold of and get excited about. Freddy and Lamar, who was now working for Hill and Range, left the room, while Elvis and Felton worked out some details of the arrangement."[151]

"The song should have been good news for everyone at the session, but apparently Freddy was not happy about doing business with Jerry Reed again," said Shilling. "As I left the listening room and headed down a hall toward the studio, I saw Reed just about pinned to the wall by Freddy and Lamar. From the bits of growled threats I picked up, the message was clear: Don't you ever, ever pitch a song again at an Elvis session. The guitarist wasn't going to back down, but he didn't have much of a chance to respond, because just then Elvis came around the corner, still looking up and energized. Freddy and Lamar backed off quickly, trying to make it look like they were shaking Reed's hand. 'Great tune, man,' Elvis said to Reed as he passed by. 'We need more of that around here.'"[152]

On January 9, the day after Elvis' thirty-third birthday, RCA released "Guitar Man" b/w "Hi-Heel Sneakers" and the album *Elvis Gold Records Vol. 4*. In February, RCA released the single "U.S. Male" b/w "Stay Away." In between those two releases, Elvis became a father on February 1 when Priscilla gave birth to a baby girl, Lisa Marie at Baptist Hospital in Memphis.

In early March, Elvis began work on his next movie, *Live a Little, Love a Little*, based on the novel *Kiss My Firm But Pliant Lips* by Dan Greenburg. Elvis' father, Vernon, had a small, nonspeaking part in the movie. The soundtrack was produced by Billy Strange at Western Recorders in L.A. *Stay Away, Joe* opened nationally and the single "You'll Never Walk Alone" b/w "We Call on Him" was released before Easter.

On April 22, 1968 the man who signed Elvis to RCA Victor and the man who convinced RCA to build a studio in Nashville, Steve Sholes, died of a heart attack while driving his car from the Nashville airport into Music Row. Sholes had been promoted to West Coast manager for RCA in 1961 and moved to Los Angeles; in 1963 he returned to New York where he was promoted to vice president for pop A&R. At the time of his death, Sholes no longer supervised Elvis' sessions, but he continued to keep close tabs on Elvis' recordings and stayed in contact with Colonel

Tom Parker. Sholes served on the Boards of Directors for the Country Music Association and the Country Music Foundation; in the latter role he was instrumental in the opening of the Country Music Hall of Fame and in 1967, the year before his death, was inducted into that Hall of Fame.

In mid-May, Elvis finished his work on *Live a Little, Love a Little* and the single "Your Time Hasn't Come Yet Baby" b/w "Let Yourself Go" was released from the *Speedway* soundtrack; the *Speedway* album was also released that month.

With his appeal as a movie star declining and the movies becoming less lucrative at the box office, Colonel Tom Parker worked out an agreement with NBC for a television special starring Elvis. Originally conceived as a Christmas special, the show was directed by Steve Binder, produced by Bob Finkel, and sponsored by the Singer Sewing Machine Company. On Monday, June 3, Elvis began rehearsals for the TV show, which was written by Chris Beard and Allan Blye. Pre-recording for the TV special was done at Western Recorders.

Binder asked vocal arranger Earl Brown to write a song that captured the idealism of the 60s. Brown wrote "If I Can Dream" overnight and it was decided that song would end the show. The format was no longer to showcase the contemporary Elvis singing Christmas songs. Colonel Parker had wanted Elvis to only say "Good evening" at the beginning of the show and "Good night" at the end and sing Christmas songs in between.

On Saturday, June 22, Scotty Moore and D.J. Fontana arrived from Nashville for an informal sequence where Elvis, dressed in a black leather outfit, performed on a small stage in front of a live audience. Taping for the show was finished on Sunday, June 30. The next day, Elvis went to Palm Springs for a week of rest.

In June, *Speedway* opened nationally; in July, Elvis began work on *Charro!* in Apache Junction, Arizona and finished that movie at the end of August, then spent most of September in Palm Springs. In September the single "A Little Less Conversation" b/w "Almost in Love" was released; in October, *Live a Little, Love a Little* opened nationally and did as poorly at the box office as *Speedway* did in June.

On October 22 Elvis began work on his last film for MGM, *The*

Trouble With Girls (And How To Get Into It). In October the album *Singer Presents Elvis Singing Flaming Star and Others* was released; this was an album the Singer Sewing Machine Company sold in their stores exclusively for three months, leading up to the television special.

In November, the single "If I Can Dream" b/w "Edge of Reality" was released and on November 22 the album *Elvis,* which came from the TV special, shipped, all leading up to the NBC Special on December 3. The hour-long special aired at 9 p.m. EST and was seen by 42 percent of the viewing audience and was the number one rated show for the season. This gave a huge boost to Elvis' career; both the single and album went Gold.

On December 18, Elvis completed work on *The Trouble With Girls* then went to Memphis, where he spent Christmas and New Year's Day.

In early January, Elvis and Felton Jarvis discussed a future recording session in Nashville but George Klein and Marty Lacker pushed the idea of recording in Memphis at the American Studio owned by Chips Moman. Chips was heavily involved in Stax Records, which had released a number of hit "soul" records. The studio was located close to Graceland—just a few miles away and, after thinking it over, Elvis felt it would give him a fresh sound.

There were no Nashville musicians on the Memphis sessions; instead, Memphis studio musicians Reggie Young, Tommy Cogbill, Mike Leech, Gene Chrisman, Bobby Wood, Bobby Emmons, John Hughey and Ed Kollis recorded with him in the studio. Ironically, a number of these musicians later moved to Nashville and became in-demand studio musicians in that city.

The material included the Hank Snow song, "I'm Movin' On," "Gentle On My Mind" by John Hartford which became a hit when Glen Campbell sang it on each episode of his television show, and the Ned Miller hit from 1962 "From a Jack to a King." Elvis recorded two Eddy Arnold songs, "I'll Hold You in My Heart" and "After Loving You," the Johnny Tillotson song, "It Keeps Right on A'Hurtin'" and three new songs, "Suspicious Minds" written by Mark James, "Kentucky Rain" written by Eddie Rabbitt and "In The Ghetto" written by Mac Davis.

In February, RCA released the single "Memories" from the TV

special b/w "Charro!" On March 5, Elvis began work on his last feature film, *Change of Habit*, co-starring Mary Tyler Moore. He recorded the soundtrack in Los Angeles at the Decca Universal Studio.

In March, the single "His Hand in Mine" b/w "How Great Thou Art" was shipped in time for Easter. "How Great Thou Art" came from his 1967 gospel album while "His Hand in Mine" was from his 1960 gospel album. A budget album on the Camden Label *Elvis Sings Flaming Star,* which was the album marketed exclusively by Singer during its first three months, was shipped nationally in March and went Gold.

In March, *Charro!* opened nationally and on April 29 Elvis completed work on *Change of Habit*. In April, "In the Ghetto" b/w "Any Day Now," his first single from the Memphis sessions, was released and sold 1.2 million copies. In June, the single "Clean Up Your Own Backyard" b/w "The Fair is Moving On" was shipped; "Clean Up" came from *The Trouble With Girls* soundtrack.

The album *From Elvis in Memphis* was released and went Gold and Elvis put together a band for Las Vegas consisting of James Burton, guitar; Larry Muhoberac, piano; Ronnie Tutt, drums; Jerry Scheff, bass, John Wilkinson, rhythm guitar and two vocal groups: The Imperials and the Sweet Inspirations. On Friday, July 18 he began rehearsals for his Las Vegas opening on July 31 at the International Hotel. In addition to his band, Elvis was backed by a 30-piece orchestra. To solve the problem of RCA needing more recordings, the shows were taped. On August 28, Elvis ended his first Las Vegas engagement.

In August, the single "Suspicious Minds" b/w "You'll Think of Me" was released and "Suspicious Minds" became his first number one on the *Billboard* Hot 100 chart since "Good Luck Charm" in 1962. In September, *The Trouble with Girls* opened nationally; on the twenty-fifth Elvis and Charlie Hodge flew to Nashville for vocal overdubs on "Let Us Pray" and "A Little Bit of Green."

After the successful Vegas run in August, Colonel Parker signed an agreement for Elvis to perform at the International Hotel for four weeks, seven nights a week, with two shows a night for $100,000 a week; Elvis was responsible for paying his band and backup group.

In October, the double album *From Memphis to Vegas/From Vegas to Memphis* was shipped. The album contained live recordings from the International Hotel as well as recordings from the Memphis sessions. On Monday, November 10 *Change of Habit* was released nationally and the next day the single "Don't Cry Daddy" b/w "Rubberneckin'" was released; this third single from the American Studio sessions sold 1.2 million copies.

Once again, Elvis came back to Graceland for Christmas and New Year's.

Chapter 16: 1970 - 1971

Elvis flew to Los Angeles on January 6, 1970 to begin rehearsals for his next Las Vegas engagement; the rehearsals were held at the RCA Studio on Sunset Boulevard. Since his previous Vegas engagement, drummer Ronnie Tutt had left and was replace by Bob Lanning; pianist Larry Muhoberac left and was replaced by Glen D. Hardin and Cissy Houston of the Sweet Inspirations left and was replaced by Ann Williams.

Another live album was planned as Elvis and the Colonel realized the commitment to RCA to record three albums per year could be accomplished with albums of live performances. The only problem was that Elvis needed a new set of songs to sing.

Dissatisfied with the sound in Vegas, Elvis hired Bill Porter, the former RCA studio engineer who now had a studio in Las Vegas, to run the sound when the show, scheduled to run for four weeks, opened on Monday, January 26.

Three days after the Vegas engagement opened, RCA released the fourth single from the Memphis sessions, "Kentucky Rain" b/w "My Little Friend." Shows in February were taped for the *On Stage* album under the production supervision of Felton Jarvis.

Elvis had not performed in a concert outside Las Vegas since 1961 but on February 25 he took the stage at the Astrodome for the Houston Livestock Show and Rodeo. This show proved to him that he was still a major concert attraction. After those shows, Elvis returned to Los Angeles and in April, "The Wonder of You," from the live Vegas show, b/w "Mama Liked the Roses" was shipped. RCA released the budget album, *Let's Be Friends* and in May, Elvis came back to Memphis.

Felton Jarvis resigned as staff producer at RCA on June 1 to devote his full attention to Elvis. On Thursday, June 4, Elvis came to RCA Studio B in Nashville to record and brought some new musicians to the sessions. On guitars were James Burton, Chip Young and Elvis (who played acoustic), Norbert Putnam was on bass, Jerry Carrigan on drums, David Briggs on piano, Charlie McCoy on organ and harmonica; and Charlie Hodge did vocals on "This Is Our Last Dance" and "Heart of Rome."

Since the recording process had changed with new technology in-stalled—RCA Studio B now had a 16-track board, up from the four and eight track boards that Elvis had previously recorded on—there were overdub sessions that involved musicians James Burton, Jerry Carrigan, Farrell Morris, Weldon Myrick, Bobby Thompson, Buddy Spicher, The Imperials, The Jordanaires, and female vocalists Millie Kirkham, Mary Greene, Mary and Ginger Holladay, Temple Riser, June Page, Sonja Montgomery, Dolores Edgin, and Joe Babcock.

The session began with "Twenty Days and Twenty Nights," then proceeded to "I've Lost You," "I Was Born About Ten Thousand Years Ago," "The Sound of Your Cry," "The Fool," and some bluegrass songs, "A Hundred Years From Now" by Lester Flatt and Earl Scruggs, "Little Cabin on The Hill" by Bill Monroe and Lester Flatt, and the first night ended with Elvis recording "Cindy Cindy." On the next night, Elvis re-corded the Paul Simon song "Bridge Over Troubled Water," a medley of "Got My Mojo Working"/"Keep Your Hands Off Of It," "How the Web Was Woven," "It's Your Baby, You Rock It," "Stranger In the Crowd," "I'll Never Know" and "Mary In the Morning."

On the third day of sessions Elvis recorded "I Didn't Make It On Playing Guitar," "It Ain't No Big Thing (But It's Growing)," "You Don't Have to Say You Love Me," "Just Pretend," "This Is Our Dance," "Life" and "Heart of Rome." The fourth day of sessions saw Elvis record "When I'm Over You" and a series of country songs. "I Really Don't Want to Know" was an Eddy Arnold hit, "Faded Love" came from Bob Wills, "Tomorrow Never Comes" was a hit for Ernest Tubb, a new song, "The Next Step Is Love," then the Eddy Arnold hit "Make the World Go Away," Willie Nelson's "Funny How Time Slips Away," the Stonewall Jackson hit from 1955 "I Washed My Hands in Muddy Water" and finished the evening with "Love Letters."

On June 8, Elvis began his fifth day of recording with the Jack Greene hit written by Dallas Frazier, "There Goes My Everything," then "If I Were You," "Only Believe," "Sylvia," and finished with "Patch It Up," a song written by Eddie Rabbitt and Rory Burke; Rabbitt had written

"Kentucky Rain."

It was a remarkably productive set of sessions; Elvis recorded 37 songs over the five day period. On June 23, Elvis flew back to Nashville to listen to the sessions and make some vocal repairs.

Elvis' album *On Stage* was released in June and during the rehearsals for Las Vegas held at the MGM Studios in Culver City, filming began on the documentary *That's The Way It Is*. On August 10, 1970, Elvis began his next engagement at the International Hotel in Las Vegas; those performances ended on September 7. During August a four album set *Worldwide 50 Gold Award Hits Vol. 1* was released and two days after his Las Vegas engagement ended, Elvis embarked on a six city tour, performing in Phoenix, St. Louis, Detroit, Miami, Tampa, and Mobile, Alabama before he returned to Memphis.

On September 21, Elvis came to Nashville with Priscilla and entered RCA Studio A—the new, big facility—where he worked with musicians David Briggs and Norbert Putnam in a mock session so that Priscilla, who badgered him to let her attend a recording session, could be satisfied. "I love that woman but I don't want her at my recording sessions," said Elvis to Putnam and Briggs as they pretended to overdub some instrumental parts on songs already recorded.[153]

"Elvis only knew one thing on the bass guitar," said Putnam, "and that was a slide up the neck into a note. So he played that and told me 'I want you to do this.'" Putnam complied as Priscilla watched.

The next day, Elvis came to the recording studio in a bad mood; apparently Priscilla had confronted him about his drug use. During this session he recorded four songs, the Anne Murray hit "Snowbird," "Where Did They Go, Lord," the Jerry Lee Lewis hit "Whole Lotta Shakin'" and "Rags to Riches."

In October, the single "You Don't Have to Say You Love Me," a song made famous by British singer Dusty Springfield, was released b/w "Patch It Up" as well as the budget album *Almost In Love*. On November 10, Elvis opened a tour in Oakland, California, then performed in Portland, Oregon, Seattle, San Francisco, Los Angeles at the Inglewood Forum, San Diego, Oklahoma City and Denver.

In November *Elvis' Christmas Album* was released as a budget album; it was the original album from 1957 with four gospel songs dropped and "Mama Liked The Roses" added. The album *That's The Way It Is* —his eighth in 1970–was released at the same time as the documentary. The single "I Really Don't Want To Know" b/w "There Goes My Everything" was released in December.

On December 17 Elvis flew to Memphis for his Christmas break; however, on December 19, after an argument over his spending habits with Vernon and Priscilla, Elvis boarded a plane to Washington, then to Los Angeles and Dallas before he went to the White House in Washington to meet with President Richard Nixon and FBI Director John Ingersoll in order to obtain a special narcotics badge. He then flew back to Memphis and remained there until January 9.

On January 16, 1971 Elvis attended a Junior Chamber of Commerce breakfast; the Jaycees named him one of the nation's "Ten Outstanding Young Men of the Year for 1970." Elvis hosted a reception at Graceland for the award winners and Jaycee officials, then hosted a formal dinner that evening. The awards ceremony was held at Ellis Auditorium and, as he accepted the honor, Elvis said, "When I was a child, ladies and gentlemen, I was a dreamer. I read comic books, and I was the hero of the comic book. I saw movies, and I was the hero in the movie. So every dream that I ever dreamed has come true a hundred times. 'Without a song the day would never end/Without a song a man ain't got a friend/Without a song the road would never bend/Without a song' ...So I keep singing a song.'"[154]

On Tuesday, January 26, Elvis opened at the International Hotel in Las Vegas; that engagement lasted until February 23. In January, the album *Elvis Country* was released and on the day his Las Vegas engagement ended, the single, "Rags to Riches" b/w "Where Did They Go, Lord" was released.

RCA needed albums of pop, gospel and Christmas material and pressed Elvis to arrange time for sessions to do these. Colonel Parker was especially keen that Elvis do another Christmas album. On March 15, 1971, Elvis drove his blue deluxe Mercedes to Nashville and parked in the lot behind RCA Studio B where approximately 40 women waited for him.

Security was tight; there were several policemen and a newspaper reporter was on hand to cover the event. RCA promotion executive Wally Cochran told those assembled, "He'll be here several days—that's all I can say."

The women gathered in the parking lot were loyal fans. A Mrs. Hardison said, "He could burp on a record and it would be music to me. I remember him when he came to Nashville for the disc jockey convention, signing autographs and getting his picture taken before he made it, when he was still with Sun Records in Memphis."

After some debate amongst the women and police, Mrs. Hardison went in search of Wally Cochran to try to get herself and some girl friends into the studio and missed the arrival of Elvis. Mrs. Hardison asked the policemen what Elvis was wearing; it seems Elvis had on a blue, wide-collared shirt, black "wet looking" pants, "cutaway" shoes and yellow tinted sunglasses "because he has had a little eye problem–but it's not supposed to be anything serious," she said.

"I'm no screaming teenager," said Mrs. Hardison. "He's the only man there is that I'd walk from here to Memphis to see. You should see his eyes. They're wide like mine, but they're kind of green and sort of half-awake-looking. The sexiest eyes you ever saw."

It would be an all-night job for the three guards assigned to keep fans out of the studio.[155]

Initial plans called for 40 songs to be recorded during the sessions so Freddy Bienstock submitted over 30 demos from his British publishing company. The Aberbachs sent songs as well but Elvis picked some songs on his own and submitted a list to Bienstock, who attempted to get publishing deals on them. Elvis did not require that every song have a favorable publishing arrangement for him, but if it could be obtained, then so much the better.

Songs that Elvis told the organization he wanted to record included "Help Me Make It Through The Night" and "Sunday Morning Coming Down" by Kris Kristofferson, the Frank Sinatra hit, "My Way," "The First Time Ever I Saw Your Face" and "The Impossible Dream," which he used to close his show in Las Vegas. Religious songs he listed included "Lead Me, Guide Me," "Just A Closer Walk With Thee" and "An Evening

Prayer," which was in the public domain.[156]

Elvis had a runny nose and his eyes ached when he came into the studio, but he was determined to go forward. He had been listening to the folk music albums of Peter, Paul and Mary and loved their harmonies and their songs.

During the first evening, Elvis recorded "The First Time Ever I Saw Your Face," which he had learned from a Peter, Paul and Mary record (not the Roberta Flack version, which was a number one single for her the next year), the gospel standard "Amazing Grace," and two songs by Gordon Lightfoot, "Early Morning Rain," and "That's What You Get For Lovin' Me" that he had also learned from a Peter, Paul and Mary album. He wanted to record the Kris Kristofferson song, "Sunday Morning Coming Down," but Freddy Bienstock was unable to secure a publishing arrangement. Still, Elvis was determined to record it, but, at 1:30 in the morning he called it quits because his eye was giving him problems; it felt like it was burning.

Back in his hotel room, the discomfort did not get any better so early the next morning his regular physician, Dr. Nichopoulos and Dr. David Meyer flew in from Memphis, examined his eye and Dr. Meyer gave him a shot of Demerol, then a shot of cortisone directly into the eyeball to relieve some of the built-up pressure. They sent him to Baptist Hospital on Church Street where he was diagnosed with iritis and secondary glaucoma. Priscilla was in Los Angeles, decorating their new house, so Elvis called actress Barbara Leigh, who flew in to comfort him in the hospital.

The Nashville newspapers kept the public informed about Elvis' stay in the hospital. They told readers he was in a private suite, then that he had been moved to another area which "placed Presley's room in a 'quieter part of the building' and an area which is 'More easily guarded.'" The hospital was "deluged with telephone calls, flowers and callers attempting to convey their wishes" to Elvis.[157]

On Friday evening, Tennessee Governor Winfield Dunn came by for a visit; a little later Elvis "was presented an 180-inch long moleskin-bandage get well 'card' signed by several hundred hospital employees." The card was presented to Elvis by David Stringfield, hospital executive vice president and Elvis "presented a gold American Flag pin to Mrs. Jeane Beasley, head nurse of one of the hospital units." There were reports that Elvis was eating "bran, half-and-half milk, bananas, biscuits, pancakes, cheese omelet, bacon, sausage, orange juice and chocolate ice cream." The hospital was overwhelmed with telegrams, phone calls and letters. When Elvis was moved to his new suite, he was "'on parade' as staff members lined up to watch the star take his stroll to the new suite. They appeared impressed by Presley's black lounging clothes and large belt." Out in the hospital parking lot, fans gathered around Elvis' Mercedes-Benz, with many posing for pictures beside it and some even kissing it and leaving messages.[158]

Elvis was discharged from the hospital on Friday, March 19. Barbara Leigh had returned to California so he flew Joyce Bova in from Washington to accompany him back to Memphis.[159]

Since the studio time and musicians were already booked and paid for, Felton Jarvis did some mixing and overdubbing for an album and guitarist James Burton used the time Elvis was in the hospital to record a solo album for A&M Records.[160]

RCA released the album *You'll Never Walk Alone*, comprised of gospel songs, on their budget label in March; the following month the single "Life" b/w "Only Believe" was shipped for the Easter season. Elvis was in Los Angeles for most of April.

Two months later—on May 15—Elvis returned to RCA Studio B for the re-scheduled sessions; walking into the studio, he saw a Christmas tree with wrapped presents underneath and Lamar Fike dressed like Santa Claus. This was Felton Jarvis' way of getting Elvis into the mood to record Christmas songs. Elvis, who always dressed the part of a rock star, wore a black cape and carried a lion's head cane with diamonds and rubies encrusted. Colonel Parker sent a Christmas card wishing him success in the recordings. Everything was designed to get Elvis in a Christmas mood and do a lot of recording.

It worked. That first day he recorded "Miracle of the Rosary," "It Won't Seem Like Christmas," "If I Get Home on Christmas Day," "Padre," "Holly Leaves and Christmas Trees," "Merry Christmas, Baby," and "Silver Bells." By the time he quit at four in the morning, Elvis had finished half his Christmas album.

The next day, drummer Kenny Buttrey replaced Jerry Carrigan, who failed to show up because he overslept. On that evening Elvis recorded "The Lord's Prayer," "I'll Be Home on Christmas Day," "On a Snowy Christmas Night," "Winter Wonderland" and "Don't Think Twice, It's All Right."

The most interesting thing about this session is that in the midst of recording Christmas material—which he was not excited about—he and the studio band jammed for 11 minutes on the Bob Dylan song "Don't Think Twice, It's All Right," made famous by Peter, Paul and Mary. A break in the session occurred after he recorded "Winter Wonderland," a song he disliked and Priscilla called him from Los Angeles because the power had gone off in the house and she could not find the flashlight. After he hung up, guitarist James Burton hit a chord and Elvis started singing the Dylan song. After singing "Don't Think Twice" for an extended time, Elvis left the studio and the studio musicians recorded three instrumental tracks: "O Come, All Ye Faithful," "The First Noel" and "The Wonderful World of Christmas."

On Monday, May 17, Elvis recorded "Help Me Make It Through the Night," "Until It's Time for You to Go," "Lady Madonna" and "Lead Me, Guide Me." After the gospel song, with Elvis backed by the Imperials, Elvis demonstrated how to disarm a gunman by demonstrating a karate kick to a gun held by Red West and kicked the gun through the hand-crafted Conde-Hermanos guitar of Chip Young. That ended that session.

The sessions moved along quickly—almost too quickly—and arranger Glen Spreen was struck by the feeling that "It was not enjoyable: we did the songs too quick. It was just, 'Let's get it over with.'" Bassist Norbert Putnam was "more than a little disappointed that things appeared to be getting worse rather than better" and the bassist "took little satisfaction in an atmosphere that he was beginning to see as fundamentally uncreative, with Elvis more interested in telling his stories and showing off his guns than he was in singing, and the Memphis Mafia always at full howl."

Drummer Jerry Carrigan noted that "All of a sudden nobody cared. We

all felt, 'What can we do to get this over with?' He'd settle for anything."
The musicians became bored with the sessions and "disappointed by what
they saw as an almost total abdication of responsibility on Felton's part"
they took long breaks in a Winnebago owned by Jerry Shook that was
parked outside. Shook, a studio guitar player, was not on those sessions
but his Winnebago "came equipped with all the comforts of home: girls,
dope, and booze."[161]

Elvis was increasingly distracted and the control room was so crowded
with the backup singers and Elvis' entourage that there weren't enough
chairs to sit in. Out in the Winnebago, the musicians were smoking dope
when the policemen assigned to security duty walked in and said "Hey,
boys, what are ya'll smoking that stuff for? It's gonna put you to sleep.
Let's give you something to keep you awake" and then gave them some
amphetamines, explaining that "they had just confiscated them from
somebody, took them to jail, took their dope, and brought it to us."

Elvis always proclaimed loudly that he was against drugs and those
who used them; he had an armload of police and narcotics badges to bolster
those claims. It was ironic that the musicians on Elvis' session sat outside
imbibing dope and joked, "Can you imagine being arrested by Elvis?"[162]

On Tuesday, May 18, Elvis recorded "Fools Rush In," "He Touched
Me," "I've Got Confidence" and "An Evening Prayer." The next day he
began the session with a vocal overdub on "Miracle of the Rosary," then
recorded "Seeing is Believing" and "A Thing Called Love." Around four
or five in the morning, with almost everyone gone from the studio, Elvis
sat down at the piano and recorded two Ivory Joe Hunter songs, "It's Still
Here" and "I Will Be True" and the classic "I'll Take You Home Again,
Kathleen" accompanied only by Norbert Putnam on bass.

On Thursday Elvis recorded "I'm Leavin'," "We Can Make the Morning," "I Shall Be Released" and "It's Only Love."

Elvis called Joyce Bova, a girlfriend he met in Las Vegas in 1969,
and flew her in to join him on the last day. Elvis showed her around the
studio, explained the process of recording and the sound board and, as she
watched, he recorded "Love Me, Love the Life I Lead" and recorded the
vocals for the three Christmas songs the musicians had recorded on the

Sunday evening session that extended into Monday morning.

Despite the musicians feeling the sessions were rushed and short of inspiration, Elvis' week in the studio resulted in 30 songs.

Early on Saturday morning, Elvis woke up in his hotel suite in pain so he called one of his bodyguards, Sonny West, to arrange a chartered jet and flew to Memphis and went straight to Dr. Nichopoulos' house.

Elvis returned to Nashville on June 8 and stayed at the Quality Court Motel. On the first session, which ran from six in the evening until two the next morning, he re-recorded "Until It's Time For You to Go," then did "Put Your Hand in the Hand" and "Reach Out to Jesus." The next evening he worked until 4:30 in the morning on four songs, which completed his gospel album: "He Is My Everything," "There is No God But God," "I John," and "The Bosom of Abraham."

On Thursday evening, June 10 he recorded "My Way" and then re-recorded "I'll Be Home on Christmas Day." He ended the session by storming out, apparently frustrated with the background singers.

During these sessions the musicians increasingly "spoke openly among themselves about his weird fluctuations of mood, about why he would have his bodyguards cordon off the bathroom when he was in there so that no one else could even go in and take a leak," noted Peter Guralnick in his biography of Elvis. "The female backup singers were a constant source of annoyance, maintaining a steady stream of chatter among themselves, seemingly oblivious to Elvis' increasing irritation with them...the musicians' own pill taking and toking went on, even as the session continued to focus on Jesus."

During the recording of "My Way," when the female singers were working on their vocal overdubs, Elvis' frustration hit its peak and he told the singers, "I've run this damn song fifty times, and you still don't know your parts!" then threw his headphone down and angrily left the studio, followed by his entourage. He never returned.[163]

In June, the single "I'm Leavin'" b/w "Heart of Rome" and the album *Love Letters From Elvis* were released.

Some honors came his way in 1971; on June 29, Highway 51 South in front of Graceland was renamed "Elvis Presley Boulevard" and in August the National Association of Recording Arts and Sciences, the organization that awards the Grammys, gave Elvis their "Bing Crosby Award for Lifetime Achievement" in the music industry.

Elvis opened at the Sahara in Lake Tahoe on June 20 and during this engagement, orchestra conductor Joe Guercio adapted "Also Sprach Zarathustra," also known as the "Theme from 2001," as the music that played when Elvis took the stage. "Can't Help Falling In Love," from the *Blue Hawaii* movie and soundtrack, was established as Elvis' closing number. Elvis finished his Lake Tahoe engagement on August 2 and opened at the Hilton in Las Vegas a week later and continued until September 6. On the final show, he wore a cape for the first time on stage.

RCA continued to release recordings. In July an album of movie songs, *C'mon Everybody*, was released on their budget Camden label; in August, the four album set comprised mostly of "B" sides, *The Other Sides—Elvis Worldwide Gold Award Hits Volume 2* was released and in September the single "It's Only Love" b/w "The Sound of Your Cry" was released. In October RCA released movie songs on the budget album *I Got Lucky* and the Christmas album, *Elvis Sings the Wonderful World of Christmas* was released. In November, the single, "Merry Christmas Baby" b/w "O Come, All Ye Faithful" was shipped.

On Friday, November 5, Elvis went on tour, starting in Minneapolis, then went to Cleveland, Louisville, Philadelphia, Baltimore, Boston, Cincinnati, Houston, Dallas, Tuscaloosa, Alabama, Kansas City and Salt Lake City. On this tour, he hired J.D. Sumner and the Stamps and this group continued to tour and record with him.

When not on the road, Elvis spent most of his time in Los Angeles or Las Vegas but back home at Graceland for Christmas, he told those close to him that Priscilla was leaving.

Chapter 17: 1972 - 1973

The year 1972 began with Elvis' single "Until It's Time For You To Go" b/w "We Can Make the Morning" shipped on January 4, four days before his thirty-seventh birthday; on January 26, Elvis opened at the Las Vegas Hilton. Elvis received some radio airplay on his singles, but had no big hit. "Until It's Time For You To Go" entered the *Billboard* Hot 100 Chart in January but only reached number 40; it entered the *Billboard* country chart in March but only lasted two weeks, peaking at number 68. In February, the single "He Touched Me" b/w "Bosom of Abraham" was shipped for the Easter season but did not chart. The album *Elvis Now* was released and reached number 45 on the country chart but did not reach the pop charts.

During his Las Vegas engagement Elvis sang several songs with Nashville roots in his show: "You Gave Me a Mountain," was written by Marty Robbins and "An American Trilogy," was written by Mickey Newbury. During his recording sessions in Hollywood on March 27 and 28, Elvis recorded several songs with a Nashville connection, including "For the Good Times" by Kris Kristofferson and "Burning Love," written by Dennis Linde. He also recorded "Always On My Mind" written by Wayne Carson, Mark James and Johnny Christopher. On this session, Elvis recorded for the first time with Nashville-based J.D. Sumner and the Stamps and with the band he used during his live performances except for bassist Jerry Scheff, who was replaced by Nashville musician Emory Gordy.

Increasingly, Elvis recorded songs whether or not he received a favorable publishing deal. Since his record sales were not as strong as in the past, there was little incentive to give up publishing money for an Elvis cut and publisher Bob Beckham refused to give breaks for the Kristofferson songs he published or for Dennis Linde's "Burning Love," a song which Elvis was reluctant to cut and had to be cajoled into doing by the studio musicians and Felton Jarvis. During those sessions, Elvis recorded "Where Do I Go From Here," "For the Good Times" and "Separate Ways," a song written for and about Elvis by his long time friend Red West. The next day he recorded "Burning Love" and on the third day of recording did "Always On My Mind."

On Thursday, March 30, the documentary *Elvis On Tour* began filming; it began with a simulated recording session and the filming was completed by the end of April. In April, the single "An American Trilogy" b/w "The First Time Ever I Saw Your Face" was shipped; Roberta Flack's version of "First Time Ever I Saw Your Face" had entered the pop chart and was the hit version of that song. "An American Trilogy" came from a live performance and the record reached number 66 on the pop chart in *Billboard* but did not reach the Country Chart.

The album *He Touched Me* was released in April and reached number 32 on the *Billboard* Country Album chart but did not enter the *Billboard* Hot 100. Although the album did not receive a great deal of sales immediately, it became a catalog item that sold consistently through the years. This album won Elvis a Grammy Award.

On March 30, Elvis began a tour which took him to Buffalo, Detroit, Dayton, Knoxville, Hampton Roads, Virginia, Richmond, Roanoke, Indianapolis, Charlotte, Greensboro, North Carolina, Macon, Georgia, Jacksonville, Florida, Little Rock, San Antonio and Albuquerque; after completing the tour, Elvis flew home to Memphis

On Saturday and Sunday, May 10 and 11, Elvis performed in New York at Madison Square Garden in three concerts—two on Saturday and one on Sunday—that were recorded and released about a month later. The album, *Elvis As Recorded Live at Madison Square Garden*, went Gold in two months and was his most successful album in nine years. After the New York shows, Elvis performed concerts in Fort Wayne, Indiana, Evansville, Indiana, Milwaukee (two days), Chicago (two days), Fort Worth, Wichita and Tulsa, Oklahoma.

RCA continued to mine the vault of recordings of Elvis they had; they released an album of movie songs, *Elvis Sings Hits From His Movies*, then released the single "Burning Love" b/w "It's a Matter of Time." On August 4 he opened at the Las Vegas Hilton for a series of shows.

In October, Elvis made a surprise, unannounced appearance at the National Quartet Convention, a gathering of Southern gospel groups, in

Nashville with J.D. Sumner. Elvis did not perform but greeted a number of the Southern gospel performers.

The concert documentary *Elvis On Tour* opened on November 1 and received a Golden Globe Award for "Best Documentary of 1972." On November 8, Elvis began another tour that took him to Lubbock, Texas, Tucson, El Paso, Oakland, San Bernardino (2 days), Long Beach, California, (2 days), then on Thursday, November 16 flew to Hawaii where he prepared for a worldwide broadcast from the Honolulu International Center. At this point, Elvis had pretty much cut his creative ties to Nashville; he no longer used the "A Team" musicians and did not record in Nashville, although J.D. Sumner and other members of his musical entourage lived in Nashville and he continued to record songs written by Nashville songwriters and published by Nashville publishing companies.

As the 1970s progressed, rock music splintered into southern rock, hard rock, heavy metal and various other permutations. Elvis, who began as a country performer because he was white and from the South, then became the "King of Rock and Roll" and, within country circles, was considered by many to be the "enemy" of country music. But he found himself accepted more in the country world than in the world of pop and rock in terms of his audience and radio airplay as the 1970s progressed.

The day after his thirty-eighth birthday, Elvis arrived in Honolulu, 25 pounds lighter after a crash diet, to perform three shows at the International Convention Center. The shows began on Friday, January 12, and continued on Saturday and Sunday. The performance just after midnight on Saturday was carried live via satellite to Japan, Korea and Hong Kong; 28 European countries saw the show on a delayed broadcast while the American audience did not view it until April. After the Honolulu performances, Elvis opened at the Las Vegas Hilton on January 26 but some of the shows had to be cancelled because of sickness.

In February, Elvis' *Aloha from Hawaii Via Satellite* album—a two record set—was released worldwide and quickly reached number one on the Pop charts, two months before American audiences had a chance to see the show. His last number one album, *Roustabout*, had been eight years earlier. The single, "Steamroller Blues" b/w "Fool" came from the

Hawaii album.

In March, Nashville newspapers reported that Elvis' grandfather, Jessie Presley, had died in Louisville, Kentucky, where he moved after he left Tupelo in 1943. Jessie was the husband of Minnie—who lived with Elvis—and the father of Vernon, but Minnie did not have much use for Jessie after he left her. Elvis was not close to his grandfather, although he visited him shortly after he shot to fame. His grandfather tried to capitalize on his grandson's success by recording some songs but they were never released.[164]

On April 4, 1973, 57 percent of the people watching television that evening tuned into the NBC broadcast of "Elvis: Aloha From Hawaii," including Elvis himself, who watched from his home in Los Angeles. His album had entered the *Billboard* pop LP charts on March 10 and rose to number one, remaining on the chart for 19 weeks. On the *Billboard* Country Album chart, the album entered on March 3 and remained in the number one position for four weeks and on the chart for 31 weeks.

In May, 1973, Nashville *Banner* reporter Red O'Donnell informed readers that Elvis Presley would—for the first time—appear in concert in Nashville. Elvis would give two shows—at 3 in the afternoon and 8:30 that evening—on Sunday, July 1 at Municipal Auditorium. O'Donnell also informed his readers that "The deal for Elvis' appearances was consummated late Tuesday afternoon by his manager, Col. Tom Parker, Bob Parkhill of RCA Tours (which is booking and promoting the shows) and auditorium manager Floyd Rice. Bob Parkhill, representing Elvis and The Colonel, is in charge of the booking."

The article stated that tickets would probably go on sale on June 1, but there was no information on how much they'd cost.

O'Donnell talked with Parker by phone from Lake Tahoe where Elvis was headlining at the Sahara Hotel and the Colonel told the reporter, "Elvis—and this is no malarkey—has been wanting to perform for the public in Nashville for a long time and he is pleased that the booking is set. We have been working on it for about two weeks. Naturally, I'm happy. Although I now live in Palm Springs, California, I still consider Nashville my home and maintain a residence and office on Gallatin Road in Madison. I don't get back there as often as I would like to."

O'Donnell stated that, although Elvis had never performed in concert in Nashville, "he has done numerous recording sessions at RCA studio, [and] 'took a bow' at the gospel music convention last fall, and has visited his record producer Felton Jarvis and wife Mary Lynch of Williamson County.[165]

The day before the concert, Nashville *Banner* reporter Bill Hance informed his readers that "A personal interview with Elvis Presley these days is at a premium—about as hard to come by as a John W. Dean III For President campaign button" before stating that in Jackson, Mississippi during the summer of 1955, "Banner managing editor Pinckney Keel granted the lanky singer his very first interview." Hance quoted Keel talking about that hot July night, saying "I was the police reporter for the *Clarion-Ledger* newspaper and writing a record review column once a week. There was an all night cafe on the main drag in Jackson where a bunch of us would hang out and on the jukebox was Elvis' first record, "That's All Right, Mama." Every time I would drop by there, someone would be playing it. It must have played 100 times a day. One night, while making my police rounds, I got a call from some fellow telling me Elvis Presley was at the corner service station and asked me if I would like to interview him. At first, I didn't know who he was talking about. But then it dawned on me he was the same guy whose song kept blaring over the jukebox."

Keel stated that when he arrived at the station in his used 1962 convertible, Elvis was standing beside his new grey Cadillac. When Keel got out of his car, Elvis "walked over, stuck out his hand and said, "Hi. You must be Pinckney Keel. I'm Elvis Presley." Keel said he and Presley talked for about 15 minutes and during the conversation he told Keel that his new single coming out was "Hound Dog." Keel said he "forgot to take my camera with me" and couldn't find a picture of Elvis back at the office. Keel's story, in the next day's edition of the paper, "was about five paragraphs long on the inside of the paper," according to Hance, who noted that in that story, Keel was the person who named the singer "Elvis the Pelvis."[166]

The Nashville *Tennessean* reported that "About $300,000 in mail order requests for tickets" for the two Elvis shows were being returned because "there weren't enough seats to satisfy the demand for tickets." Lon Varnell, local promoter of the shows, told reporters that requests for tickets had come from as far away as California and West Virginia.[167]

On the day of the show, an article by Kathy Sawyer in the *Tennessean* told readers that "When Elvis Presley materializes for two shows at the Municipal Auditorium today, security will be 'like the Normandy invasion,' according to the Nashville promoter. 'They're not telling anybody anything,' said Lon Varnell, of Varnell Enterprises."

Elvis was on a concert tour and had performed in Atlanta two days before his Nashville performance and was scheduled to perform in Oklahoma City after Nashville.

The reporter stated that "Col. Tom Parker, Presley's manager, lays the ground rules for the singer's appearances and they do not traditionally include interviews or other exposure outside the contractual obligations." Lon Varnell was quoted saying "I know Col. Parker has talked with the police here and gone over every detail. He put in a private line in my office and we talked about the tickets. But they don't let one group know what the others are doing."

According to Varnell, there was only one advertisement—in the "Sunday Showcase" (a magazine inserted into the *Tennessean* that printed the TV schedule and local entertainment) and that had "Sold Out" stamped across it because the 9,601 seats were all sold before the ad ran.

Varnall, who promoted concerts for a wide variety of acts, including the Carpenters, Charley Pride, Tom Jones and Lawrence Welk, stated that Elvis had "more appeal to more people than any in the 26 years I've been a promoter. Elvis draws the people who were kids when he first became a rock and roll star in the '50s and he gets the fans of all those movies he's made and he gets today's young rock fans; and he draws a lot of religious people because of his gospel singing and especially a 30-minute radio show he does at Christmas time. He draws everybody. We realized all this in a big way when we started trying to handle the calls for tickets."

The ticket prices for the Elvis show were $10, $7.50 and $5."[168]

An interview with J.D. Sumner appeared in the Nashville *Tennessean* on the day of the show and Sumner stated that Elvis "always wanted to be a gospel singer. Once he even tried out for a quartet. They turned him down because he wasn't good enough."

The reporter noted that during a concert, "the largest part of his audience will be women with 'heaven' on their minds."

Sumner was interviewed after a recording session and wanted to set the record straight. "You just can't class Elvis as a rock'n'roll singer," said Sumner. "After Elvis started hitting it big in rock'n'roll, one of the quartets called him back and offered him a job. Elvis went to his father and said, 'Daddy, what am I going to do?' His father said, 'Well son, you're doing alright the way you're going now, so I would just keep it up.' But Elvis' intention is to really do something for gospel music."

Sumner noted that when he began working with Elvis, The Imperials, another gospel group, sang with him but there was a conflict in dates and they couldn't perform so Sumner agreed to step in. "At first I was just going to take my boys up to sing while I took a little vacation," said Sumner. "But then Elvis said he wanted me to sing and he would get me a microphone by myself. You see, he used to listen to me back in his younger days when I was a gospel star and he was just a country boy. He remembered how I used to sing and he said he wanted some of those old endings I used to do—some of those '56 endings is what he called them. I used to go DOOOOooo and slur down to a low note. So he made me sing."

"Sometimes Elvis puts us on the stage to sing gospel music to people who have never before heard it," continued Sumner. "Each night after a concert, we go up to Elvis' room and sit around singing gospel music. I've had a chance to sing to Red Skelton, Tom Jones and Sammy Davis Jr.—stars like that. They dig it very much. They just can't believe this kind of music exists and they hadn't heard it before. This is sort of important to us that they dig our music."[169]

The day after the show, a short article titled "His Popularity Reaches Across Three Generations" appeared in the *Tennessean*, The article informed readers that 19,202 fans saw Elvis perform in Nashville, 76,000 could not get tickets which sold for $10 tops but there were reports that scalpers got $100 for a ticket.[170]

A review of the show by Kathy Sawyer in the Nashville *Tennessean* began, "Like a truck driver hauling a load of TNT, Elvis Presley gave a demonstration of restraint in the use of power twice yesterday at the Municipal Auditorium."

The opening act was comedian Jackie Kahane, then The Sweet Inspirations did some songs before "Thus Spake Zarathustra (Theme from 2001: A Space Odyssey)" came over the speakers and the crowd "roared and screamed and the flashbulbs exploded into the shafts of the spotlights. Presley strolled casually from behind a curtain to the center of the stage, nodded to the crowd and the musicians, grabbed the mike by the throat and began to sing. Except for a few persistent screamers, the crowd quieted to listen. He talked occasionally between songs. 'It's a pleasure to play this town,' he told the rapt audience. 'I've worked here but never played here. So, uh, I hope y'all have a good time.'"

Later, he introduced his musicians and acknowledged Felton Jarvis, Chet Atkins and the Jordanaires in the audience. Elvis was "shoulder heavy in a white suit crusted with silver, gold and iridescent metallic studs, jeweled rings glittering on both hands," stated the reporter as Elvis "punctuated his songs with a controlled version of the hip gyrations and erotic guitar thrusts which scandalized the nation in the 1950s but which now seem just the least he could do. He could draw a shrill burst from any section of the auditorium with a wiggle of his index finger or a tilt of his head in that direction. But he didn't do it often. To one determined and loud admirer in the balcony he said, 'I'll be up there in a minute, honey. It takes me a few minutes to make the rounds.'"

After performing for about 30 minutes "and working up a good sweat" Elvis "unraveled a white scarf from around his neck, revealing a bare chest hung with an ivory tooth on a glittering chain and a cross on another. He used the scarf to mop his brow and flung it to a lucky lady in the front row." During the rest of the show, his buddy Charlie Hodge, who sang harmony with him, "dogged his steps keeping him supplied with fresh scarves, usually blue, and glasses of water to sip from." Fans threw things on stage; Elvis picked up a lavender lei and put it around his neck, and "a pair of white panties, which he picked up, contemplated and then threw back into the crowd."

The musical selections covered a wide spectrum, everything from the country classic "Faded Love" to "Shake, Rattle and Roll" but "most memorable, perhaps, was a chillingly beautiful rendering of the gospel song 'How Great Thou Art,' with J.D. Sumner supporting Presley with his patented inhumanly low-range bass. During pauses in the song, the audience was so quiet that the summer rain could be heard, drumming on the auditorium roof."

Commenting that Elvis sang "Love Me," "Blue Suede Shoes," "Hound Dog" and "Fever," the reporter noted that "except for some lines around the eyes and a few more pounds above the belt, the boy from Mississippi looked the same as when he first sang them to some of these same people on records in another time."

Elvis sang the Kristofferson song, "Help Me Make It Through the Night," "Something" by the Beatles, Don Gibson's "I Can't Stop Loving You" and Mickey Newbury's "American Trilogy," which pulls together "Dixie," "The Battle Hymn of the Republic" and "All My Trials, Lord."

Toward the end of his hour and 15 minute performance, Elvis requested the house lights be turned up so "I can have a look at you." He concluded the show with "Love Me Tender" and "I Can't Help Falling in Love With You," then "laid down the microphone and it snaked off the stage. Raising his arms under a white cloak, he walked to each corner of the stage and saluted the crowd and was gone. About one second after he had left the stage, an announcer with a very emphatic voice said, 'Ladies and Gentlemen, Elvis has left the building.'"

The reporter observed that the quick exit "didn't stop some die-hards from trying to catch a glimpse of the great man as he sped off in his black limousine surrounded by security guards. Presley headed back to the Sheraton South for a rest leaving a satisfied crowd. As one old fellow, who said he had grown up with Elvis Presley records, put it, 'The boy still sings good.'"[171]

An article in the Nashville *Banner* on the day after the show opened with the statement, "There's talk in the tight-lipped Elvis Presley compound that the famed 38-year-old entertainer is becoming 'bored' with his personal appearance tour" although the article went on to state, "If he is, he hides his feelings well because both of his Nashville concerts Sunday were loaded with excitement from start to finish."

The writer continued with a review of the show, stating, "Presley hip-swiveled and karate-chopped his way through a long string of songs" beginning with 'C.C. Rider' and 'Mean Woman Blues,' then cut the pace with 'Love Me Tender' and 'You Gave Me A Mountain.'" The audience was "three to one female" and Elvis "seemed to feel each drum and guitar beat with a body shake he's seemingly perfected over the years."

The review stated that "a line of Metro policemen lined the front of the stage to ward off any approaching females who might try to come in contact with the former truck driver. Some did. One young woman went charging down the center aisle just as Elvis swung into '(A hunka hunka) Burning Love.' 'I've got to get up there,' she screamed. 'He wants me up there with him.' 'No, he doesn't, lady,' calmly replied Lt. Richard Ordway." Another female fan "spoke with Patrol Sgt. L.I. Miller before the show started, trying to convince him he should deliver a folded pair of undergarments to Presley before show time. 'I didn't know what to do at first,' said Miller. 'Then I told her as politely as possible, 'no.'"

According to the reviewer, Elvis escaped in "a waiting green Cadillac" which carried him to his motel room. The article concluded that "Whether Presley is becoming disenchanted with his highly pressurized tour still remains in question, although rumors are circling. But it looks as though he will remain in the public eye at least until his shows fail to be sellouts."[172]

On July 20, Elvis began a series of recording sessions at Stax Studios in Memphis. Drummer Jerry Carrigan noted it was "the first time I saw him fat" and musicians were generally shocked at Elvis' attitude and appearance. Producer Felton Jarvis and engineer Al Pachucki came down from Nashville to oversee the sessions.

In August, his album *Elvis* was released and reached number eight on the *Billboard* Country chart but did not make the pop chart. On Monday, August 6 Elvis opened at the Las Vegas Hilton; he performed there until September 3. During this period of time Elvis spent a lot of time in either

Las Vegas or Palm Springs.

In September, the single "Raised on Rock" b/w "For Ol' Times Sake" from the Stax sessions was released and the next month the album *Raised on Rock/For Ol' Times Sake"* was released.

On October 9 Elvis' divorce from Priscilla was finalized at the Los Angeles County Superior Courthouse in Santa Monica.

In December, Elvis did more sessions at the Stax Studios. He recorded a number of songs with Nashville roots; "I Got a Feeling in My Body" was written by Dennis Linde, "It's Midnight" was written by Billy Edd Wheeler and Jerry Chesnut, "You Asked Me To" was written by Waylon Jennings and Billy Joe Shaver, "If You Talk In Your Sleep" was written by Red West and Johnny Christopher, "Love Song of the Year" was written by Chris Christian, "Help Me" was written by Larry Gatlin, "Talk About the Good Times" was written by Jerry Reed, "Your Love's Been a Long Time Coming" was written by Rory Bourke, "There's a Honky Tonk Angel" was written by Troy Seals and Danny Rice, "If That Isn't Love" was written by Dottie Rambo, and "She Wears My Ring" was written by Boudleaux and Felice Bryant.

Chapter 18: 1974

On January 8, 1974, Elvis turned 39; three days later his single, "I've Got a Thing About You Baby" b/w "Take Good Care of Her" was released. The album *Elvis: A Legendary Performer Vol 1*" was released and entered the *Billboard* Country Chart in February and rose to number one, staying in that position for two weeks and remaining on the chart for 47 weeks; it sold 750,000 units. The album contained his first recording "That's All Right, Mama," his first number one, "Heartbreak Hotel," some excerpts from interviews he had granted as well as more of his earlier hits, such as "Love Me Tender," "Don't Be Cruel" and "Can't Help Falling In Love."

An article by Jerry Bailey in the Nashville *Tennessean* informed readers, "Elvis Presley will return to harm the women of Middle Tennessee March 14, but if you didn't already know about it, there's little chance of getting tickets now. The announcement that the 'King of Rock and Roll' would be playing Middle Tennessee State University's Murphy Center went out yesterday morning, and tickets are being claimed with the usual madness that surrounds Elvis' appearance. An estimated 800 early birds got the secret beforehand and had their mail orders waiting when the folks at Sound Seventy Productions reported for work yesterday morning. By mid-afternoon, the constant ringing of telephones had Sound Seventy staff members thinking they worked in a bell factory." The prices for the tickets were $10, $7.50 and $5.

This clamor for tickets to an Elvis Presley concert happened wherever Elvis played; the audience may have gotten tired of his movies, but they were certainly not tired of seeing him perform live.

The reporter spoke with Colonel Parker, who said he "knew little of Presley's personal activities during recent months, 'because I just haven't had a chance to be around him,'" although he added, "He's healthy, though. Some of the boys told me he was running up a sizeable grocery bill."

The Murphy Center in Murfreesboro held 12,400 people and there was one show scheduled for 8:30 p.m. Colonel Parker informed the reporter that Elvis would appear for two shows at the Astrodome—which seats

40,000—in Houston during the annual livestock show, that Elvis would do a network television gospel show later in the year and that another movie was in the works. *Remnants of the Old West* was scheduled to be filmed in New Mexico, although it had been postponed twice because of weather and scheduling problems.[173]

Three days later, the *Tennessean* reported "Elvis Presley will be giving a second show at MTSU's Murphy Center, but the second show "was sold out before it was announced." According to the promoter, they had orders for 30,000 tickets after they had booked the first show.[174]

On January 26, Elvis opened a two week stand at the Las Vegas Hilton, which finished on February 9, then toured March 1 to 20.

A concert review in the Nashville *Tennessean* the day after the show on March 14 in Murfreesboro reported Elvis' show "was a carbon copy of those at Nashville's Municipal Auditorium last summer. Breezy and easy, clean fun with a hairy chest to thrill the ladies, he stood cool and suave while they screamed his name in what could have been mistaken for a final breath. 'Hey, I'll be around,' he assured one worshiper who sounded critical."

Elvis opened with "C.C. Ryder," then moved quickly through "I Got A Woman," "All Shook Up," "Amen," and "I'm a Steam Roller Baby." The outfit he wore was a "shoulder heavy in high collared, sequined, white sateen suit."

The reporter noted that musical highlights included "American Trilogy" and J.D. Sumner's rumbling low bass voice on Kristofferson's "Why Me, Lord." The review concluded that "The concert was short and sweet, for Elvis fans possibly the world's shortest 75 minutes."[175]

The review in the Nashville *Banner* stated, "It doesn't look like anyone will ever unseat the king of rock and roll, Elvis Presley. But, if anyone wants to try, now's the time to start. Presley looks like he's slowing down a bit."

The reporter noted that "Despite the security guards, there was an almost constant stream of women dashing to the stage, either to hand their idol flowers, a handkerchief or become the lucky recipient of one of his pale blue neck scarfs. Midway through the show, a little girl was hoisted to the stage armed with a lei of roses. She got a kiss in return. Moments later two midddle-aged women broke through the guard line and presented him with two more leis, both made of paper. 'Are we in Hawaii?' Presley asked his band."

In addition to the Sweet Inspirations and J.D. Sumner and the Stamps Quartet, Elvis had added the vocal trio, Voice, to his shows. The review reported that Elvis had "performed 24 shows in the last 20 days. All of them were sellouts. The entertainer was visibly tired. Except for three songs, the show was the same as those he staged in Louisville and Knoxville two years ago and Nashville last summer. The only difference was a seeming lack of energy. But apparently, he wants to keep up with the times."[176]

After Elvis left town, the Nashville *Tennessean* reported that "Little Michael Bowen got a special package this weekend from his favorite singing idol and now his bed in Vanderbilt Hospital's intensive care unit is draped with Elvis Presley pictures and buttons. "He doesn't take his eyes off of them," said Mrs. Frank Bowen of Lebanon, whose son underwent brain surgery March 4 and since then had responded more to the mention of Elvis than anything else. Mrs. Bowen and her husband said last Tuesday they wished Michael, eight, would "just get a simple card" from the Memphis rock and roll king. Saturday, Michael received a package filled with autographed photos and buttons with Elvis' picture on them, sent from Col. Tom Parker, the star's manager.[177]

Performing with Elvis on the tour that included the Murfreesboro date was Tony Brown, who played piano for Voice. "We stayed at the Ramada Inn," remembered Tony. "After the show Elvis always flew to the next town while the band always stayed in town but every woman thought that Elvis was at the hotel. We'd say, 'No, he's not here' but they wouldn't believe us. 'I know he's up there!' they'd say. And, of course, there were a few guys who used that thought as bait."[178]

Tony Brown had a strong background in gospel music. He played piano for the Oak Ridge Boys during the period when they were making the transition from being a gospel group to a country act. The Oaks toured Sweden where Tony met Pete Keleen, who played piano for the Samuelson Brothers, a southern gospel act in Sweden. "I had just discovered Elton John and Billy Joel and those were the pop stars that really influenced my life," remembered Brown. "I also knew who Herbie Hancock and Keith Jarrett were although I wasn't that good but I was fascinated with that ability so Pete Keleen and I became close friends because he would sit around and play unbelievable stuff. I would say 'can you do some Elton John' and he would do 'Country Comfort' or anything else I'd ask him to do. He did Billy Joel's 'Piano Man' and songs by Keith Jarrett. He also wrote songs that I thought were as good as any pop songs on the radio."

Elvis hired J.D Sumner and the Stamps as his back-up group and in that group was J.D.'s nephew, Donnie Sumner, but "J.D. fired Donnie over something and hired Dave Rowland," remembered Tony. After the firing, "Elvis had someone from his office call Donnie Sumner because Elvis wanted someone to sing gospel songs around the house because he always wanted to sing gospel songs." According to Tony, Donnie was told by Elvis to "get a couple of other guys and a piano player and I'll give you guys a job as my house group."

"The Imperials had just let Shirl Neilson—or Shawn Neilson, as he called himself then—go and Shirl was Elvis' favorite tenor singer because he sounded like Roy Orbison," said Tony. "Donnie needed a baritone singer and Tim Batey was a good baritone singer so they hired Tim and then they needed a piano player so Donnie called me, because I used to play with the Stamps, and asked if I knew a good piano player who could play this gig. I said, 'I know just the guy. I met him in Sweden, his name is Pete Keleen and he will rock your world."

It was arranged for Pete to fly over and audition and he got the job. One night Pete called Tony from Elvis' home in Beverly Hills and thanked Tony for recommending him for the job. "This job is amazing," Pete told Tony. "Today we were driving down Sunset Boulevard in his Mercedes limo and he was firing a 9 mm out the sunroof." As Tony listened to Pete he thought "Man, I should have taken that job!"

Tony got the opportunity to play piano for Voice when Pete Keleen could not get his Green Card to stay in the United States and had to return to Sweden. Donnie Sumner called Tony and said, "Why don't you quit the Oak Ridge Boys and take this job?" Tony thought "Why not?" and that's how he got the job.[179]

In March, the album *Good Times* was released and Elvis did a short tour in California before he opened at the Sahara in Lake Tahoe on May 16 for a ten day series of shows. The single "If You Talk In Your Sleep" b/w "Help Me" was released and Elvis toured from June 15 to July 2. In July, his album *Elvis Recorded Live on Stage in Memphis* was released; in that album was his live version of "How Great Thou Art," which won him his third Grammy for "Best Inspirational Performance." On August 19, he opened at the Hilton; that same month *Having Fun With Elvis On Stage,* which was comprised solely of pieces of onstage monologues, was released on the Boxcar label. "Boxcar" was Colonel Parker's label and he sought to capitalize on the fact that Elvis' recording contract did not cover him talking on stage.

Elvis' last night at the Hilton was September 2 and on the twenty-eighth he began a 15-day tour; the day before the tour the single "Promised Land" b/w "It's Midnight" was released from the Stax sessions. Another stint at the Sahara Hotel in Lake Tahoe followed his tour as Elvis began to suffer problems with his health. During Christmas and New Year's he was once again in Memphis at Graceland.

By 1974 Music Row was well-defined. At the head of "the Row" on 16th Avenue South stood the Country Music Hall of Fame with offices for the Country Music Association in the basement. Next door to the Hall of Fame was BMI and headed south were offices for Columbia and Epic Records, Capitol, MCA (formerly known as Decca) and, just off the Row were the offices for MGM Records. At the head of 17th Avenue South was ASCAP with RCA Records further South. The offices for record and publishing companies were located in former residential homes which had been converted. "Music Row" was a legendary place, but it did not look very impressive to a visitor driving down those two streets; however, the real activity was behind closed doors and in the studios located up and down that street.

The downtown area was a victim of urban blight and the once central Broadway was filled with "adult" shops and run-down buildings. Opryland had opened and the Grand Ole Opry was now in the new Opry House, about 15 miles away from the downtown Ryman, which was shuttered and in danger of being bulldozed.

Chapter 19: 1975 - August, 1977

On January 8, 1975, Elvis Presley turned 40 years old. Five days before, his single "My Boy" b/w "Thinkin' About You" was shipped; both the single "My Boy" and the *Good Times* album had been successful in England. Later that month the *Promised Land* album, consisting of material recorded at the Stax studio, was released.

Elvis was suffering health problems; on January 29, he was admitted to Baptist Hospital in Memphis then, about a week later, Vernon Presley suffered a heart attack and was placed in a room next to his son. Still, his schedule of concerts continued to move forward and in the *Tennessean* newspaper it was reported that Elvis was scheduled to appear at Middle Tennessee State University's Murphy Center on April 29 and it was expected to be an early sellout.

The article stated that Elvis remained in Baptist Hospital in Memphis, undergoing treatment for "an intestinal blockage," according to his doctor. Concert promoter for the event was Joe Sullivan of Sound 70 Productions, who noted that "There will be only one show this time because there are no other dates open." However, two days later the newspaper informed readers that a second show would be held on May 6 at the Murphy Center.[180]

The *Tennessean* then reported that, because of the huge demand for tickets, a third show was added for May 7. A spokesperson for Sound 70 told the reporter that they "haven't been able to get to the bottom of the pile' of ticket requests" despite two 12,250 seat sellouts already.[181]

Elvis must have been listening to a lot of country music on the radio because he recorded recent country hits as well as songs published in Nashville during his recording sessions in Hollywood on March 10-12. On those dates he recorded "Fairytale" by the Pointer Sisters, "Green Green Grass of Home" by Curly Putman, "I Can Help" by Billy Swan, "Susan When She Tried" by Don Reid of the Statler Brothers, "T-R-O-U-B-L-E" and "Woman Without Love" by Jerry Chesnut, and "Pieces of My Life" by Troy Seals.

On February 18 Elvis opened at the Las Vegas Hilton; on the twenty-ninth he was visited backstage by Barbra Streisand and her husband, Jon Peters, who wanted him to co-star in the re-make of the movie *A Star Is Born*. Although he was initially enthusiastic about the role, Elvis eventually turned it down and the role intended for him went to Kris Kristofferson.

Elvis finished at the Hilton on April 1 and his tour began on April 24 and ran through June 10 with a three week break in May.

Just prior to the first Nashville area concert on April 29, an interview over the telephone with Linda Thompson, Elvis' girlfriend, appeared in the Nashville *Banner*. In the article Linda defined marriage as "having two children." She elaborated that "I'd like to have a boy and a girl—and the boy first. I think most people do. I always have wanted it that way since I was small."

The 24-year old Memphis State University graduate who won a number of beauty contests—including Miss Tennessee Universe and Miss Liberty Bowl—had been "a constant companion of Elvis Presley for two-and-a-half years."

She "spends much of her time with Elvis at his home" and said of their romance "I've never been more excited in my life," continuing that "I'm so very much in love with Elvis. He's such a very fine person...and he's in love with me," then added, "After two and-a-half years together if he's not, he should be doing something about it."

When asked about their plans to marry, she said "We don't talk in definite terms, you know. We just kind of leave everything open and let time tell. I think that's the best way. There are no plans for the immediate future, anyway. We're very happy with the way things are now. We have a very, very good relationship. We understand each other very well. We really have a good relationship. I wouldn't trade our relationship—and he wouldn't either. Our romance is flourishing. It's doing just great!," then added, "I like to keep our lives together pretty private. So does Elvis. But it's never really private..." Her voice trailed off, then she laughed and said, "You want to know what I mean by 'not in the immediate future,' don't you? Well, tomorrow. The next day. I'm only 24 years old."

Talking about Elvis, she said there was "something about him that makes you glow. And around me he just acts natural. We don't have arguments like many couples. And he is never critical of me. He has that certain magic and charm any girl looks for in a man. He calls you by your name—not, 'Hey, Darling.' Elvis thinks so much of my safety that he taught me a few important moves in Karate. He says I should protect myself at all times. He said the five moves I learned are basic ones, and will keep any wolves away. I'm not really into the art of Karate, however. You see, I don't want to develop muscles—and Elvis doesn't want me to either. It's not the most feminine thing in the world."

According to the article, Linda stated she is Elvis' "true love—and not one of those girls mentioned in fan and pulp magazines. 'You just really can't believe anything that you read. That's why I want you to know the truth,'" she said. "You read about so many different things—and so many different girls. It's so false it's funny. Elvis and I have had so many laughs over it. But I have learned to expect it. Even if a girl doesn't need the publicity, she tries to latch onto Elvis just for her own ego trip."

At home in Graceland, "We always keep a pot of coffee brewing, and a cooked roast is ready at all times," said Linda. "In addition to roast or steak, Elvis enjoys vegetables and fresh fruits. He reads a lot and listens to the recordings of all popular stars, some of whom are among his friends. Elvis is dedicated to his music. He has become an expert on all types of guitars, drums and woodwinds. And he has a video machine like Sammy Davis, Jr. He has the Advent. It's a super, super large screen. It's like watching a movie. I guess it's five feet by five feet. It's in the den, where we can munch on a sandwich, sip a soft drink, and watch a football game. Ah, that's what we love to do—watch football on television. We do that real often. I like football. He loves football. He watches all of the pro games. You name it. If it's on television, he watches it. I sit right there and watch—right along with Elvis. He gets so excited sometimes. You know, he enjoys touch football himself. It's all like a regular home atmosphere at Graceland."[182]

Four days before Elvis appeared in the Nashville area concert, the *Banner* ran a story that stated, "He has the waistline the world is waiting to see. 'What a waist! one confided.' Is King Elvis really a blimp? Has he really ballooned to 219 pounds like reports indicate? Hope not. It just wouldn't seem right to have your teenage singing idol come out looking like Fatty Arbuckle."

Mrs. Georgia Harper, who worked as a secretary in the Metro Police Department and admitted being an "Elvis freak" told the reporter "I don't believe a word of it. Two other secretaries, Mrs. Iva Hullett and Mrs. June Burgess, and I go to all of Elvis' shows. There's no way you can convince me he's fat." There were no comments from the inner circle around Elvis but it was noted that during his Las Vegas engagement someone observed he was "pudgy" and another observed his figure was "not unlike Henry Kissinger." A "Music Row secretary" stated she met Elvis three years ago and "The first thing he told me when we met was that he was on a diet. He said he had been on once since he was 17 years old."

The article concluded that Elvis will perform in Murfreesboro and asked the question: "Will he be Elvis the Trim or Elvis the Tub?"[183]

In a review of the show, headlined "Chubbier Elvis Still Sports Pelvis That Crowd Adores," Nashville *Banner* reporter Bill Hance wrote, "Elvis now 'weighs a ton.' Well, maybe not a ton, but he's a lot bigger than he was this time a year ago. Instead of bouncing on stage dressed in sequined body suits, capes and scarves, King Elvis appeared much more subdued Tuesday night in Murfreesboro. He walked up a small flight of stage steps, bowed in all directions to the audience, picked up his guitar and began singing. The Presley movements were still there, but slower. His eyes appeared puffy as he started out with 'C.C. Rider' and halfway through the song propped his right eyelid open with his fingers and told his band 'I just woke up.' No more snazzy, light colored hip huggers for Elvis. At least not until he joins Weight Watchers, or something similar."

Elvis wore a Navy blue suit for this concert "but the suit had class," said the review. "A tunic collar single button double vent and red, orange, yellow and gold stripes around the neck and down the pant legs. The pants, however, appeared baggy," then added "but the Presley magnetism still is there and it still is strong enough to pack the 12,000 person capacity" venue.

The reviewer stated that Elvis had always "handed out neck scarves to the girls in the audience, or those lucky enough to catch one when he tosses it. But this time, Presley ended his show by handing out dozens of them, and in turn, caused a near riot next to the stage. Four girls almost got into a fist fight over one of the scarves, a bright red number."

The show began with the vocal trio "Voice," then comedian Jackie Kahane did his routine before the Sweet Inspirations sang some songs, followed by J.D. Sumner and the Stamps Quartet, who performed before Elvis appeared.

"The show was much more relaxed than it ever seemed before, maybe more mature, just as Elvis himself appears," the review stated. "Relax, Elvis. Just because you're 40 now and a little heavier, you're still good. In fact, the rosy cheeks are reminiscent of when you first started out. Your 'gain' is not bad. In fact, it's a little becoming. At least you're not wearing funny clothes anymore and looking like a ballet dancer. You know what they say. The bigger you are, the more there is to love. Girls, take note."[184]

In the *Tennessean*, reviewer Eve Zibart noted, "Neither overweight nor age nor familiarity can dim Elvis Presley's appeal, according to reactions to his Tuesday night concert." She quoted fan Polly Bell who said, "I'm still madly in love with him. I would say he seems to have sung much better, his voice seemed deeper" although she admitted she was "very disappointed" by the amount of weight Elvis had gained. Another fan, Judy Wray, "dismissed the question of Presley's weight," stating "His appearance doesn't mean that much to me. I love his music."

I attended that concert and was quoted in the *Tennessean* review saying the concert was "rather a disappointment. Elvis had a paunch on him, obviously. He wasn't on and his band wasn't on all that much. His act hasn't changed much at all—he had to read the words to his latest release" before adding, "What can you say about the King? He can have a bad day but he's still the King. He's still pretty—just a little more hefty." It was noted that I "tended to be a little more critical" because I was a male.[185]

An article in the Nashville *Banner* stated, "The time has come for Elvis Presley to face facts. Time has come when it's getting a little boring to keep asking, 'Where's Elvis? Anybody seen Elvis? Wonder how long he's going to keep on hiding? Elvis, don't cha' think it's time you quit playing hide and seek with your admirers, the people that have spent piles of money on you?'" The article continued that Elvis "has got to be the all-time best kept secret. More is made public of the Central Intelligence Agency than the singer's personal life. What does he eat? What does he do for recreation? Doesn't he get tired of being a recluse? What does he feel he has missed most in his life because of the Colonel's tight rein? Has he ever walked into McDonald's and ordered a double cheeseburger (hold the ketchup)? Wouldn't he like to get out of his Graceland mansion in Memphis and meet some people, go to a movie, have a beer and pizza with the guys and gals, go to the lake, things like that?"

The reporter then quoted "a friend" who stated, "People think Elvis is miserable. He's anything but miserable. Elvis does everything he wants to do, maybe more. One of his big things is riding his motorcycle and very often he cranks it up and takes out driving through Memphis. Even in Las Vegas. Elvis' secret is that once he does go outside, he doesn't stay in one place too long. Some girls might see Elvis dashing around, but all they'll be able to say is 'Wasn't that Elvis?' He goes to all the movies he wants to see but he doesn't do it in the conventional manner. Elvis rents theaters most of the time after midnight and takes his friends with him. If he doesn't like the show, he'll usually get up and leave during the performance. Everybody else goes out, too."

The "friend" then related a story. During one of his appearances in Las Vegas, Elvis wanted to take a sauna so Colonel Parker called the hotel manager and relayed this request. The manger reportedly replied, "Well, sir, you have the entire third floor rented. There's a sauna bath at the end of the hall," whereby the Colonel replied, "I don't think you understand. Mr. Presley wants it in the next room." According to the article, a sauna was being installed in the next room about an hour later."[186]

Before the next show in Murfreesboro, *Banner* reporter Larry Brinton interviewed Elvis' long time friend and bodyguard, Red West, for an article. West stated that "Our biggest problem is in a crowd or when he's leaving for a big concert or coming from a concert. Fans just don't think and they go into a frenzy trying to grab Elvis. It's just like the spreading of a prairie fire. When someone breaks a police line, everyone breaks it. They just don't realize that one of them might get hurt or that they can hurt one of us. Sometimes they'll punch you in the eye with their finger. That's why Elvis always wears glasses now when he is in a crowd. He has been caught quite a few times with fingernails. People don't try to hurt him, but they do. It's just that they don't realize the danger."

Elvis' security detail consisted of four personal bodyguards who were joined by a number of local policemen. "It takes a lot of time going over the entire security plans to make sure everything will go off just right and that Elvis won't get mobbed," said West, who then talked about the concert at Madison Square Garden. West stated that "after the show we hurried out of the Garden and jumped in a car to make a quick getaway back to our hotel. We went out the back door and pulled off, but the traffic flow required us to drive beside the building and then turn back in front of Madison Square Garden. People were just leaving after Elvis' performance and they spotted us and surged towards the car. The New York policemen were on horses and as the crowd came at us, some of the horses fell. Cars were going everywhere. Five of us were in the car and I was in the back seat with Elvis. It got kind of scary until the horses and policemen brought the crowd under control and we could get out of there."

West related that a humorous incident occurred before a show in Abilene, Texas when they were gathered in two rooms. "This guy came up with a tray full of weird looking drinks," said West. "I initially suspected something was wrong and asked him, 'Who ordered these?' The guy had a waiter's coat on and everything. He said, 'Somebody in the room here, Mr. Presley's room.' There were different kinds of glasses and the drinks looked real weak. I later found out by talking to him he was just a fan of Elvis' and had gone around the motel gathering up any kind of glasses he could find that had been used and just poured water in them to fill them up. He did all this just to get in the room. I let him stay a little while because he had shown a lot of nerve. I talked with him as long as I could, but I never did let him see Elvis."

West said that some girls "go to almost all extremes" to meet Elvis. "Two girls even mailed themselves to his home in Memphis," said West. "They'll do anything, sometimes even acting like waitresses and cleaning women."[187]

In April, the single "T-R-O-U-B-L-E" b/w "Mr. Songman" and the album *Today* was released. Elvis' third tour in 1975 began on July 8 and ended on August 24; on September 18 he opened in Las Vegas but, two days later, cancelled the engagement and entered the hospital with chronic intestinal and bowel problems, high cholesterol, fatty liver and depression. On September 30 the single "Bringing It Back" b/w "Pieces of My Life" was released and he returned to the Las Vegas Hilton on December 2 and performed there until December 15.

Just before midnight on Christmas Day, Elvis made a quick trip to Nashville, staying about 45 minutes. "He wanted to show some of his Memphis friends his new Convair 880 (four engine jet that resembles a 707)," wrote Red O'Donnell in the Nashville *Banner*. "So they all got in and flew up here, landing at a private airstrip. Elvis got out of the plane, got into the car of his longtime friend Lamar Fike of Madison and drove away." When some of his friends yelled, 'Where are you going?' Elvis laughed and said, 'I'll be seeing you guys later,'" the friends said. The friends just stood there while the car with Elvis and Lamar breezed down the runway of the private airport. However, it was all a joke—and Elvis loves to play jokes on his friends—because the car soon turned around and came back to the hangar. They then boarded the 880—and it is a deluxe craft—and returned to Memphis."[188]

On New Year's Eve Elvis performed at the huge Silverdome in Pontiac, Michigan.

On January 3, 1976—five days before his birthday—an article in the Nashville *Banner* by Red O'Donnell noted that Elvis will probably spend his forty-first birthday playing racquet ball and that "Elvis has had a court built on the grounds of his Memphis home and has gone nuts about the game," according to a friend. The article quoted producer Felton Jarvis, who attended the Silverdome concert and said that during the show, which he described as "fantastic," Elvis' "pants split during one of his on-stage numbers. It happened once before (the pants splitting incident) when he was performing in Memphis. Some of the guys on the show kidded Elvis, telling him 'We believe that is now part of your act.'"[189]

In January the album *Elvis: A Legendary Performer, Vol 2* was released by RCA, and the label set up recording equipment at Graceland to do more recording, which was done February 2-8. Songs recorded during those sessions were "Bitter They Are, Harder They Fall," "She Thinks I Still Care," "The Last Farewell," "Solitaire," "Moody Blue," "I'll Never Fall in Love Again," "For the Heart," "Hurt," "Danny Boy," "Never Again," "Love Coming Down" and "Blue Eyes Crying in the Rain." Elvis toured March 17-22 and again April 21-30. In April the album *From Elvis Presley Boulevard, Memphis, Tennessee* was released.

In April, an article in the Nashville *Banner* reported that "Elvis Presley and a team of Nashville businessmen will construct three racquetball complexes in Nashville costing more than $2 million." The first facility was scheduled for construction on Trousdale Avenue near Harding Place where Elvis and his partners "have purchased a one-acre tract there for $80,000." The article noted that "this is Presley's first step into the promotional world outside his field of entertainment. The singer will serve as chairman of the board of Presley Center Courts Inc., based in Memphis."

Plans were in place for two more racquetball complexes—containing ten racquetball courts—in Nashville, three in Memphis and two each in Chattanooga and Knoxville. Each facility would reportedly cost $700,000. Elvis was cited as an "excellent player" in the article who "reportedly took up the sport at the advice of his personal physician, Dr. George Nichopoulos in an effort to lose weight. "Elvis plays racquetball every day," he said. "He's lost a considerable amount of weight by doing it." The new business will have Nichopoulos as president and, in addition to racquet ball courts, will also feature "pro shops, child care centers, sauna baths, locker rooms, exercise rooms and teaching facilities."

It was noted that Elvis "will not be involved in the day-to-day management of the business."[190]

In March, the Nashville *Banner* published an article which stated that Elvis was planning another appearance in the Nashville area at the Murphy Center in Murfreesboro in mid-August. At the time of the article, Elvis was finishing his current tour in Johnson City, Tennessee. There were two new musicians playing keyboards in Elvis' band, Nashvillians David Briggs and Shane Keister. It was also reported that Elvis included "a batch of new songs" in his shows. The reporter interviewed a fan, Mrs. Faye Bailey, who, with her friends, had traveled to Knoxville, Nashville and Murfreesboro to see him perform. They were in Johnson City trying to spot him but "We never found him," said Mrs. Bailey, who stated that she and her friends had gone to Las Vegas twice to see Elvis. "We got the money together by having yard sales," she said. "It's taken 20 years but we're finally getting upset about this. We're going to try one more time—Friday night."[191]

An edition of the *Banner* reported that there were rumors floating about another Elvis show in Murfreesboro during August but Harold Smith, who was in charge of booking concerts at Murphy Center said, "If they're going to have it here, they had better get on the ball and let us know." Nobody in the Presley camp was talking but there was a mid-summer tour scheduled to begin on July 23 and Elvis had "several open dates in the near future." The article noted that "bookings are not made more than six weeks in advance" so the concert was a possibility. Harold Smith stated that "Throughout the year we get 12-25 phone calls a day asking about Elvis and when he's coming back, plus about 10 or 12 pieces of mail a day. A lot of the letters have money inside or checks asking us to hold them tickets 'just in case.' I don't mean from people in Tennessee—but all over the country." The same was true in Nashville, according to Hal May of Sound Seventy. "We get calls almost every day," he said. "And every time an Elvis movie comes on TV, they start calling wanting to know when he's coming for a show."[192]

Elvis toured June 25-July 5, July 23-August 5, August 27-September 8, and October 14-27—but did not perform in the Nashville area for any of these shows. Two days after his October tour, Elvis recorded four songs at Graceland: "It's Easy For You," "Way Down," "Pledging My Love" and "He'll Have To Go." He toured again November 24-30, then opened a ten day stand at the Las Vegas Hilton and toured again at the end of the year, finishing with a New Year's Eve Show at the Civic Center Arena in Pittsburgh.

On January 8, 1977, Elvis celebrated his forty-second birthday and the final trip of Elvis to Nashville occurred about two weeks later, on January 21. Felton Jarvis, Elvis' Nashville producer, had arranged for Elvis to record at Creative Workshop, a new state-of-the art studio owned by Buzz Cason in Berry Hill, a suburb of Nashville. Elvis registered at the Sheraton South Hotel but remained in his room, complaining of a sore throat while the musicians waited in the studio. The next day, he returned to Memphis without ever going into the studio. Jarvis completed the overdubs on material recorded at Graceland the previous October at the studio.

Elvis recorded in the "Jungle Room" at Graceland and when Felton mixed the songs in Nashville he invited Tony Brown over to listen and Tony remembered that "in a recording studio there are these big microphones mounted on huge mic stands. The mic hangs down and has a protection cover around them to keep the words from popping. Elvis had unscrewed his mike and taken it off the boom—which you're not supposed to do—and was holding the thing like a hand mike, walking around the room singing 'Way Down' and I was playing that boogie woogie thing on the piano and his hand was over my left hand while he was singing 'Way Down' and I had to play around his hand. Then he would walk all around the room—he wanted to make eye contact with James Burton, with Ronnie Tutt. Felton soloed Elvis' microphone and you could tell where he was in the room—walking in front of Tutt's drum kit, then walking in front of Burton's amp, then over by me and the piano. Most producers get the singer to sing a song four or five times but Elvis only did one vocal and that was live. If there was a session now where a singer took the microphone off the boom I think we'd just stop everything and say 'hold it, guys.' But that was E.P."[193]

Elvis was on tour February 12-21, then took a vacation in Hawaii March 4-12, toured again March 23-31 then spent time in the hospital in April before he toured again April 21-May 1 and May 3-June 26. On June 6, the single "Way Down" b/w "Pledging My Love" was released and in July the album, *Moody Blue*, comprised of recordings from the Graceland sessions, was shipped.

The band wore "those horrible polyester suits," remembered Tony Brown. "We had a baby blue one, a dark blue one, a maroon one, a white one and a black one. Elvis wore the sunburst suit every night during that last year of his life because that was the only one that would really fit him.[194]

On August 4, the book *Elvis: What Happened?*, written by former bodyguards Red West, Sonny West and Dave Hebler was published; it exposed Elvis' extensive drug use and bizarre behavior.

Chapter 20: August 16 - 17, 1977

On Tuesday afternoon, August 16, 1977, Tony Brown was at the Nashville airport, waiting for the plane to take him, Felton Jarvis, the six members of the Stamps Quartet, Bobby Ogden and a few others to Elvis' scheduled concert in Portland, Maine.

"There were four planes on tour—the band had a plane, the sound crew had a plane, Elvis had a plane and the Colonel had a plane," said Tony. "The Colonel flew a few days ahead and set things up, Elvis flew the day of the show and the band flew the day of the show. If the tour started on the East Coast the planes started in Los Angeles and picked up James Burton, Ronnie Tutt, Jerry Scheff and the other band members that lived there and then stopped in Las Vegas and picked up Joe Guercio and his horn players. The next stop was Nashville where they picked up the rest of us. If the tour originated on the West Coast, we would take commercial flights to wherever the first show was and then the show plane would go from there."

"We had to be at the airport an hour or hour and a half early because there was a bunch of us," continued Tony. "When that plane landed—it was the big plane—they didn't want any stragglers because they didn't want anything to slow things down. They'd land and then take off pretty quickly. It was always exciting to go on tour."

"It was a real pretty afternoon, gorgeous, when all of a sudden this big storm out of nowhere came up and the wind started blowing," remembered Tony. "It almost looked like a hurricane." Tony and the other musicians were in the section of the Nashville airport where the private planes landed, next to the hangers for the National Guard.

"The storm got so crazy that I noticed six or seven National Guard guys came running into this private waiting area where the Elvis entourage was waiting," continued Tony. "I guess just to get out of the rain. This was back before cell phones, back when cell phones were portable phones, like a little suitcase in your hand, and I remember these National Guard guys walking in and I overheard the leader talking over his portable phone and I heard him say 'So is he dead?' He listened and then he said, 'So are they waiting to pronounce Mr. Presley dead?' My first thought was that Vernon had passed away."

"I'd been on the Elvis show for three years but I still felt like a newbie so I kept my mouth shut, I didn't say much," said Tony. "I kept quiet and then the storm subsided, the National Guard guys left, and Felton Jarvis, who was Elvis' producer and, at that time the tour manager, walked up to all of us and said, 'Hey, guys, the tour is off. Go home; we'll give you a call.' That's all he said. On my way home, on the radio, I heard that Elvis Presley was on his way to the Memphis Hospital. He had not been pronounced dead, officially, but they found him in his bathroom in Graceland. Then, in just a few more minutes, they said 'Elvis has been pronounced dead.' My first thought was 'I can't believe they didn't tell us. Maybe pull us aside and say 'Hey, guys, something really awful has happened. Say prayers or whatever.' But the Colonel was so private that I'm not surprised now when I look back on it that he didn't tell us. But that still flabbergasted me because Felton was such a sweet, compassionate man, I mean, one of my favorite people I ever met in my life. Why didn't he just pull us aside and say 'Hey guys, say a prayer for Elvis,' but no one said that."

As he drove towards his home Brown "burst out crying in my car and then I went to a bar and had lots of adult beverages." David Briggs had played electric piano in Elvis' band but left the tour and was replaced by Bobby Ogden. Tony and Briggs had met for a drink at Julian's, a restaurant and bar located on West End, near Centennial Park, about three days before and talked about the book, *Elvis: What Happened?*

"I remember telling David Briggs 'This is going to kill Elvis. It's unbelievable—it's going to kill him. I can't believe that those guys did that,'" said Tony. "Elvis was not a happy guy. He had a lot of demons with him during the last few years that I was with him. Everyone said that after his Mom passed away, he was not the same and then after he and Priscilla broke up he was never the same and he was constantly struggling with his weight so he was in a very depressed state. In hindsight I was not surprised that he had a heart attack and died. But, still, it was just a strange, strange moment with the National Guard guy and what happened and how impersonal it all was. I don't hold it against Felton or anybody because I knew that's how it worked."[195]

The next morning the *Tennessean* had two front page stories on Elvis. The first, headlined "Elvis' Death at 42 Called Heart Attack; No Drugs Found" was from wire reports. It stated that Elvis "died yesterday afternoon of heart failure" at 3:30 p.m. at Baptist Hospital in Memphis and that "Dr. Jerry Francisco, medical examiner for Shelby County, said the cause of death was 'cardiac arrythmia,' an irregular heartbeat. He said, 'That's just another name for a form of heart attack.'"

Francisco told the reporters that "a three-hour autopsy uncovered no sign of any other diseases, and there was no sign of any drug abuse," adding that "the only drugs he had detected were those that had been prescribed by Presley's personal physician for hypertension and a blockage of the colon for which the singer had been hospitalized twice in 1975." Memphis Police Captain John McLaughlin "denied an earlier report that detectives were investigating a possible drug overdose while Presley's personal physician, Dr. George Nichopoulos, stated the singer "was in 'respiratory distress' when he was brought into the emergency room."

The article noted that road manager Joe Esposito discovered the body and attempted resuscitation efforts, then called Dr. Nichopoulos and an ambulance. The article quoted Nichopoulos saying "Come on Presley, breathe. Breathe for me," in the ambulance as it drove to the hospital.

The article also stated that twenty-year old Ginger Alden was at Presley's home at the time of his death.

The phone lines of newspapers, radio and TV stations in Memphis were deluged with calls and the article pointed out that Elvis "had been hospitalized at Baptist in April when he cut short a tour in Louisiana and returned to Memphis." He was reportedly suffering "from exhaustion and intestinal flu at that time" although during the past two years he was "hospitalized for eye problems and for what doctors described as a twisted colon."

Elvis was scheduled to leave the day he died for an eleven day tour to start in Portland, Maine. The venue announced it would refund the 17,000 tickets that were sold for the two scheduled performances.

It was noted that Vernon Presley "was taking his son's death 'very badly.'" Radio stations responded by playing Elvis records; Radio Luxembourg in Europe played "a long program of his music."

The article presented a brief biography of his career, from his birth in Tupelo to his recordings at the Sun Studio, early fame, time in the Army, marriage, divorce and movie career.[196]

The second front page story in the *Tennessean* that day was written by two Nashville reporters, Laura Eipper and Alice Alexander, who quoted Jordanaire Ray Walker who stated, "I think Elvis was always looking for happiness, but he once said to me: 'I've come too far, and I don't know how to get back. I doubt I'll ever live to be fifty.'"

The reporters stated that "reports of the singer's death were met with stunned disbelief, at first, in the music community" in Nashville and quoted Country Music Association Executive Director Jo Walker, who said, "We've all heard so many rumors about his health. Of course we prayed they weren't true. It's hard to believe. We're distressed and shocked. The world of music has lost one of its finest exponents." Frances Preston, head of the performance rights organization BMI stated, "I met him when I worked at WSM, probably 25 years ago. I remember it distinctly. It was at the first WSM celebration and people pointed to Elvis' blue rhinestone cuff links and wondered who on earth he was. He was just a young kid, a country music fan—long before he'd ever come here to record."

Joe Galante, head of the Nashville division of RCA, stated, "His death reminds me of when I read about Valentino—it has touched so many people, everywhere. I don't know if we'll ever be able to fill the musical void he has left." Galante was at Hilton Head Island with Ronnie Milsap, who was getting ready for a show when they heard of Elvis' death. He continued, "We were all amazed and terribly upset. A tremendous part of our music is gone, and with it a man responsible for helping Nashville enormously."

Ray Walker countered that Elvis' death "wasn't really sudden. Elvis had been in bad health for the past two or three years. In fact, more serious than he knew himself."

Eipper and Alexander quoted Nancy Anderson, a reporter for the Copley news service who claimed to be "among the last admitted backstage for interviews in the dressing room" who stated "He would tell a lot of people, me included, about the time he was still with Priscilla. He would suffer from nightmares, he said, from which he would awake in a cold sweat—all the money was gone, the Colonel was gone, the girls at the fence—everything. The last time I spoke with him he said the nightmares were still coming."

"Elvis always wanted to amount to something," remembered Ray Walker. "He did not underestimate his impact, but I don't think he ever accomplished what he wanted to."

The article quoted Pat Boone, "a contemporary of Presley whose white buck shoes and smooth demeanor contrasted with Presley's leather jackets and gyrating hips" who stated, "The void he will leave is impossible to gauge. The one thing I regret is that he never made his tour of Europe and the Orient, because of his fear of flying, which would have made him a world-wide success all over again. He died young, like James Dean. And perhaps that's the best way for the public to remember him," adding that no one "could imagine an old Elvis."

Creative Workshop owner Buzz Cason was quoted saying, "He was a major influence on those of us who grew up in that era—a poor American boy who made it to the top. He gave us all the drive to do what we're doing. His impact was too great to narrow it down to just to Nashville; Elvis affected the entire world."[197]

On Thursday, August 18, the *Tennessean* reported that "Elvis Presley lay in state yesterday in the quiet dimness of his Graceland mansion as thousands of his fans crushed against the wrought iron gates, weeping, screaming, fainting and nearly trampling one another. Hundreds were treated for heat prostration. Inside, Elvis' body lay in an open copper seamless coffin, dressed in a white suit with a pale blue shirt and white tie."

Crowds started gathering outside Graceland as soon as news of Elvis' death was broadcast. Some drove thousands of miles; some slept overnight in their cars until by mid-afternoon there were people lined up four deep on the Boulevard in front of his house. The column of people extended past the sight of Graceland and traffic was so congested that cars just sat. A police officer estimated there may have been 75,000 gathered during the course of the day.

It was announced that a private service would be held that afternoon and Elvis would be buried in the Forest Hill midtown Cemetery Mausoleum close to where his mother was buried "exactly 19 years ago yesterday." Like his mother, Gladys, Elvis also died when he was 42.

The scene on Elvis Presley Boulevard in front of Graceland was chaotic as police tried vainly to impose a semblance of order among the fans, many of whom seemed to be almost hysterical. Ambulances appeared regularly to carry away those who had fainted or fallen and by late afternoon, Memphis authorities estimated that over 300 people had been treated for heat prostration.

Every three to four minutes, on average, another semi-conscious victim of the afternoon's heat was carried through the gates to a makeshift emergency station. The *Tennessean* reporters stated that "Among the most distressed mourners was Ginger Alden, who was Elvis' current girlfriend. It was she who found him, near death, on the floor of a bathroom at Graceland. They had just completed a rigorous game of racketball."

According to Ginger's mother, Mrs. Joe Alden, Elvis and Ginger "had planned to announce a wedding date August 27 at a Memphis concert" and that "Elvis was going to build a studio at Graceland" for her daughter, who was described as "an art student."[198]

At three in the afternoon on the day after his death, the press walked single-file up the driveway to Graceland which, according to the Nashville reporters, "seemed less impressive than one would expect the home of a 'king' to be—a graceful stone colonial building with four white pillars in front, shuttered windows on each of the two floors and elaborate iron grill work designed, presumably, to insure the seclusion that had been so important to Elvis in his last years. To the right of the house the turquoise sparkle of a swimming pool seemed oddly festive for the occasion."

Along the path were armed guards who checked to assure that no cameras were taken into the house. In front of the house were dozens of flower arrangements, some inscribed "Elvis the King," "Elvis, We Love

You" and "Now and Forever, Love."

After the press viewed the body, fans were allowed to enter in small groups where they were allowed to glimpse Presley's body for a few seconds where he lay in a coffin lined with white satin in the hallway draped in red velvet, surrounded by nearly 20 protective friends and guards. White sheets were laid over the home's plush red carpeting to protect it from the large number of visitors.

The reporters noted that Elvis' "hair seems a bit darker than many remember" and he appeared "definitely heavier than in his prime as America's rock'n'roll idol, but he is still undeniably a handsome man."

"Most strikingly, he seems finally at peace," wrote the reporters, "something that apparently had eluded him in life."

Many of those who saw him in the casket "came away from the experience shaken, many supporting one another during the long walk away from the mansion," although "only a small fraction of the crowd ever got near the mansion before the gates were closed at 6:30 p.m.," which was 90 minutes later than originally scheduled. There were an estimated 15,000 fans waiting outside the gates that day when they were closed as a light rain started to fall.

The newspaper reporters quoted a fan who said "I don't believe this is really happening" while another stated, "It's just impossible to believe he's really gone. I've loved him my whole life. He's a part of my life like my brother. He can't be gone."

Hysterical fans jammed the gates, which kept those who had viewed the body from leaving. One fan complained, "These people are maniacs. Don't they have any respect? This is horrible! I loved Elvis for 20 years and I didn't even get a chance to see him because I was pushed out of the way. Elvis would just be sickened by the whole thing."

In the early evening, those gathered went to grocery stores and fast food outlets for something to eat, although food and drinks were hard to find. Elvis song and picture books and post cards of Graceland sold out quickly while six lanes of traffic on Elvis Presley Boulevard were at a standstill.

It was announced that Elvis would be placed "in the family crypt of a marble mausoleum destined to become a shrine for adoring fans." The reporters also noted that rumors of drug problems continued to circulate although Medical Examiner Dr. Jerry Francisco stated, "There was no evidence of any abnormal illegal drug use" after he had conducted a three hour autopsy shortly after Elvis died. "Francisco's preliminary findings contradicted published reports that the singer was a heavy user of drugs that, it was said, had affected his health and his ability to function normally." [199]

In the *Tennessean*, an article quoted Perry Como saying that Elvis "was a gentle boy, mischievous but most generous, who had turned angry and frustrated at the world of stardom that he lived in."

"I felt sorry for the man," said Como, who also recorded for RCA, Elvis' record label. "I don't think he lived two years as himself. At first, he was happy about success, but as the years wore on, a sadness came, because Elvis was unable to do the things he wanted to do. Maybe he was too protected, who is to say? It was only lately he became angry with the world. He didn't go anywhere. It was as though he had become completely frustrated with his life."

Como added, "His death is a tremendous loss whether you liked him or not. We're all going to miss him."

There was a story about Elvis' generosity with several Denver policemen; he purchased a Lincoln Continental Mark IV for an officer, then bought cars for two of the police officer's subordinate officers and one for the policeman's friend.

In Hartford, Connecticut, where Elvis was scheduled to perform on his upcoming tour, there was a booth set up for refunds, but most who purchased a ticket were keeping it. Those who came to get a refund found a group surrounding the booth ready to purchase the ticket from them.

In Longview, Washington, it was reported that a 30-year old woman told her husband, after hearing of the death of Elvis, "Honey, now you're number one."[200]

In Nashville, Governor Ray Blanton ordered all state flags to fly at half mast in Presley's memory. The Governor issued a press release extolling Elvis and was invited to attend the funeral.[201]

Lon Varnell, a Nashville concert promoter who had worked with Colonel Tom Parker for years and promoted several Elvis concerts stated that the singer's "aloofness with the public came from his manager's efforts to make the singer/actor a myth. Colonel Tom Parker wouldn't let him be exposed," said Varnell.

"Colonel Tom had tremendous control over him," continued Varnell. "He felt that if he kept him under wraps people would come to see him. People are funny—they want what they think they can't have." Varnell noted that this probably took a toll on the performer because, although Parker and Presley may have profited financially, "I think it took a great deal out of Elvis in his everyday life. Elvis lived a very secluded and lonely life."

Varnell predicted that "Presley's appeal will continue long after his death. He was a legend in his own time [and] I predict he'll sell many more records in the next five years than anyone. He'll be remembered for the great entertainer that he was. People will buy his records to re-live those moments they spent at Elvis' concerts."

"You'll never know an old Elvis Presley," said Varnell. "Like James Dean, Presley will be remembered at his peak for a long time to come. There is no question that Presley's the greatest entertainer that's come across the horizon since entertainment began. He was one of a kind. I doubt that you'll ever see another Elvis Presley."[202]

The death of Elvis caused people to rush out and buy his records. Within an hour after most record stores opened on the day after Elvis died, they were sold out of Elvis records, both albums and 45s as well as 8-track tapes. One woman reportedly burst out crying when she came into a store to purchase an album and was told there were none left.

One record store manager stated that "most of the people searching for Elvis recordings bought anything they could find, although some customers admitted they had never heard of some of the songs."[203]

An Editorial in the Nashville *Tennessean* two days after his death observed that "He didn't invent rock-and-roll, but he made it roll with songs like 'Heartbreak Hotel,' recorded at the RCA studios here" and that "whatever else may be said of his talent, timing had something to do with his success." The Editorial noted that Elvis "could still pack them in at age 42, although there were those who thought that age and success had taken something from him. Perhaps they did. Those who knew him well talked of his restlessness, his poor health and his emotional insecurity. Perhaps only he knew the price he paid for fame and fortune, but he gave his fans their money's worth and a lot of happy memories."[204]

In England the Associated Press reported that "Britain's favorite disc jockey" asserted that the death of Elvis was "a global disaster" and "weeping fans of the rock'n'roll king besieged European record stores to buy vintage Presley albums and his hits once again jammed the airwaves from Peru to Israel."

The British Elvis Presley Fan Club's 21st annual convention was scheduled for the coming weekend and it would go on, although the two scheduled Elvis movies would not be shown because "I don't believe anybody could bear to see them now," said an organizer, who noted that a memorial service would be held and attendees were buying black arm bands to wear.

It was reported that on the Champs Elyses in Paris a woman waited at the door of a record store the morning after Elvis' death and bought two albums "with tears in her eyes." At the end of the day, an estimated $1,000 worth of Elvis records had been sold. There were reports that fans cried outside record stores in Brussels, radio disc jockeys all over Europe broke into regular programming for the news of the singer's death, and in Spain the government owned television station made Presley's death a major news feature. Newspapers all over Europe as well as Mexico, Brazil, and Israel had the news of Elvis' death on their front pages and articles analyzing the impact of Elvis on music were a common feature. In the Soviet Union, the Communist owned newspaper *Izvestia* used Presley's death to criticize capitalism, stating, "Enterprising businessmen transformed Presley into the 'Idol of rock'n'roll,' putting his talent and renown to work in the service of profits."[205]

Meanwhile, the Palmer House in Chicago was set to host a Beatles Convention for 2,000 Beatlemaniacs. By 1977, the Beatles had not performed together for over eight years but 29-year old Mark Lapidos organized Beatlefests because "The Beatles are as important today as they were in 1964 when they were on Ed Sullivan."

Lapidos and his wife worked full time organizing and promoting Beatlefests and believed it was a long-term commitment. "I think we'll be having Beatlefests 10 years from now...for as long as people want to celebrate the greatest rock and roll band ever. I don't know if anything will ever replace the Beatles."[206]

Chapter 21: August 18 - 24, 1977

On the morning that Elvis was buried—Thursday, August 18—over 6,000 people gathered outside the gates of Graceland. The crowd was smaller than the estimated 80,000 who lined Elvis Presley Boulevard on the day the singer died. On this day, cars drove slowly by, people took pictures of the house and hawkers peddled t-shirts and ice cream in the 98 degree heat.

There were those who stood silent in the crowd while others cried openly. A woman from Raleigh, North Carolina lamented, "I just don't think the whole thing has hit me yet. He was so vital, so lively. He did so much for people of every generation. It's impossible for me to imagine that he's dead."

Another woman told a reporter, "We're here because we loved him. We cared about him so much we named our son after him." A woman from Baltimore said, "I'm still in shock. When I heard the news I just drove around stunned for about three hours and then we got on a plane and came here. This all seemed like a dream."

A Shriner's Convention was held in Memphis during the week of Elvis' death and one Shriner noted that many of their wives "stood in the lobby of our hotel and cried this morning and told Elvis stories. It made me feel bad and I don't even like rock'n'roll."[207]

In addition to the overwhelming sadness on the day of Elvis' burial, there was also anger because two 19-year-old women from Monroe, Louisiana, Joanne Johnson and Alice Marie Hovartar, had been killed by a drunk driver who drove into the crowd of mourners at 3:45 Thursday morning and then sped away.

The young women were in a group of about 2,000 people who kept an all-night vigil outside Graceland Wednesday night and Thursday morning. Police managed to stop the car after a block long chase and arrested the 18-year old man, who came out fighting as the crowd screamed "Lynch him! Hang him up!" In the car with him were three girls, all 17 or younger.[208]

All during the day, family members and dignitaries arrived and went through the gates. Eddie Fadal, described as a "lifelong friend," came outside the house and told reporters assembled that "Things are very quiet, people are sitting around the coffin in the living room. Some are crying, but everyone is pretty subdued," adding that Elvis' fiance Ginger Alden "was taking his death well" but ex-wife Priscilla Presley and daughter Lisa were "taking it very, very hard." Fadal told the reporters that "Lisa doesn't seem to know what has really happened. She's sitting and playing with her toys around the pool. She has seen the body but is just oblivious to what this is all about."

The funeral was scheduled for two that afternoon in the music room at Graceland, which adjoined the living room. A little after 3:30 the car carrying Vernon Presley led the procession to Forest Hill Cemetery. Behind Vernon's car was the white hearse carrying Elvis in an undraped coffin; behind the hearse was the car carrying Priscilla, who held nine year old Lisa Marie. Security was tight and the procession was delayed because of the thousands gathered at the cemetery, pushing against the cemetery's gates.

There were over 3,000 floral tributes, including displays from Debbie Reynolds, O.J. Simpson, Glen Campbell, the Carpenters, Donna Fargo, Conway Twitty, President Jimmy Carter's White House, and even one from the Soviet Union. The florists in Memphis had run out of flowers and had to have more rushed in as they stayed up all night preparing floral tributes to Elvis from all over the world. The florists had to use skills they had previously not used as they created displays of a six-foot guitar, a five-by-four foot hound dog, hearts, crowns and crosses.

It was almost an hour after the hearse left Graceland before it drove through Forest Lawn and up to the mausoleum where the coffin, covered in red roses, was lifted from the hearse and carried inside by pall bearers that included Elvis' personal physician Dr. George Nichopoulos, guitar player and friend Charlie Hodge, record producer Felton Jarvis, long time friend Lamar Fike, and his cousin, Billy Smith.

The service was conducted by C.W. Bradley, minister of the Woodvale

Church of Christ in Memphis. Bradley was described as an old family friend with a Nashville connection; he graduated from David Lipscomb College in Nashville in 1942. Noted TV minister Reverend Rex Humbard also spoke at the service.

Elvis was buried a little after 4:30 p.m. in the Forest Hills Cemetery in Memphis following services attended by 200 family members, close friends and entertainment business associates. Joe Esposito was quoted saying "The service lasted longer than was expected because everyone filed by to say goodbye to Elvis." He was laid to rest wearing a diamond ring with the inscription "TCB," which stood for "Taking Care of Business," a favorite phrase of Elvis and his entourage.

After Elvis was laid to rest, "the crypt in the mausoleum where the body was placed was sealed and mortared over, then covered with a marble slab. Attending the service was Chet Atkins, who produced Elvis' early recordings for RCA. [209]

At 8:30 on Friday morning, the day after Elvis was buried, about 700 fans ran, walked and jogged up the mile-long road leading into Forest Hills Cemetery hoping to find a flower from the funeral to keep as a memento. The Presley family had announced they wanted the flowers to be distributed, so fans waited all night, some sleeping in cars, others in pitched tents in the field across from Graceland. There were about 3,000 floral displays and the original plan was to give each fan a flower; however, in the chaos some fans took entire arrangements, including one who escaped with the two foot tall Bible comprised of white carnations.

Fans were not allowed inside the mausoleum but many took pictures. One woman expressed hope that the Presley family "will build a monument to him here. He deserves it, because he really was a king. We'd like to have some place we could come back to visit again."

Some could not be consoled in their grief. "He's really gone," cried a fan from New York. "He's gone and I'll never see him again. God, why did he have to die? I came all the way from New York to give him a crown I had made for him out of crystal and velvet. I finished it on the day he died."

"I gave it to his cousin and told him to give it to Lisa," she added. "I wanted her to know her father is worth everything."

A teenager sobbed over and over "My life is over, my life is over," as police and guards expressed concern that someone might commit suicide.

After the funeral, police attempted to move the crowd away, but they lingered, seemingly unable to leave. Inside the mausoleum, a drapery of "Forever Yours" red roses that had covered his coffin was laid on the floor while a three foot tall cross of white carnations and red roses stood next to the vault; on a streamer were the names of Priscilla and his daughter Lisa Marie.[210]

The day after the funeral, the *Tennessean* reported that Colonel Tom Parker "will remain in charge of the late singer's affairs for the time being." That announcement was made by Joe Esposito while Parker avoided the press and kept a low profile during the funeral.

Parker had learned of Elvis' death while in New England, working on details for the upcoming tour. After he was informed, he went immediately to the Graceland mansion in Memphis. Parker attended the funeral and entombment. The paper reported that although Parker usually kept a low profile, he "did break his silence in late April this year to deny a report published in another Nashville newspaper that he was about to sell his Elvis contract and that he and Elvis were estranged. 'That whole story is a complete fabrication,' said Parker. 'I'm here, I'm working for Elvis. I'm in good health.'"[211]

On Friday in Nashville two movie theaters—the Tennessee and Belcourt—showed the film *Elvis On Tour*. The theaters were both crowded with fans, who left in silence or sobbing.

A woman who attended the film stated, "The realization just hasn't hit me yet that he is dead," while another said, "It is too hard to believe. We're the same age, so it really hit home," then added, "When he started out, I thought he was dirty but he grew on me and I've been a fan ever since. He could look at you and make you want to die,"

A third woman lamented, "I loved the movie, I loved Elvis. Why did he have to die? It is so sad to sit there and see him. I had to go though—I wanted to see him so bad. There will always be a sadness when I think of him."[212]

In the Sunday *Tennessean* an interview with Felton Jarvis, Elvis' producer since 1962, summarized the life of the singer, saying "Elvis Presley was a man who lived for the times he could perform onstage for the people who were his fans, a man who gave and gave until there was nothing inside left to give."

Speaking of the past week, Jarvis stated, "It weighs you, it shakes you. This is not a comfortable thing for me; Elvis was never comfortable talking to the press, and I'm not either," but he wanted "to set the record straight."

Confronting the allegations of drug use by Elvis, Jarvis stated, "Elvis took medications his doctors prescribed for him. He wasn't a bad patient. But if the doctors say lose weight today, most of us tend to put it off until tomorrow. And he was no different. But that was all."

Sitting in an office at RCA, Jarvis stated that Elvis "was really two people. There was the private Elvis, the man I was privileged to know as a friend. And then there was that other Elvis onstage. Presley lived to be that person on the stage. He loved it, loved to be out there singing and looking at the people in the audience. You know that Big Song effect he began to go for...with that Big Orchestra backing it up, the way it would put the cold chill on you: well, he loved that too."

The reporter noted that Jarvis "spoke, sometimes with difficulty and with apparent effort to keep control, of a fantasy and the quasi-destructive fantasy world that bound performer to audience."

"I remember the times when, night after night, there would be five women at the show in Boston: then the next night in New York, there they'd be again," said Jarvis. "And again the next night in Atlanta. They weren't groupies, or anything. They were...just happy to be near him. They wouldn't even have the money to buy a ticket. They were happy if they could stand in his hotel lobby. It's so hard to explain."

Felton remembered that Elvis performed "when he was dog sick, with 103-degree fever; there was a night his voice had gone, and he walked out, sick, and tired. He got so angry with himself, and he said to the crowd, 'I'm sorry. This isn't right.'"

Jarvis recounted that he and Elvis "would go into what he called his 'trophy room' at Graceland. There all over the walls would be the records, the awards and the plaques. And Elvis would stare at them and say, 'Felton, this isn't me. This all belongs to somebody else.'"

Talking about Elvis in the studio, Jarvis stated that "the chief thing was that it had to feel right. I could say, 'look here, this song'll make you a million bucks!' But if Elvis didn't like the song, well, he just wouldn't bother."

Jarvis recounted "a hot, steamy day last summer when Presley was booked to begin work on what would prove to be his last Christmas album." "How in the world can I sing about snow and Santa Claus when it's 100 degrees outside, Felton?" asked Elvis. "This doesn't feel like Christmas." So, as a "joke," Jarvis found a fir tree and decorated it with Christmas lights, dressed Lamar Fike as Santa Claus, and waited for Elvis to enter the studio. According to Felton, Elvis came in, look at the set-up and burst out laughing. "You win, Felton," said Elvis. "Let's get to work here."

Discussing his role as producer, Felton stated, "Elvis produced Elvis: I was just there to help out." Jarvis talked about Elvis' generosity and stated, "It was as if he really believed you could make people happy by spending a bunch of money. You just can't buy happiness. I guess I felt sorry for Elvis in that respect."

Jarvis told the story of when he was in the hospital on a kidney machine while Elvis was scheduled to record a live album at Madison Square Garden in New York. As they negotiated the concert and recording with executives at RCA, "he and the Colonel told RCA that they could record this concert live. That was the plan, on one condition. That I be paid just as if I were there." Meanwhile, Jarvis was "laid up in a hospital bed with tubes up my nose and half-dead. Now that's the way Elvis was."

Jarvis noted that there was some unreleased material that Elvis had recorded which would be released later before stating, "That man was my life. My whole life, since 1962." He continued, "I believe God put Elvis on this earth for one purpose: to entertain people. Yes, I think he felt the same. He told me one time, 'Felton, don't you worry. Because I'm doing this my way.' It was the way he chose."[213]

Exactly one week after Elvis died, the *Tennessean* reported that Elvis' will "gives full estate to family" and noted that his father, Vernon, had total control of the estate. The will had been drawn up and signed on March 3, five months before he died.

The newspaper noted that the estate "included his 18-room mansion, Graceland, valued at $500,000; several parcels of land in Memphis worth about $260,000, and a fleet of aircraft and luxury automobiles" but sources in the music industry stated that "the lion's share of his estate would be enormous royalties from dozens of Presley recordings and residuals from his films" which were expected to gather millions of dollars.[214]

On August 24, eight days after Elvis died, a letter to the editor of the *Tennessean* from Nashville resident Sarah Taylor Holley said, "When did it happen? We have been busy, building careers, raising families, doing all the things that adults do, in a timeless dream. There have been clues—but we were too busy to notice, too confident to care. Wasn't it only yesterday that it was 1957, and we were immortal? And now, the 'King' is dead. He is gone, taking with him a part of ourselves, as we used to be. The pony tails, the white bobby sox, the black elastic waist-cinchers, the still crinolines, the ducktails, the black leather jackets; the innocence, the 'cool.' Forgotten gym doors spring open in our minds, emitting echoes of music. It is too soon. We were not ready. Elvis is gone, and we are not immortal, after all. We have been busy growing old."[215]

"I wouldn't take anything for the three years I spent with Elvis," said Tony Brown. "Even as the piano player with Voice because that was the year and a half I was around him at his three homes in Palm Springs, Beverly Hills and Graceland. We flew on his plane and I got to know him. I also got to know Vernon and I knew them as human beings. And then playing with Elvis on stage with a band gave me that bigger than life experience of playing with someone who is iconic as an entertainer. It was just unbelievable—the rush I felt when Elvis came on stage. We'd play the "Space Odyssey" theme and it would give me chills and then we would go into 'Mystery Train' and Ronnie Tutt would just lay down that jungle beat and the flashbulbs from the audience—my hair is standing up right now as I tell this—it was unbelievable. I wouldn't trade it for anything."

Tony Brown became one of the hottest—and most influential—producers in the music industry. He produced Brooks and Dunn, Wynonna, Vince Gill and George Strait and has accumulated a house full of gold and platinum records but playing piano for Elvis "elevated my status as a musician," said Tony, and "definitely defined my life because no matter what I have done in my career it never fails that in an interview I can always count on them saying, 'Do you mind if I just ask you a couple of Elvis questions?'"

"He was truly a down-to-earth, southern guy," said Tony. "But he was also Elvis Presley. When I was at his house with him it was Voice and then it was usually either Linda Thompson or Sheila Ryan, his girl friend after Linda, or Dave or Red or Sonny or Sam, Linda Thompson's brother, those kind of people. He was in casual clothes but Elvis always dressed like Elvis 24/7. Even his pajamas had the big collars. They didn't stand up well—that silk doesn't really hold that collar very well—but they were made with a high collar. And the belts, always he had on those big belts. Elvis was always Elvis 24/7."

When Elvis walked into a room "everything changed, even the temperature changed," said Tony Brown. "And if he walked into a room and there were 20 people he'd always pick just one person and impulsively go to them, say 'Hey, what's going on?' I remember that once during the last tour we weren't on stage when he got there and as we walked towards the stage—he was a ways behind the band—he called out 'Tony!' and my heart just got huge. When he called my name it felt like I was a chosen one. He just had that kind of impact on you."[216]

Elvis had a huge impact on Nashville as well. Thousands still come to the city each year to visit RCA Studio B, where Elvis recorded, and the Country Music Hall of Fame, where he is enshrined and where his Cadillac and gold piano are on display.

The heart of Elvis was filled with music; the same can be said of Nashville. The greatest singer of all time and the greatest music town of all time are linked. So much heart and so much music; that's the story of Elvis and that's also the story of Nashville.

- End -

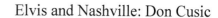

APPENDIX

Elvis in Nashville

These are documented visits of Elvis Presley to Nashville.

October 2, 1954: Ryman Auditorium. His first and only—performance on the Grand Ole Opry

October 3, 1954: Ernest Tubb Record Shop for the Midnight Jamboree.

1955: Carl Smith and June Carter's house; no one was home so he and Red West broke in and spent the night where Carl found them the next day in bed.

November 10, 1955 for the Disc Jockey Convention. At the Andrew Jackson Hotel, located where the Tennessee Performing Arts Center is now, he heard "Heartbreak Hotel," his first number one hit, for first time.

January 10, 1956: Methodist TV, Radio and Film Commission offices, 1525 McGavock Street, which had a studio that RCA used. Here is where his first recording session for RCA was held.

January 11, 1956: His second recording session for RCA at 1525 McGavock.

January 18, 1956: Drove to the Nashville Airport, the flew to New York to appear on TV on "Stage Show."

Early 1956: At Colonel Tom Parker's house, 1225 Gallatin Pike.

March 5, 1956: Parker's House

April 13, 1956: McGavock Studio for RCA session

November 27, 1956: Colonel Parker's house

November 27, 1956: Tic Toc Restaurant, 133 7th Avenue North. He stopped in to get something to eat but it was closing.

November 27, 1956: On his way out of Nashville, Elvis' car broke down and he had to put it in a shop and spent the night at the Andrew Jackson Hotel, Room 940

March 21, 1957: Parker's house and then Union Station to catch a train

October 11, 1957: Parker's House

December 20,1957: After picking up his draft notice in Memphis, Elvis drove to Parker's house, where he gave him a sports car for Christmas.

December 21, 1957: Elvis conferred with Colonel Parker during the day, then spent time in Nashville with Gordon Stoker of the Jordanaires and attended the Grand Ole Opry that evening where he socialized, posed for pictures but did not sing.

June 10, 1958: RCA Studio at the corner of 17th Avenue South and Hawkins. This is his first recording session at the new RCA Studio, which opened on November 7, 1957. After RCA built a new building and bigger studio in 1967, this became known as RCA Studio B. This session occurred after Elvis

Documented Nashville Visits

finished basic training with the Army and was on leave before being sent to school for tank training.

March 20, 1960: RCA Studio. This was Elvis' first recording session after his discharge from the Army.

March 21, 1960. After his session ended, Elvis went to Union Station and slept in a sleeping car parked under the Broad Street Bridge. The next day he awoke and took the train to Miami, where he appeared on a Frank Sinatra TV show.

April 3, 1960: RCA Studio. This recording session, which lasted until the early morning hours of April 4, saw Elvis record 12 songs for his first album since his Army discharge.

October 30, 1960: RCA Studio. Elvis recorded a gospel album on this session. Like most of Elvis' sessions, this did not end until the next morning.

March 8, 1961. Elvis drove to Nashville in his Rolls Royce and spoke before the Tennessee General Assembly. Governor Buford Ellington presented him with a certificate honoring him as a "Colonel." Elvis was quite taken with Ellington's daughter, Ann, On his way back to Memphis, Elvis stopped at the Tennessee State Prison and visited with Johnny Bragg, who led the group The Prisonaires and wrote the song, "Just Walkin' in the Rain," which they recorded for Sun Records.

March 11, 1961: Elvis visited Ann Ellington at the Governor's Mansion on Curtiswood Lane; they sat up late talking until the Governor sent security guards to deliver a message to "the hound dog" that it was time to leave.

March 12, 1961: RCA Studio. Elvis recorded 12 songs during this all night session.

June 25, 1961: RCA Studio. Elvis recorded five songs.

July 2, 1961: RCA Studio. Elvis recorded songs for his movie *Follow That Dream* and, when he finished, checked into the Anchor Motel on West End Avenue.

October 15, 1961: RCA Studio. Elvis recorded five songs this evening.

March 18, 1962: RCA Studio. Elvis recorded 11 songs this evening, then checked into the Anchor Motel.

May 26, 1963: RCA Studio. Elvis recorded eight songs, including one for his movie *Kissin' Cousins*.

May 27, 1963: RCA Studio. Elvis recorded six songs this evening and early morning.

September 29: RCA Studio. The soundtrack for Elvis' movie *Kissin' Cousins* was recorded, but only the music tracks; Elvis had a cold and did the vocals later in Los Angeles.

Documented Nashville Visits

January 12, 1963: RCA Studio. Elvis recorded three songs.
February 24, 1965: Elvis only recorded one song this evening for the soundtrack to his movie *Harem Scarem.*
February 25, 1965: RCA Studio. Elvis recorded five songs for the *Harem Scarem* soundtrack.
February 26, 1965: Elvis recorded the final five songs for the *Harem Scarem* soundtrack.
May 25, 1966: Elvis recorded six songs this evening; four were for a gospel album, including "How Great Thou Art." This is the first session where Felton Jarvis was Elvis' producer.
May 26, 1966: RCA Studio. Elvis recorded six more songs, including four for his gospel album.
May 27, 1966 : RCA Studio. Elvis recorded four songs for his gospel album.
May 28, 1966: RCA Studio. Elvis recorded two songs.
June 10, 1966: Albert Pick Motel, 320 Murfreesboro, Road. Elvis stayed in his motel room in a foul mood while Red West stood in for him at the RCA Studio, recording four songs.
June 11, 1966: Elvis remained at the Albert Pick Motel.
June 12, 1966: RCA Studio. Elvis went into the RCA Studio and, within a short time, recorded the vocals for the three songs recorded on June 10.
February 21, 1967: RCA Studio. Elvis recorded four songs for his movie *Clambake.*
February 22, 1967: RCA Studio. Elvis recorded four more songs for the *Clambake* soundtrack.
February 23, 1967: Elvis recorded the final song for the *Clambake* soundtrack.
March 20, 1967: RCA Studio B. Elvis recorded one song this evening.
September 10, 1967: RCA Studio B. Elvis recorded five songs this evening.
September 11, 1967: RCA Studio B. Elvis recorded five songs during this evening.
October 1, 1967: RCA Studio B. Elvis recorded three songs for his movie, *Stay Away, Joe.*
January 15, 1968: RCA Studio B. Elvis recorded two songs, then checked into the Jack Spence Hotel off Murfreesboro Road.
January 16, 1968: RCA Studio B. Elvis recorded two songs.
September 25, 1968: RCA Studio B. Elvis recorded vocal overdubs on two songs.
June 4, 1970: RCA Studio B. Elvis recorded nine songs during this all night session.

Documented Nashville Visits

June 5, 1970: RCA Studio B. Elvis recorded seven songs during this session

June 6, 1970: RCA Studio B. Elvis recorded six songs as well as a song listed as "I Didn't Make It on Playing Guitar," which was Elvis clowning around in the studio.

June 7, 1970: RCA Studio B. Elvis recorded nine songs during this all night session.

June 8, 1970: RCA Studio B. Elvis recorded five songs this evening.

September 21, 1970: RCA Studio A. Elvis' wife, Priscilla, wanted to attend one of his recording session; Elvis did not want her in the studio when he recorded but relented and set up this "mock" session where he pretended to overdub some instruments and vocals.

September 22, 1970: RCA Studio B. Elvis recorded four songs this evening.

March 15, 1971: RCA Studio B. Elvis recorded four songs this evening before he had to quit because of problems with his eye.

March 16, 1971: Baptist Hospital on Church Street. Elvis checked into the hospital with "irititus," a burning of his eye. Two doctors were called from Memphis to attend to him.

March 17, 1971: Baptist Hospital on Church Street.

March 18, 1971: Baptist Hospital on Church Street

March 19, 1971: Elvis was discharged from Baptist Hospital on Church Street and went back to Memphis.

May 15, 1971: RCA Studio B. Elvis returned to Nashville to continue the recording sessions originally scheduled in March. Elvis recorded six Christmas songs this evening.

May 16, 1971: RCA Studio B. Elvis recorded eight songs this evening; seven of them were Christmas songs.

May 17, 1971: RCA Studio B. Elvis recorded four songs this evening.

May 18, 1971: RCA Studio B. Elvis recorded four songs this evening; three were gospel songs.

May 19, 1971: RCA Studio B. Elvis recorded six songs this evening.

May 20, 1971: RCA Studio B. Elvis recorded four songs this evening.

May 21, 1971: RCA Studio B. Elvis recorded one song this evening.

June 8, 1971: RCA Studio B. Elvis recorded three songs this evening.

June 9, 1971: RCA Studio B. Elvis recorded four songs this evening—all gospel.

June 10, 1971. RCA Studio B. Elvis recorded two songs this evening, including

Documented Nashville Visits

"My Way." He grew frustrated with the backup singer during the session, threw down his ear phones and stormed out of the studio; this was the last time that Elvis recorded at RCA Studio B in Nashville.

October, 1972: Elvis came to Nashville and attended the National Quartet Convention with J.D. Sumner at the Municipal Auditorium. Elvis visited groups backstage, took a bow but did not sing.

July 1, 1973: Elvis gave his first concert in Nashville at the Municipal Auditorium. During his visit he stayed at the; Sheraton South Hotel.

March 14, 1974: Elvis gave a concert at the Murphy Center on the Middle Tennessee State University campus in Murfreesboro, about 35 miles southeast of Nashville.

March 19, 1974: Concert at the Murphy Center in Murfreesboro.

April 29, 1975: Concert at the Murphy Center in Murfreesboro.

December 25, 1975: Elvis flew into a private airport in Nashville in his private plane, having fun on Christmas. He spent less than an hour on the ground.

Spring 1976: It was announced that Elvis had invested in Racquetball Courts, located on Trousdale; Elvis did not come to Nashville to open them and that investment, which was announced would include a chain of racquetball courts, never materialized outside of the initial court.

January 21, 1977: Elvis was scheduled to record at Creative Workshop in Berry Hill but, upset over several issues, remained in his room at the Sheraton South Hotel. This was Elvis' last trip to Nashville.

SOURCES

CHAPTER 1

1. Moore, Scotty. Personal Interview, November 7, 2007.
2. Guralnick, Peter. *Last Train to Memphis: The Rise of Elvis Presley*. Boston: Back Bay Books, 1994. p. 95
3. Moore, Scotty as told to James Dickerson. *That's Alright, Elvis: The Untold Story of Elvis's First Guitarist and Manager, Scotty Moore*. New York: Schirmer Books, 1997. p. 78
4. Moore, p 78.
5. Guralnick, *Last Train*, p. 129.
6. Moore, p. 79

CHAPTER 2

7. Snow, Hank with Jack Ownbey and Bob Burris. *The Hank Snow Story*. Chicago: University of Illinois Press, 1994. pp. 384-385
8. Snow pp. 386-387
9. Nash, Alanna. *Baby, Let's Play House: Elvis Presley and the Women Who Loved Him*. New York: itbooks, 2010, pp. 105-106.
10. Guralnick, Peter and Ernst Jorgensen. *Elvis: Day By Day: The Definitive Record of His Life and Music*. New York: Ballantine, 1999. p. 226
11. Havighurst, Craig. *Air Castle of the South: WSM and the Making of Music City*. Urbana and Chicago: University of Illinois Press, 2007, p. 181.
12. Nash, Alanna. *The Colonel: The Extraordinary Story of Colonel Tom Parker and Elvis Presley*. New York: Simon and Schuster, 2003, p. 115.

CHAPTER 3

13. Guralnick and Jorgensen, p. 73.
14. Mercer, Charles. "Elvis The Pelvis Belongs In Jungle, New York Writer Tells Steve Allen." AP Story datelined New York. Nashville *Banner*, June 22, 1956
15. Pett, Saul. "Does His Mama Think He's Vulgar?" sub head: "Nope! He Just Puts Too Much Into His Singing." AP: New York dateline. Nashville *Tennessean* July 22, 1956.
16. Seigenthaler, John. "Tupelo Ain't Nothin' but a Town Agog: Hometowners Give Elvis Long, Tall Rally." Nashville *Tennessean*, September 27, 1956.
17. "Graham Doubtful About Elvis." Nashville *Tennessean*, October 29, 1956.

SOURCES

CHAPTER 4

18. Sharborough, Jacqueline. "Ghosts of Elvis Foul Up Festival: Teen-Age Throng Rip Disc Jockeys With Sideburns But Alas No Presley." Nashville *Tennessean*, November 10, 1956.
19. "D.J. Parley Ends Tonight At Opry." Nashville *Banner*, November 10, 1956.
20. Kleiner, Dick. NEA Feature Writer. "Elvis Tugs at the Purse Strings." Nashville *Tennessean* Nov 11, 1956.
21. Graham, Gene. "They Squealed—But Mildly; It Was Only a Movie Elvis." Nashville *Tennessean*, November 22, 1956.
22. Hieronymus, Clara. "Critic Rates Elvis Low in Acting Ability." Nashville *Tennessean*, December 2, 1956.
23. Barker, George. "Girls, You'll Cry! Elvis Was HERE!: Nashville *Tennessean*, November 27, 1956.
24. "Not Everyone Missed Elvis During Visit." Nashville *Tennessean*, November 28, 1956.
25. Creach, Ed. "The Elvis Presley Century? 'Lost' World Steeped in Own Discord." (AP story: datelined Washington) Nashville *Banner*, November 30, 1956..)

CHAPTER 5

26. "Elvis Swings—From Rope; Officers Find It's Dummy." Nashville *Tennessean*, January 7, 1957 and "Elvis Effigy Draws Crowds to 'Hanging'" Nashville *Banner*, January 7, 1957.
27. "Memphis Neighborhood Irked By Presley Fan's Request." Nashville *Banner*, February 16, 1957. (AP)
28. Gilbert, Eugene, Director Gilbert Research. "He's Nothing Anymore,' Girls Says; Pat Boone Moving Up Strongly." Nashville *Tennessean*. March 21, 1957.
29. O'Donnell, Red. "Elvis Slipping From Starry Peak? Not So's You Could Tell It: Parker." Nashville *Banner*. March 22, 1957.
30. Halberstam, David. "Elvis Still Midstate Smash, But 'Too Much' for Parents." Nashville *Tennessean* March 24, 1957.
31. Emerson, Ken. *Always Magic in the Air: The Bomp and Brilliance of the Brill Building Era*. New York: Viking, 2005. P 64
32. "Rock'n'Roll Banned, Hate Elvis Drive Launched by Iran To Save Its Youth." Tehran (UP) August 12, 1957.
33. Kirkham, Millie. Personal interview, May 8, 2010.

SOURCES

34. Kirkham Interview.

35. Halberstam, David. "Presley vs. Sinatra; Fans Of Both Here Square Off." Nashville *Tennessean*, October 30, 1957.

36. O'Donnell, Red. "Elvis 'Least Bothered' By Army Draft; Jokes On Visit." Nashville *Banner*, December 21, 1957.

37. Barker, George. "Forward Career????. Nashville *Tennessean*, December 22, 1957.

38. Stoker, Gordon. Personal Interview, October 25, 2008.

39. Nash, Alanna with Billy Smith, Marty Lacker and Lamar Fike. *Elvis and the Memphis Mafia*. New York: Harper Collins, 1995. p. 99

CHAPTER 6

40. "Draft Official Swaps Insults in Elvis' Deferment Furor." Nashville, *Tennessean*, January 6, 1959.

41. Weiser, Norman. "Elvis Not Sure He Has It Made." Nashville *Banner*, February 27, 1958. p. 30.

42. Baker, Missy. "RCA's Studio B: Memories of Little Victor." Mix, March 1990. p. 62

43. Barker, George. "Elvis Drops By—Singing's Same!" Nashville *Tennessean*, June 11, 1958.

44. O'Donnell, Red. "Elvis Here For Turn With Discs. Nashville *Banner*, June 11, 1958.

45. Jorgensen, Ernst. *Elvis Presley: A Life in Music: The Complete Recording Sessions*. New York: St. Martin's Press, 1998. pp. 107-111-)

46. Walker, Ray. Personal Interview, May 24, 2007

47. Jorgensen. pp. 107-111

48. Jorgensen. pp. 107-111

49. "Elvis' Homecoming Cheers Ailing Mother. Nashville *Tennessean*, August 14, 1958. (AP)

50. "Elvis Takes Last Look At 'Best Girl'—His Mom." Nashville *Banner*, August 15, 1958.

51. "'She's All We Lived For,' Sobs Rock'n Roll Star" Nashville *Banner*, August 15, 1958. (UPI)

52. "Grief-Stricken Elvis Remains in Mansion." (AP)

53. "'Best Girl' Gone; Elvis Weeps Openly." Nashville *Banner*, August 14, 1958. (UPI)

SOURCES

54. "Elvis' Songs Keep Seagulls Away from London Airport." Nashville *Tennessean*, Mar 19, 1959.
55. Whitburn Top Pop Singles
56. Halberstam, David. "And You Think You Send Cards." Nashville *Tennessean*, December 10, 1959.
57. Gris, Henry. "Homecoming Presley To Find He's Become A Bit Outdated." Nashville *Banner*, Dec 25, 1959.
58. Emery, Ralph, Personal interview, August 28, 2010.

CHAPTER 7
59. "Presley's All Ready For Rock'n'Roll Go." Nashville *Tennessean*, March 4, 1960.
60. "Elvis Signs Out, Draws Pay Today." Nashville *Tennessean* March 5, 1960.
61. "Will Elvis Still Rule the Roost?" Nashville *Tennessean*, March 7, 1960.
62. "Crowds Greet Elvis at Memphis." Nashville *Banner*, March 7, 1960 (UPI)
63. Jorgensen. pp. 113-114
64. Halberstadt, Alex. *Lonely Avenue: The Unlikely Life & Times of Doc Pomus* New York: Da Capo Press, 2007. p. 108
65. Rumble, John. "Behind the Board with Bill Porter: Part Three." The Journal Of Country Music, Vol. 19, No. 1, 1997. p. 25
66. Rumble, John. "Behind the Board with Bill Porter: Part Three." p. 26
67. Rumble, John. "Behind the Board with Bill Porter: Part Three." p. 26
68. Anderson, Pat. "Elvis Slips Into Nashville For Platter-Cutting Session." Nashville *Tennessean*, March 21, 1960.
69. Anderson, Pat. "Elvis Fears Nothing—But His Fans." Nashville *Tennessean* March 22, 1960.
70. McDavid, Joe. "Elvis' Star on Downgrade, Or Is It Now?" Nashville Banner, April 16, 1960 (AP))

CHAPTER 8
71. Guralnick, Peter. *Careless Love: The Unmaking of Elvis Presley*. Boston and New York: Back Bay Books, 1999. p. 64.
72. Jorgensen. pp. 126.
73. Rumble, John. "Behind the Board with Bill Porter: Part Three." p 26
74. Jorgensen. pp. 126.

SOURCES

75. Jorgensen. pp. 124

76. Rumble, John. "Behind the Board with Bill Porter: Part Three." The Journal Of Country Music, Vol. 19, No. 1, 1997. pp. 27

77. Jorgensen. pp. 126)

78. Guralnick, *Careless Love*, p.64-66

79. Rumble, John. "Behind the Board with Bill Porter: Part Three." The Journal Of Country Music, Vol. 19, No. 1, 1997. pp. 24-31.

CHAPTER 9

80. Jorgensen. pp. 138

81. Guralnick, *Careless Love*, p. 82

82. Jorgensen. pp. 138

83. Jorgensen. pp. 140

84. Walker, Ray. Personal Interview, May 27, 2009.

85. Jorgensen. p. 141

86. Jorgensen. p. 141

87. Guralnick, *Careless Love*, p. 83

88. Jorgensen. p. 142

89. Jorgensen. p. 138

90. Jorgensen. p. 142

91. Anderson, Pat. "Movie Making With Elvis Can Be Fun." Nashville *Tennessean*, December 4, 1960.

CHAPTER 10

92. Anderson, Pat. "Elvis Proves He Can Sell Discs." Nashville *Tennessean*, January 4, 1961.

93. Morrell, Ken. "Presley To Visit Assembly." Nashville *Banner*, March 6, 1961.

94. Nash, Alanna. *Baby, Let's Play House: Elvis Presley and the Women Who Loved Him*. New York: itbooks, 2010. p. 342

95. O'Donnell, Red. "Elvis Does Free Shot For Assembly." Nashville *Banner* March 8, 1961.

96. Morrell, Ken. "Presley To Visit Assembly." Nashville *Banner*, March 6, 1961.

97. O'Donnell, Red. "Elvis Does Free Shot For Assembly." Nashville *Banner* March 8, 1961.

98. Ibid

SOURCES

99. O'Donnell, Red. "Elvis Does Free Shot..."

100. Warner, Jay. *Just Walkin' in the Rain: the true story of a convict quintet, a liberal governor, and how they changed southern history through rhythm and blues.* Los Angeles: Renaissance Books, 2001. Pp 205-206

101. Nash, *Baby Let's Play House*, p. 343

102. Jorgensen, p. 149

103. Jorgensen, p. 150

104. "Presley's Hubcaps Are Stolen." Nashville *Tennessean*, March 13, 1961 and "Two of Elvis' Hubcaps Found," Nashville *Banner*, March 15, 1961.

105. Jorgensen, p. 157

106. Guralnick, *Careless Love,* p. 113

107. Guralnick, *Careless Love*, p. 150

108. Jorgensen, p. 159

109. Halberstadt, Alex. *Lonely Avenue: The Unlikely Life & Times of Doc Pomus.* New York: Da Capo Press, 2007. p. 139

110. Jorgensen, pp. 158-159

111. Jorgensen, p. 160

112. Kennedy, Jerry. Personal Interview, May 21, 2009.

CHAPTER 11

113. Jorgensen, pp. 165, 168

114. Guralnick, *Careless Love.* p. 122

115. Guralnick, *Careless Love.* p. 122

116. "Elvis Being Sued For Car Mishap." Nashville *Banner*, May 11, 1963.

117. "Cuban Elvises Get Army Duty." Nashville *Banner*, December 5, 1963.

CHAPTER 12

118. Portis, Charles. "That New Sound From Nashville, *Saturday Evening Post*, February 12, 1965.

119. Battle, Bob. "Demand For Elvis' Locks Just Got to Be Too Much." Nashville *Banner*, September 7, 1965.

120. Battle, Bob. "Elvis Presley Finds New Hobby In Race Car Set." Nashville *Banner*, January 10, 1966.

SOURCES

CHAPTER 13

121. Guralnick. *Careless Love*. p. 223
122. Guralnick. *Careless Love*. p. 229
123. Jorgensen p. 207
124. Guralnick. *Careless Love*. p. 229
125. Guralnick. *Careless Love*. p. 229
126. Guralnick. *Careless Love*. p. 230
127. Guralnick. *Careless Love*. p. 232
128. Schilling, Jerry with Chuck Crisafulli. *Me and a Guy Named Elvis: My Life-long Friendship with Elvis Presley*. New York: Gotham Books, 2006. p. 143
129. Shilling, *Me and a Guy* p. 144
130. Jorgensen, pp. 213-214
131. Guralnick. *Careless Love*. p. 233
132. Guralnick. *Careless Love*. p. 234
133. Shilling, *Me and a Guy* pp. 142-143
134. Nash et al pp 383-384
135. Shilling, *Me and a Guy* p. 146
136. Guralnick, *Careless Love* p. 236
137. Shilling, *Me and a Guy* p. 146-147
138. Nash et al p 384
139. Ibid p 386
140. Jorgensen, p. 219

CHAPTER 14

141. Battle, Bob. Personal Interview, January 21, 2008.
142. Battle, Bob. "Bing Crosby Calls Elvis 'A Spectacular Talent.'" *Nashville Banner*, Oct 5, 1966. (First of three-part series.)
143. Battle, Bob. "Show Business Defines Elvis as 'Phenomenon.'" *Nashville Banner*, October 13, 1966. (Second of three-part series.)
144. Battle, Bob. "Elvis Presley Conquered Hollywood in First Film." *Nashville Banner*, October 14, 1966. (Third of three-part series.)

CHAPTER 15

145. Nash et al p. 396
146. Guralnick, *Careless Love* p. 277

SOURCES

147. Stoker, Gordon. Personal Interview, October 25, 2008.

148. Shilling, *Me and a Guy* p. 181

149. Bradley, Harold. Personal interview, February 1, 2008.

150. Bradley interview

151. Shilling, *Me and a Guy* p. 181

152. Shilling, *Me and a Guy* pp. 181-182

CHAPTER 16

153. Putman, Norbert Personal Interview, November 14, 2009.

154. Guralnick *Careless Love* p. 429

155. Hurst, Jack. "Elvis Slips in Unnoticed, Almost." Nashville *Tennessean*, March 16, 1971.

156. Jorgensen, p. 322

157. "Elvis Moved To Quiet Area At Baptist." Nashville *Banner* March 19, 1971.

158. "Gov. Dunn Makes Visit To Presley." Nashville *Banner*, March 20, 1971.

159. Guralnick, *Careless Love* p. 433

160. Jorgensen, p. 322

161. Guralnick, *Careless Love* pp. 436-437

162. Guralnick, *Careless Love* p. 438

163. Guralnick, *Careless Love* pp. 439-440

CHAPTER 17

164. "Elvis Presley's Grandfather Dies. Nashville *Tennessean*, March 20, 1973 and "Elvis Presley's Grandfather Dies at 76." Nashville *Banner*, March 20, 1973.

165. O'Donnell, Red. "Elvis Presley to Appear Here For Two Concerts." Nashville *Banner*, May 9, 1973.

166. Hance, Bill. "At One Time Elvis Was Easy to Interview." Nashville *Banner*, June 30, 1973.

167. "Promoter Sends $300,000 Back On Elvis Tickets." Nashville *Tennessean*, June 1, 1973.

168. Sawyer, Kathy. "Elvis Slated Today But Plans Quiet." Nashville *Tennessean*, July 1, 1973.

169. Bailey, Jerry. "Elvis--Frustrated Gospel Singer." Nashville *Tennessean* July 1, 1973.

170. "His Popularity Reaches Across Three Generations." The Nashville *Tennessean*, July 2, 1973

SOURCES

171. Sawyer, Kathy. "Elvis Harnesses Power To 'Just Entertain Folks.'" Nashville *Tennessean*, July 2, 1973.

172. Hance, Bill. "If Elvis Is Bored, He Hides It Well." Nashville *Banner*, July 2, 1973.

CHAPTER 18

173. Ibid

174. Bailey, Jerry. "Elvis To Do 2nd Show At MTSU." Nashville *Tennessean*, January 19, 1974.

175. Bailey, Jerry. "As Usual, Elvis Keeps Gals Happy." Nashville *Tennessean*. March 15, 1974.

176. "Elvis Slower, But ????" Nashville *Banner*, March 15, 1974

177. "Elvis' Power Stretches To Intensive Care Unit." Nashville *Tennessean*, March 18, 1974.

178. Brown, Tony, personal interview July 23, 2009.

179. Brown interview

180. "Elvis at MTSU Set April 29." Nashville *Tennessean*, February 6, 1975.

CHAPTER 19

181. "Elvis Sets 3rd Show At MTSU." Nashville *Tennessean*. February 12, 1975.

182. Brinton, Larry. "Linda Talks of Times With Elvis. Nashville *Banner*. N.D.

183. "Controversy Bulges Around Elvis Presley: Midstaters To Get Answer Tuesday." Nashville *Banner*, April 25, 1975.

184. Hance, Bill. "Chubbier Elvis Still Sports Pelvis That Crowd Adores." Nashville *Banner*, April 30, 1975.)

185. Zibart, Eve. "'The King' Still Just That." Nashville *Tennessean*, May 1, 1975

186. Hance, Bill. "Loosen The Colonel's Reins, Elvis; Ultra-Private Presley: Miserable Or Not?" Nashville *Banner*, May 2, 1975.)

187. Brinton, Larry. "Protecting Elvis Harrowing, But Fun: West." Nashville *Banner*, May 3, 1975.)

188. O'Donnell, Red. "Elvis' Birthday: A Courtly Affair?" Nashville *Banner*, January 3, 1976.)

189. Ibid

190. Hance, Bill. "Nashville Getting Elvis' 'Racquet'." Nashville *Banner*, April 20, 1976.

191. Hance, Bill. "Presley Plans MTSU Concert." Nashville *Banner*, March 19, 1976.

SOURCES

192. Hance, Bill. "Rumors Have Elvis in Murfreesboro Again. Nashville *Banner*, June 18, 1976.
193. Brown interview
194. Ibid

CHAPTER 20

195. Brown interview
196. "Elvis' Death at 42 Called Heart Attack; No Drugs Found." from Wire Reports. Nashville *Tennessean*, August 17, 1977, pp. 1, 6
197. Eipper, Laura and Alice Alexander. "Rock'n'Roll King's Death Touches Music Community." Sub- head "Poor Health Rumors Seemingly Founded." Nashville *Tennessean*, August 17, 1977, p. 1, 6
198. Eipper, Laura. "Fans Create Tumultuous Elvis Scene." Nashville, *Tennessean*, Thursday, August 18, 1977. p. 1, 10
199. Ibid
200. "In Wake of Elvis' Death." Nashville *Tennessean*, August 18, 1977. p. 1, 10
201. "Blanton Invited." Nashville *Tennessean*. August 18, 1977. p. 10)
202. Ballard, Gloria. "Elvis 'Aloofness' Seen Managed: Vanrell Reflections." Nashville *Tennessean*, August 18, 1977. p. 4
203. Thomas, Susan. "Elvis Records All Sold Out." Nashville *Tennessean*, August 18, 1977. p. 10.)
204. "Elvis: The King Is Dead." Editorial: Nashville *Tennessean*, August 18, 1977, p. 12
205. "World Mourns Presley" by the Associated Press. Nashville *Tennessean*, August 18, 1977. p. 1, 10
206. Wilson, Marc. Associated Press Writer. "Beatlemaniacs Gather for Festival." Nashville *Tennessean*, August 18, 1977. p. 47. (Chicago AP)

CHAPTER 21

207. Eipper, Laura. "Elvis Burial Hushed, Private." Nashville *Tennessean*, August 19, 1977 p. 1
208. "Auto Deaths Shock Mourners at Mansion." The *Tennessean*, Friday, August 19, 1977. p. 15
209. Eipper, Laura. Elvis Burial Hushed, Private. Nashville Tennessean, August 19, 1977 p. 1

SOURCES

210. Ibid

211. "Colonel To Maintain Control." The *Tennessean*, Friday, August 19, 1977. p. 15

212. Crowe, Adell and Katherine Freed. "Film 'Brings Elvis Back' for Awhile." The *Tennessean*, Saturday, August 20, 1977. pp. 1, 4

213. Alexander, Alice. "He Knew the 'Private' Elvis." The *Tennessean*, Sunday, August 21, 1977. p. 6-A.

214. "Elvis' Will Gives Full Estate to Family. Father Granted Total Control." Nashville *Tennessean*, August 23, 1977, p. 1, 6 (Datelined Memphis: UPI)

215. Holly, Sarah Taylor, "Presley Fans Weren't Ready." Letters To The Editor: The *Tennessean*, August 24, 1977. p. 8

216. Brown interview

BIBLIOGRAPHY

"2nd Show Confirmed For Elvis" Nashville *Tennessean*, February 8, 1935.

Anderson, Pat. "Elvis Fears Nothing--But His Fans." Nashville *Tennessean* March 22, 1960.

Anderson, Pat. "Elvis Proves He Can Sell Discs." Nashville *Tennessean*, January 4, 1961.

Anderson, Pat. "Elvis Slips Into Nashville For Platter-Cutting Session." Nashville *Tennessean*. March 21, 1960.

Anderson, Pat. Movie Making With Elvis Can Be Fun." Nashville *Tennessean*, December 4, 1960.

Bailey, Jerry. "As Usual, Elvis Keeps Gals Happy." Nashville *Tennessean*. March 15, 1974.

Bailey, Jerry. "Elvis To Do 2nd Show At MTSU." Nashville *Tennessean*, January 19, 1974.

Bailey, Jerry. "Elvis--Frustrated Gospel Singer." Nashville *Tennessean* July 1, 1973.

Bailey, Jerry. Want To See Elvis at MTSU? Hurry!" Nashville *Tennessean*, January 16, 1974.

Barker, George. "Elvis Drops By--Singing's Same!" Nashville *Tennessean*, June 11, 1958.

Barker, George. "Forward Career???? Nashville *Tennessean*, December 22, 1957.

Barker, George. "Girls, You'll Cry! Elvis Was HERE!" Nashville *Tennessean*, November 27, 1956.

Battle, Bob. "Bing Crosby Calls Elvis 'A Spectacular Talent'" Nashville *Banner*, Oct 5, 1966.

Battle, Bob. "Col. Parker Dispels Rumors He May Quit Managing Elvis." Nashville *Banner*, Feb 16, 1966.

Battle, Bob. "Demand For Elvis' Locks Just Got to Be Too Much." Nashville *Banner*, September 7, 1965.

Battle, Bob. "Elvis Presley Conquered Hollywood in First Film." Nashville *Banner*, October 14, 1966.

BIBLIOGRAPHY

Battle, Bob. "Elvis Presley Finds New Hobby In Race Car Set." Nashville *Banner*, January 10, 1966.

Battle, Bob. "Show Business Defines Elvis as 'Phenomenon'" Nashville *Banner*, October 13, 1966.

Battle, Bob. Personal interview, January 21, 2008.

Bertrand, Michael T. *Race, Rock, and Elvis*. Urbana and Chicago: University of Illinois Press, 2005.

"Best Girl' Gone; Elvis Weeps Openly." Nashville *Banner*, August 14, 1958. (UPI)

Biszick-Lockwood, Bar. *Restless Giant: The Life and Times of Jean Aberbach & Hill and Range Songs*. Urbana and Chicago: University of Illinois Press, 2010.

Bradley, Harold. Personal interview, February 1, 2008.

Brinton, Larry. "Linda Talks of Times With Elvis. Nashville *Banner*. N.D.

Brinton, Larry. "Protecting Elvis Harrowing, But Fun: West." Nashville *Banner*, May 3, 1975.

Brown, Tony. Personal interview. July 23, 2010.

Burke, Ken and Dan Griffin. *The Blue Moon Boys: The Story of Elvis Presley's Band*. Chicago: Chicago Review Press, 2006.

Cantor, Louis. *Dewey and Elvis: The Life and Times of a Rock'n'Roll DeeJay*. Urbana and Chicago: University of Illinois Press, 2005.

Carey, Bill. *Fortunes, Fiddles and Fried Chicken: A Nashville Business History*. Franklin, TN: Hillsboro Press, 2000.

"Controversy Bulges Around Elvis Presley: Midstaters To Get Answer Tuesday." Nashville *Banner*, April 25, 1975.

Creach, Ed. "The Elvis Presley Century?" 'Lost' World Steeped in Own Discord." Nashville *Banner*, November 30, 1956. (AP story: datelined Washington).

"Crowds Greet Elvis at Memphis. Nashville *Banner* March 7, 1960 (UPI)

"Cuban Elvises Get Army Duty." Nashville *Banner*, December 5, 1963.

BIBLIOGRAPHY

"D.J. Parley Ends Tonight At Opry." Nashville *Banner*, November 10, 1956.

Doyle, Don H. *Nashville Since the 1920s*. Knoxville: The University of Tennessee Press, 1985.

"Draft Official Swaps Insults in Elvis' Deferment Furor" Nashville, *Tennessean*, Jan 6, 1959

"Ellington Introduces Presley." Nashville *Banner* March 8, 1961. (Picture of Elvis with Ann Ellington.)

"Elvis at MTSU Set April 29." Nashville *Tennessean* February 6, 1975.

"Elvis Being Sued For Car Mishap." Nashville *Banner*, May 11, 1963

"Elvis Effigy Draws Crowds to 'Hanging'" Nashville *Banner*, January 7, 1957.

"Elvis' Homecoming Cheers Ailing Mother." Nashville *Tennessean*, August 14, 1958. AP:

"Elvis Moved To Quiet Area At Baptist." Nashville *Banner* March 19, 1971.

"Elvis' Power Stretches To Intensive Care Unit." Nashville *Tennessean*. March 18, 1974.

"Elvis Presley in Hospital with 'Iritis'." Nashville *Tennessean*, March 17, 1971.

"Elvis Presley's Grandfather Dies at 76." Nashville *Banner*, March 20, 1973.

"Elvis Sets 3rd Show At MTSU." Nashville *Tennessean*. February 12, 1975.

"Elvis Signs Out, Draws Pay Today." Nashville *Tennessean*. March 5, 1960.

"Elvis Slower, But ????" Nashville *Banner*. March 15, 1974

"Elvis' Songs Keep Seagulls Away from London Airport." Nashville *Tennessean*. Mar 19, 1959.

"Elvis Swings—From Rope; Officers Find It's Dummy." Nashville *Tennessean*, January 7, 1957.

"Elvis Takes Last Look At 'Best Girl'—His Mom" Nashville *Banner*.

BIBLIOGRAPHY

August 15, 1958.

Emerson, Ken. *Always Magic in the Air: The Bomp and Brilliance of the Brill Building Era.* New York: Viking, 2005.

Emery, Ralph. Personal interview, August 28, 2010.

Escott, Colin with Martin Hawkins. *Good Rockin' Tonight: Sun Records and the Birth of Rock'n'Roll.* New York: St. Martin's Press, 1991.

Gilbert, Eugene, Director Gilbert Research. "He's Nothing Anymore,' Girls Says; Pat Boone Moving Up Strongly" Nashville *Tennessean.* Syndicated column. March 21, 1957.

"Gov. Dunn Makes Visit To Presley." Nashville *Banner*, March 20, 1971.

"Graham Doubtful About Elvis." Nashville *Tennessean*, October 29, 1956.

Graham, Gene. "They Squealed--But Mildly; It Was Only a Movie Elvis." Nashville *Tennessean*, November 22, 1956.

"Grief-Stricken Elvis Remains in Mansion." AP. N.D.

Gris, Henry. "Homecoming Presley To Find He's Become A Bit Outdated." Nashville *Banner*, Dec 25, 1959.

Guralnick, Peter and Ernst Jorgensen. *Elvis: Day By Day: The Definitive Record of His Life and Music.* New York: Ballantine, 1999.

Guralnick, Peter. *Careless Love: The Unmaking of Elvis Presley.* Boston and New York: Back Bay Books, 1999.

Guralnick, Peter. *Last Train to Memphis: The Rise of Elvis Presley.* Boston: Back Bay Books, 1994.

Halberstadt, Alex. *Lonely Avenue: The Unlikely Life & Times of Doc Pomus.* New York: Da Capo Press, 2007.

Halberstam, David. "And You Think You Send Cards." Nashville *Tennessean*, Dec 10, 1959.

Halberstam, David. "Elvis Still Midstate Smash, But 'Too Much' for Parents." Nashville *Tennessean*, March 24, 1957

Halberstam, David. "Presley vs. Sinatra; Fans Of Both Here Square

BIBLIOGRAPHY

Off." Nashville *Tennessean*, October 30, 1957.

Hance, Bill. "At One Time Elvis Was Easy to Interview." Nashville *Banner*, June 30, 1973.

Hance, Bill. "Chubbier Elvis Still Sports Pelvis That Crowd Adores." Nashville *Banner*, April 30, 1975.

Hance, Bill. "If Elvis Is Bored, He Hides It Well." Nashville *Banner*, July 2, 1973.

Hance, Bill. "Loosen The Colonel's Reins, Elvis; Ultra-Private Presley: Miserable Or Not?" *Nashville Banner*, May 2, 1975.

Hance, Bill. "Nashville Getting Elvis' 'Racquet'." Nashville *Banner*, April 20, 1976.

Hance, Bill. "Nearly Everyone In Memphis Knows Elvis." Nashville *Banner*. March 12, 1976.

Hance, Bill. "Presley Plans MTSU Concert." Nashville *Banner*, March 19, 1976.

Hance, Bill. "Rumors Have Elvis in Murfreesboro Again." Nashville *Banner*, June 18, 1976.

Harrison, Nigel. *Songwriters: A Biographical Dictionary with Discographies*. Jefferson, N.C.: McFarland & Company, Inc.: 1998.

Havighurst, Craig. *Air Castle of the South: WSM and the Making of Music City*. Urbana and Chicago: University of Illinois Press, 2007.

Hieronymus, Clara. "Critic Rates Elvis Low in Acting Ability." Nashville *Tennessean*, December 2, 1956.

"His Popularity Reaches Across Three Generations." The *Tennessean*, July 2, 1973

Hollabaugh, Jule, "Elvis Still Wows Womenfolks" Nashville *Tennessean*, March 9, 1961.

Hurst, Jack. "New Record Sounds Like Elvis But..." Nashville *Tennessean*, August 27, 1972.

Hurst, Jack. "Elvis Slips in Unnoticed, Almost." Nashville *Tennessean*, March 16, 1971.

"I'll Be A Houn' Dog, Elvis Slips In For A Visit." Nashville *Banner*,

BIBLIOGRAPHY

November 27, 1956.

Jorgensen, Ernst. *Elvis Presley: A Life in Music: The Complete Recording Sessions*. New York: St. Martin's Press, 1998.

Kennedy, Jerry. Personal interview, May 21, 2009.

Keogh, Pamela Clarke. *Elvis Presley: The Man. The Life. The Legend*. New York: Atria books, 2004.

Kirkham, Millie. Personal interview, May 8, 2010.

Kleiner, Dick. NEA Feature Writer. "Elvis Tugs at the Purse Strings." Nashville *Tennessean*, November 11, 1956.

Kosser, Michael. *How Nashville Became Music City U.S.A.* New York: Hal Leonard, 2006.

"Marine Says Presley Threatened With Toy Pistol" Nashville *Tennessean* March 24, 1957.

Mason, Bobbie Ann. *Elvis Presley: A Penguin Life*. New York: Viking, 2003.

McDavid, Joe. "Elvis' Star on Downgrade, Or Is It Now?" Nashville *Banner*, April 16, 1960 (AP)

"Memphis Neighborhood Irked By Presley Fan's Request." Nashville *Banner*, February 16, 1957. (AP)

Mercer, Charles. "Elvis The Pelvis Belongs In Jungle, New York Writer Tells Steve Allen." Nashville *Banner*, June 22, 1956 (AP Story datelined New York).

Moore, Scotty as told to James Dickerson. *That's Alright, Elvis: The Untold Story of Elvis's First Guitarist and Manager, Scotty Moore*. New York: Schirmer Books, 1997.

Moore, Scotty. Personal Interview, November 7, 2007.

Morrell, Ken. "Presley To Visit Assembly." Nashville *Banner*, March 6, 1961.

Moscheo, Joe. *The Gospel Side of Elvis*. New York: Center Street, 2007.

"MTSU Rush For Presley Tickets Seen" The Nashville *Tennessean*, February 15, 1974.

BIBLIOGRAPHY

Nash, Alanna with Billy Smith, Marty Lacker and Lamar Fike. *Elvis and the Memphis Mafia*. New York: Harper Collins, 1995.

Nash, Alanna. *Baby, Let's Play House: Elvis Presley and the Women Who Loved Him*. New York: itbooks, 2010).

Nash, Alanna. *The Colonel: The Extraordinary Story of Colonel Tom Parker and Elvis Presley*. New York: Simon and Schuster, 2003.

"Not Everyone Missed Elvis During Visit." Nashville *Tennessean*, November 28, 1956.

O'Donnell, Rd. "Elvis Does Free Shot For Assembly." Nashville *Banner* March 8, 1961.

O'Donnell, Red. "Elvis' Birthday: A Courtly Affair?" Nashville *Banner*, January 3, 1976.

O'Donnell, Red. "Elvis Here For Turn With Discs." Nashville *Banner*, June 11, 1958.

O'Donnell, Red. "Elvis 'Least Bothered' By Army Draft; Jokes On Visit." Nashville *Banner*, December 21, 1957.

O'Donnell, Red. "Elvis Presley to Appear Here For Two Concerts." Nashville *Banner*, May 9, 1973.

O'Donnell, Red. "Elvis Slipping From Starry Peak? Not So's You Could Tell It: Parker." Nashville *Banner*. March 22, 1957

Pett, Saul. "Does His Mama Think He's Vulgar?" sub head: "Nope! He Just Puts Too Much Into His Singing." AP: New York dateline. Nashville *Tennessean*, July 22, 1956.

Pierce, Patricia Jobe. *The Ultimate Elvis: Elvis Presley Day by Day*. New York: Simon & Schuster, 1994.

Ponce De Leon, Charles L. *Fortunate Son: The Life of Elvis Presley*. New York: Hill and Wang, 2006.

"Presley To Give 2nd MTSU Show." January 18, 1974 (no publication)

Presley, Priscilla Beaulieu with Sandra Harmon. *Elvis and Me*. New York: G.P. Putnam's Sons, 1985.

"Presley's All Ready For Rock'n'Roll Go" Nashville *Tennessean*, March 4, 1960.

BIBLIOGRAPHY

"Presley's Hubcaps Are Stolen." Nashville *Tennessean*, March 13, 1961.

"Presley's Hubcaps Recovered From Girl," Nashville *Tennessean*, March 15, 1961.

"Promoter Sends $300,000 Back On Elvis Tickets." Nashville *Tennessean*, June 1, 1973.

Putman, Norbert. Personal Interview, November 14, 2009.

Ritz, David, editor. *Elvis By the Presleys*. New York: Crown Publishers, 2006.

"Rock'n'Roll Banned, Hate Elvis Drive Launched by Iran To Save Its Youth." Tehran (UP) August 12, 1957.

Rumble, John. "Behind the Board with Bill Porter: Part One." *The Journal Of Country Music*, Vol. 18, No. 1, 1996. Pp. 27-40.

Rumble, John. "Behind the Board with Bill Porter: Part Three." *The Journal Of Country Music*, Vol. 19, No. 1, 1997. Pp. 24-31.

Rumble, John. "Behind the Board with Bill Porter: Part Two." *The Journal Of Country Music*, Vol. 18, No. 2, 1996. Pp. 20-30.

Sawyer, Kathy. "Elvis Harnesses Power To 'Just Entertain Folks'" Nashville *Tennessean*, July 2, 1973.

Sawyer, Kathy. "Elvis Slated Today But Plans Quiet." Nashville *Tennessean*, July 1, 1973.

Schilling, Jerry with Chuck Crisafulli. *Me and a Guy Named Elvis: My Lifelong Friendship with Elvis Presley*. New York: Gotham Books, 2006.

Seigenthaler, John. "Tupelo Ain't Nothin' but a Town Agog: Hometowners Give Elvis Long, Tall Rally." Nashville *Tennessean*, September 27, 1956.

Sharborough, Jacqueline. "Ghosts of Elvis Foul Up Festival: Teen-Age Throng Rip Disc Jockeys With Sideburns But Alas No Presley." Nashville *Tennessean*, November 10, 1956.

"'She's All We Lived For,' Sobs Rock'n Roll Star" Nashville *Banner*, August 15, 1958. (UPI)

BIBLIOGRAPHY

Snow, Hank with Jack Ownbey and Bob Burris. *The Hank Snow Story*. Urbana and Chicago: University of Illinois Press, 1994.

Stoker, Gordon. Personal Interview, October 25, 2008.

"Two of Elvis' Hubcaps Found" Nashville *Banner*, March 15, 1961.

Vellenga, Dirk and Mick Farren. *Elvis and the Colonel: The True and Shocking Story of the Man Behind 'The King.'* London: Grafton Books, 1990.

Walker, Ray. Personal Interview, May 27, 2009.

Walker, Ray. Personal Interview. May 24, 2007.

Warner, Jay. *Just Walkin' in the Rain: the true story of a convict quintet, a liberal governor, and how they changed southern history through rhythm and blues*. Los Angeles: Renaissance Books, 2001.

Weiser, Norman. "Elvis Not Sure He Has It Made." Nashville *Banner*, Feb 27, 1958. p. 30.

Whitburn, Joel. *Hot Country Songs: 1944-2008*. Menomonee Falls, Wisconsin: Record Research Inc., 2008.

Whitburn, Joel. *The Billboard Albums: 6th Edition*. Menomonee Falls, Wisconsin: Record Research Inc., 2006.

Whitburn, Joel. *Top Pop Singles, 12th Edition*. Menomonee Falls, Wisconsin: Record Research Inc., 2009.

"Will Elvis Still Rule the Roost?" Nashville *Tennessean*, March 7, 1960

Zibart, Eve. "'The King' Still Just That." Nashville *Tennessean*, May 1, 1975 (Thursday)

ELVIS PRESLEY RECORDING SESSIONS IN NASHVILLE

January 10, 1956:
RCA Studio in Methodist TV, Radio and Film Commission,
1525 McGavock Street

Producer: Steve Sholes
Engineer: Bob Ferris
Guitar: Scotty Moore
Guitar: Chet Atkins
Guitar: Elvis Presley
Bass: Bill Black
Drums: D.J. Fontana
Piano: Floyd Cramer
Vocals: Gordon Stoker, Ben & Brock Speer

I Got a Woman (Ray Charles)
Heartbreak Hotel (Mae Boren Axton-Tommy Durden-Elvis Presley)
Money Honey (Jesse Stone)

January 11, 1956 :
RCA Studio in Methodist TV, Radio and Film Commission,
1525 McGavock Street
Producer: Steve Sholes
Engineer: Bob Ferris
Guitar: Scotty Moore
Guitar: Chet Atkins
Guitar: Elvis Presley
Bass: Bill Black
Drums: D.J. Fontana
Piano: Floyd Cramer
Vocals: Gordon Stoker, Ben & Brock Speer

I'm Counting on You (Don Robertson-Ross Jungnickel)
I Was the One (Schroeder-DeMetrius-Blair-Peppers-Ross Jungnickel)

April 13, 1956:
RCA Studio in Methodist TV, Radio and Film Commission, 1525 McGavock Street

Producer: Steve Sholes
Engineer: Bob Ferris
Guitar: Scotty Moore
Guitar: Chet Atkins
Guitar: Elvis Presley
Bass: Bill Black
Drums: D.J. Fontana
Piano: Marvin Hughes
Vocals: Gordon Stoker, Ben & Brock Speer

I Want You, I Need You, I Love You (Maurice Mysels-Ira Kosloff)

June 10, 1958:
RCA Studio B:

Producer: Steve Sholes
Engineer: RLJ
Guitar: Hank Garland
Guitar: Chet Atkins
Guitar: Elvis Presley
Bass: Bob Moore
Drums: D.J. Fontana
Piano: Floyd Cramer
Bongos: Buddy Harman
Vocals: Jordanaires

I Need Your Love Tonight (Sid Wayne-Bix Reichner)
A Big Hunk o' Love (Aaron Schroeder-Sid Wyche)
Ain't That Loving You Baby? (Clyde Otis-Ivory Joe Hunter)
A Fool Such as I (Bill Trader-Bob Miller)
I Got Stung (Aaron Schroeder-David Hill)

March 20, 1960:
RCA Studio B:

Producer: Steve Sholes & Chet Atkins
Engineer: Bill Porter
Guitar: Scotty Moore
Guitar: Elvis Presley
Bass: Bob Moore
Electric Bass: Hank Garland
Drums: D.J. Fontana
Drums: Buddy Harman
Piano: Floyd Cramer
Vocals: Jordanaires

Make Me Know It (Otis Blackwell)
Soldier Boy (David Jones-Theodore Williams, Jr.)
Stuck on You (Aaron Schroeder-S. Leslie McFarland)
Fame and Fortune (Fred Wise-Ben Weisman)
A Mess of Blues (Doc Pomus-Mort Shuman)
It Feels So Right (Fred Wise-Ben Weisman)

April 3, 1960:
RCA Studio B:

Producer: Steve Sholes & Chet Atkins
Engineer: Bill Porter
Guitar: Scotty Moore
Guitar: Hank Garland
Guitar: Elvis Presley
Bass: Bob Moore
Drums: D.J. Fontana
Drums: Buddy Harman
Piano: Floyd Cramer
Sax: Boots Randolph
Vocals: Jordanaires
Harmony Vocal on "I Will Be Home Again" Charlie Hodge

Fever (John Davenport-Eddie Cooley)
Like a Baby (Jesse Stone)
It's Now or Never (Aaron Schroeder-Wally Gold)
The Girl of My Best Friend (Beverly Ross-Sam Bobrick)
Dirty, Dirty Feeling (Jerry Leiber-Mike Stoller)
Thrill of Your Love (Stanley Kesler)
I Gotta Know (P. Evans-M. Williams)
Such a Night (Lincoln Chase)
Are You Lonesome Tonight? (Roy Turk-Lou Handman)
The Girl Next Door Went A'Walking (Bill Rise-Thomas Wayne)
I Will Be Home Again (Benjamin-Leveen-Singer)
Reconsider Baby (Lowell Fulsom)

October 30, 1960:
RCA Studio B:

Producer: Steve Sholes
Engineer: Bill Porter
Guitar: Scotty Moore
Guitar: Hank Garland
Guitar: Elvis Presley
Bass: Bob Moore
Drums: D.J. Fontana
Drums: Buddy Harman
Piano: Floyd Cramer
Sax: Boots Randolph
Vocals: Jordanaires
Harmony Vocal on "His Hand in Mine," I Believe in the Man In the Sky" and
"He KNows Just What I Need"
Vocal: Millie Kirkham:

Milky White Way (arr Elvis Presley)
His Hand in Mine (Mosie Lister)
I Believe in the Man in the Sky (Richard Howard)
He Knows Just What I Need (Mosie Lister)
Surrender (Doc Pomus-Mort Shuman)
Mansion Over the Hilltop (Ira Stamphill)
In My Father's House (Ailecne Hanks)

Joshua Fit the Battle (arr Elvis Presley)
Swing Down, Sweet Chariot (arr Elvis Presley)
I'm Gonna Walk Dem Golden Stairs (Cully Holt)
If We Never Meet Again (Albert Brumley)
Known Only to Him (Stuart Hamblen)
Crying in the Chapel (Artie Glenn)
Working on the Building (W.O. Hoyle-Lillian Bowles)

March 12, 1961:
RCA Studio B:

Producer: Steve Sholes
Engineer: Bill Porter
Guitar: Scotty Moore
Guitar: Hank Garland
Guitar: Elvis Presley
Bass: Bob Moore
Drums: D.J. Fontana
Drums: Buddy Harman
Piano: Floyd Cramer
Sax: Boots Randolph
Vocals: Jordanaires
Vocal: Millie Kirkham:

I'm Coming Home (Charlie Rich)
Gently (Murray Wisell-Edward Lisbona)
In Your Arms (Aaron Schroeder-Wally Gold)
Give Me the Right (Fred Wise-Norman Blagman)
I Feel So Bad (Chuck Willis)
It's a Sin (Fred Rose-Zeb Turner)
I Want You With Me (Woody Harris)
There's Always Me (Don Robertson)
Starting Today (Don Robertson)
Sentimental Me (Jimmy Cassin-Jim Morehead)
Judy (Teddy Redell)
Put the Blame on Me (Twomey-Wise-Blagman)

June 25, 1961:
RCA Studio B

Producer: Steve Sholes
Engineer: Bill Porter
Guitar: Scotty Moore
Guitar: Hank Garland
Guitar: Neal Matthews
Bass: Bob Moore
Drums: D.J. Fontana
Drums: Buddy Harman
Piano, Organ: Floyd Cramer
Piano: Gordon Stoker
Claves: Boots Randolph
Vocals: Jordanaires
Vocal: Millie Kirkham

Kiss Me Quick (Doc Pomus-Mort Shuman)
That's Someone You Never Forget (Red West-Elvis Presley)
I'm Yours (Don Robertson)
(Marie's The Name Of) His Latest Flame (Doc Pomus-Mort Shuman)
Little Sister (Doc Pomus-Mort Shuman)

July 2, 1961:
RCA Studio B:

Producer: Hans Salter
Engineer: Bill Porter
Guitar: Scotty Moore
Guitar: Hank Garland
Guitar: Neal Matthews
Bass: Bob Moore
Drums: D.J. Fontana
Drums: Buddy Harman
Piano: Floyd Cramer
Sax: Boots Randolph
Vocals: Jordanaires
Vocal: Millie Kirkham:

Angel (Sid Tepper-Roy C. Bennett)
Follow That Dream (Fred Wise-Ben Weisman)
What a Wonderful Life (Sid Wayne-Jerry Livingston)
I'm Not the Marrying Kind (Mack David-Sherman Edwards)
A Whistling Tune (Sherman Edwards-Hal David)
Sound Advice (Giant-Baum-Kaye)

October 15, 1961:
RCA Studio B:

Producer: Steve Sholes
Engineer: Bill Porter
Guitar: Scotty Moore
Guitar: Jerry Kennedy
Bass: Bob Moore
Drums: D.J. Fontana
Drums: Buddy Harman
Piano: Floyd Cramer
Sax: Boots Randolph
Accordion: Gordon Stoker
Vocals: Jordanaires
Vocal: Millie Kirkham:

For the Millionth and the Last Time (Roy C. Bennett-Sid Tepper)
Good Luck Charm (Aaron Schroeder-Wally Gold)
Anything That's Part of You (Don Robertson)
I Met Her Today (Don Robertson-Hal Blair)
Night Rider (Doc Pomus-Mort Shuman)

March 18, 1962:
RCA Studio B

Producer: Steve Sholes
Engineer: Bill Porter
Guitar: Scotty Moore
Guitar: Harold Bradley
Guitar, Vibes: Grady Martin
Bass: Bob Moore
Drums: D.J. Fontana
Drums: Buddy Harman
Piano: Floyd Cramer
Sax, Vibes: Boots Randolph
Accordion: Gordon Stoker
Vocals: Jordanaires
Vocal: Millie Kirkham:

Something Blue (Paul Evans-Al Byron)
Gonna Get Back Home Somehow (Doc Pomus-Mort Shuman)
Easy Question (Otis Blackwell-Winfield Scott)
Fountain of Love (Bill Giant-Jeff Lewis)
Just for Old Time's Sake (Sid Tepper-Roy C. Bennett)
Night Rider (Doc Pomus-Mort Shuman)
You'll Be Gone (Red West-E. Presley-Charlie Hodge)
I Feel That I've Known You Forever (Doc Pomus-Alan Jeffreys)
Just Tell Her Jim Said Hello (Mike Soller-Jerry Leiber)
Suspicion (Doc Pomus-Mort Shuman)
She's Not You (Doc Pomus-Mike Stoller-Jerry Leiber)

May 26, 1963:
RCA Studio B

Producer: Steve Sholes
Engineer: Bill Porter
Guitar: Scotty Moore
Guitar: Grady Martin
Guitar: Harold Bradley
Guitar: Jerry Kennedy

Bass: Bob Moore
Drums: D.J. Fontana
Drums: Buddy Harman
Piano: Floyd Cramer
Sax, Vibes, Shakers: Boots Randolph
Vocals: Jordanaires
Vocal: Millie Kirkham:

Echoes of Love (Bob Roberts/Paddy McMains) (Kissin' Cousins)
Please Don't Drag that String Around (Otis Blackwell-Winfield Scott)
(You're the) Devil in Disguise (Giant/Baum/Kaye)
Never Ending (Buddy Kaye-Phil Springer)
What Now, What Next, Where To (Don Robertson-Hal Blair)
Witchcraft (Dave Bartholomew-P. King)
Finder Keepers, Loser Weepers (Dory Jones-Ollie Jones)
Love Me Tonight (Don Robetson)

May 27, 1963:
RCA Studio B

Producer: Steve Sholes
Engineer: Bill Porter
Guitar: Scotty Moore
Guitar: Grady Martin
Guitar: Harold Bradley
Guitar: Jerry Kennedy
Bass: Bob Moore
Drums: D.J. Fontana
Drums: Buddy Harman
Piano: Floyd Cramer
Sax, Vibes, Shakers: Boots Randolph
Vocals: Jordanaires
Vocal: Millie Kirkham:

Memphis Tennessee (Chuck Berry)
(It's a) Long Lonely Highway (Doc Pomus-Mort Shuman)
Ask Me (Modugno-Giant-Baum-Kaye)
Western Union (Sid Tepper-Roy C. Bennett)

Slowly But Surely (Sid Wayne-Ben Weisman)
Blue River (Paul Evans-Fred Tobias)

September 29, 1963:
RCA Studio B

Kissin' Cousins soundtrack

Producer: Gene Nelson & Fred Karger
Engineer: Bill Porter
Guitar: Scotty Moore
Guitar: Grady Martin
Guitar: Harold Bradley
Guitar: Jerry Kennedy
Bass: Bob Moore
Drums: D.J. Fontana
Drums: Buddy Harman
Banjo: Jerry Kennedy on "Smokey Mountain Boy"; Harold Bradley banjo on
"Barefoot Ballad)
Piano: Floyd Cramer
Sax and Jug: Boots Randolph
Sax: Bill Justis
Fiddler: Cecil Brower
Vocals: Jordanaires
Vocal: Millie Kirkham, Winnifred Brest, Dolores Edgin

There's Gold In the Mountains (Giant-Baum-Kaye) (Kissin' Cousins movie)
(Just tracks--no vocal)
One Boy, Two Little Girls (Giant-Baum-Kaye) (Kissin' Cousins movie) (Just
tracks--no vocal)
Once Is Enough (Sid Tepper-Roy C. Bennett) (Kissin' Cousins movie) (Just
tracks--no vocal)
Tender Feeling (Ginat-Baum-Kaye) (Kissin' Cousins movie) (Just tracks--no
vocal)
Kisisn' Cousins No. 2 (Giant-Baum-Kaye) (Kissin' Cousins movie) (Just
tracks--no vocal)
Smokey Mountain Boy (Rosenblatt-Millrose) (Kissin' Cousins movie) (Just
tracks--no vocal)

Catchin' On Fast (Giant-Baum-Kaye) (Kissin' Cousins movie) (Just tracks--no vocal)
Barefoot Ballad (Dolores Fuller-Lee Morris) (Kissin' Cousins movie) (Just tracks--no vocal)
Anyone (Could Fall In Love With you) (Benajimin-Marcus-DeJesus) (Kissin' Cousins movie) (Just tracks--no vocal)
Kissin' Cousins (Fred Wise-Randy Starr) (Just tracks--no vocal)

January 12, 1964:
RCA Studio B

Producer: Chet Atkins
Engineer: Ron Steele
Guitar: Scotty Moore
Guitar: Grady Martin
Guitar: Harold Bradley
Bass: Bob Moore
Drums: D.J. Fontana
Drums: Buddy Harman
Piano, Organ: Floyd Cramer
Sax and Vibes: Boots Randolph
Sax: Bill Justis
Fiddler: Cecil Brower
Vocals: Jordanaires
Vocal: Millie Kirkham

Memphis, Tennessee (Chuck Berry)
Ask Me (Modugno-Giant-Baum-Kaye)
It Hurts Me (Joy Byers-Charles E. Daniels)

February 24, 1965: RCA Studio B
Sessions for MGM's "Harum Scarum"

Producer: Fred Karger & Gene Nelson
Engineer: n/a
Guitar: Scotty Moore
Guitar: Grady Martin
Guitar: Charlie McCoy

Bass: Henry Strzelecki
Drums: D.J. Fontana
Drums: Kenneth Buttrey
Piano: Floyd Cramer
Tambourine: Hoyt Hawkins
Congas: Gene Nelson
Flute: Rufus Long
Oboe: Ralph Strobel
Vocals: Jordanaires

Shake That Tambourine (Giant-Baum-Kaye) (Harum Scarum movie)

February 25, 1965:
RCA Studio B
Sessions for MGM's "Harum Scarum"

Producer: Fred Karger & Gene Nelson
Engineer: n/a
Guitar: Scotty Moore
Guitar: Grady Martin
Guitar: Charlie McCoy
Bass: Henry Strzelecki
Drums: D.J. Fontana
Drums: Kenneth Buttrey
Piano: Floyd Cramer
Tambourine: Hoyt Hawkins
Congas: Gene Nelson
Flute: Rufus Long
Oboe: Ralph Strobel
Vocals: Jordanaires

So Close, Yet So Far (From Paradise) (Joy Byers) (Harum Scarum movie)
My Desert Serenade (Stanley Gelber) (Harum Scarum movie)
Wisdom of the Ages (Giant-Baum-Kaye) (Harum Scarum movie)
Kismet (Sid Tepper-Roy C. Bennett) (Harum Scarum movie)
Hey Little Girl (Joy Byers) (Harum Scarum movie)

February 26, 1965:
RCA Studio B
Sessions for MGM's "Harum Scarum"

Producer: Fred Karger & Gene Nelson
Engineer: n/a
Guitar: Scotty Moore
Guitar: Grady Martin
Guitar: Charlie McCoy
Bass: Henry Strzelecki
Drums: D.J. Fontana
Drums: Kenneth Buttrey
Piano: Floyd Cramer
Tambourine: Hoyt Hawkins
Congas: Gene Nelson
Flute: Rufus Long
Oboe: Ralph Strobel
Vocals: Jordanaires

Golden Coins (Giant-Baum-Kaye) (Harum Scarum movie)
Animal Instinct (Giant-Baum-Kaye) (Harum Scarum movie)
Harem Holiday (P. Andreoli-V. Poncia, Jr.-J. Crane) (Harum Scarum movie)
Go East, Young Man (Giant-Baum-Kaye) (Harum Scarum movie)
Mirage (Giant-Baum-Kaye) (Harum Scarum movie)

May 25, 1966:
RCA Studio B:

Producer: Felton Jarvis
Engineer: Jim Malloy
Guitar: Scotty Moore
Guitar: Chip Young
Guitar, Bass, Harmonica: Charlie McCoy
Bass: Bob Moore
Drums: D.J. Fontana
Drums, Tympani: Buddy Harman
Piano: Floyd Cramer
Piano, Organ: Henry Slaughter
Steel Guitar: Pete Drake
Sax: Rufus Long
Sax: Boots Randolph
Vocals: Jordanaires
Vocals: The Imperials
Vocals: Millie Kirkham, June Page, Dolores Edgin

Run On (Arr Elvis Presley)
How Great Thou Art (Stuart K. Hine)
Stand By Me (Arr Elvis Presley)
Where No One Stands Alone (Mosie Lister)
Down in the Alley (Jesse Stone and the CLovers)
Tomorrow Is a Long Time (Bob Dylan)

May 26, 1966:
RCA Studio B:

Producer: Felton Jarvis
Engineer: Jim Malloy
Guitar: Scotty Moore
Guitar: Chip Young
Guitar, Bass, Harmonica: Charlie McCoy
Bass: Bob Moore
Drums: D.J. Fontana
Drums, Tympani: Buddy Harman

Piano: Floyd Cramer
Piano, Organ: Henry Slaughter
Piano, Organ: David Briggs
Steel Guitar: Pete Drake
Sax: Rufus Long
Sax: Boots Randolph
Vocals: Jordanaires
Vocals: The Imperials
Vocals: Millie Kirkham, June Page, Dolores Edgin

Love Letters (E. Heyman-V. Young)
So High (arr Elvis Presley)
Farther Along (arr Elvis Presley)
By and By (arr Elvis Presley)
In the Garden (C.A. Miles)
Beyond the Reef (J. Pitman)

May 27, 1966:
RCA Studio B:

Producer: Felton Jarvis
Engineer: Jim Malloy
Guitar: Scotty Moore
Guitar: Chip Young
Guitar, Bass, Harmonica: Charlie McCoy
Bass: Bob Moore
Drums: D.J. Fontana
Drums, Tympani: Buddy Harman
Piano: Floyd Cramer
Piano, Organ: Henry Slaughter
Steel Guitar: Pete Drake
Sax: Rufus Long
Sax: Boots Randolph
Vocals: Jordanaires
Vocals: The Imperials
Vocals: Millie Kirkham, June Page, Dolores Edgin

Somebody Bigger Than You and I (J. Lange-H. Heath-S. Burke)
Without Him (Mylon LeFevre)

If the Lord Wasn't Walking By My Side (Henry Slaughter)
Where Could I Go But To The Lord (J.B. Coats)

May 28, 1966:
RCA Studio B:

Producer: Felton Jarvis
Engineer: Al Pachucki
Guitar: Scotty Moore
Guitar: Chip Young
Guitar, Bass, Harmonica: Charlie McCoy
Bass: Henry Strzelecki
Drums: D.J. Fontana
Drums, Tympani: Buddy Harman
Piano: Floyd Cramer
Steel Guitar: Pete Drake
Sax: Rufus Long
Sax: Boots Randolph
Trumpet: Ray Stevens
Vocals: Jordanaires
Vocals: Millie Kirkham, June Page, Dolores Edgin

Come What May (Tableporter)
Fools Fall in Love (J. Leiber-M. Stoller)

June 10, 1966:
RCA Studio B

Producer: Felton Jarvis
Engineer: Jim Malloy
Guitar: Scotty Moore
Guitar: Chip Young
Guitar: Harold Bradley
Bass: Bob Moore
Drums: D.J. Fontana
Drums, Tympani: Buddy Harman
Piano: David Briggs

Organ: Henry Slaughter
Steel Guitar: Pete Drake
Sax: Rufus Long
Vocals: Jordanaires
Vocals: The Imperials (not 5/28)
Vocals: Millie Kirkham, June Page, Dolores Edgin

Indescribably Blue (Darrell Glenn) (TRACKS)
I'll Remember You (KuiokalaniLee) (TRACKS)
If Every Day Was Like Christmas (Red West) (TRACKS)

June 12, 1966:
RCA Studio B

Indescribably Blue (Darrell Glenn) (VOCAL)
I'll Remember You (Kuiokalani Lee) (VOCAL)
If Every Day Was Like Christmas (Red West) (VOCAL)

February 21, 1967:
RCA Studio B

Movie Company Producer: Jeff Alexander
Producer: Felton Jarvis
Engineer: Jim Malloy
Guitar: Scotty Moore
Guitar: Chip Young
Guitar, Harmonica: Charlie McCoy
Bass: Bob Moore
Drums: D.J. Fontana
Drums: Buddy Harman
Piano: Floyd Cramer
Piano: Hoyt Hawkins
Steel Guitar: Pete Drake
Sax: Norm Ray
Vocals: Jordanaires
Vocals: Millie Kirkham

The Girl I Never Loved (Randy Starr) (Clambake movie)

How Can You Lose What You Never Had (Ben Weisman-Sid Wayne)
(Clambake movie)
You Don't Know Me (Cindy Walker-Eddy Arnold)
A House That Has Everything (Sid Tepper-Roy C. Benentt) (Clambake
movie)

February 22, 1967:
RCA Studio B

Movie Company Producer: Jeff Alexander
Producer: Felton Jarvis
Engineer: Jim Malloy
Guitar: Scotty Moore
Guitar: Chip Young
Guitar, Harmonica: Charlie McCoy
Bass: Bob Moore
Drums: D.J. Fontana
Drums: Buddy Harman
Piano: Floyd Cramer
Piano: Hoyt Hawkins
Steel Guitar: Pete Drake
Sax: Norm Ray
Vocals: Jordanaires
Vocals: Millie Kirkham

Who Needs Money? (Randy Starr) (Clambake movie)
Confidence (Sid Tepper-Roy C. Bennett) (Clambake movie)
Hey, Hey, Hey (Joy Byers) (Clambake movie)
Clambake (Ben Weisman-Sid Wayne) (Clambake movie)

February 23, 1966:
RCA Studio B

Clambake (reprise (Ben Weisman-Sid Wayne)

March 20, 1967:
RCA Studio B

Producer: Felton Jarvis
Engineer: Jim Malloy
Guitar: Scotty Moore
Guitar: Chip Young
Guitar: Grady Martin
Bass: Bob Moore
Drums: D.J. Fontana
Drums: Buddy Harman
Piano: David Briggs
Steel Guitar: Pete Drake
Harmonica: Charlie McCoy
Vocals: Jordanaires
Vocals: Millie Kirkham

Suppose (Sylvia Dee-George Goehring)

September 10, 1967:
RCA Studio B:

Producer: Felton Jarvis
Engineer: Jim Malloy
Guitar: Scotty Moore
Guitar: Chip Young
Guitar: Harold Bradley
Guitar: Jerry Reed
Bass: Bob Moore
Drums: D.J. Fontana
Drums: Buddy Harman
Piano: Floyd Cramer
Steel Guitar: Pete Drake
Organ: Hoyt Hawkins
Organ, Guitar, Harmonica: Charlie McCoy
Vocals: Jordanaires
Vocals: Millie Kirkham

Guitar Man (Jerry Reed)
Big Boss Man (Smith-Dixon)
Mine (Sid Tepper-Roy C. Bennett) (Speedway movie)
Singing Tree (A.L. Owens-Solberg)
Just Call Me Lonesome (Griffin) (Clambake movie)

September 11, 1967:
RCA Studio B

Producer: Felton Jarvis
Engineer: Jim Malloy
Guitar: Scotty Moore
Guitar: Chip Young
Guitar: Harold Bradley
Bass: Bob Moore
Drums: D.J. Fontana
Drums: Buddy Harman
Piano: Floyd Cramer
Piano: Elvis Presley (on "You'll Never Walk Alone")
Steel Guitar: Pete Drake
Organ, Guitar, Harmonica: Charlie McCoy
Vocals: Jordanaires
Vocals: Millie Kirkham

Hi-Heel Sneakers (Higginbotham)
You Don't Know Me (Walker-Arnold)
We Call On Him (Fred Karger-Ben Weisman-Sid Wayne)
You'll Never Walk Alone (Rodgers-Hammerstein)
Singing Tree (A.L. Owens-Solberg) (Clambake movie)

October 1, 1967:
RCA: Studio B

MGM Producer: Jeff Alexander
Producer: Felton Jarvis
Engineer: Al Pachucki
Guitar: Scotty Moore
Guitar: Chip Young
Bass: Bob Moore
Drums: D.J. Fontana
Drums: Buddy Harman
Piano: Floyd Cramer
Fiddle: Gordon Terry
Harmonica: Charlie McCoy
Vocals: Jordanaires

Stay Away Joe (Ben Weisman-Sid Wayne)
All I Needed Was the Rain (Sid Wayne-Ben Weisman)
Dominick (Sid Wayne-Ben Weisman)

January 15, 1968:
RCA Studio B:

Producer: Felton Jarvis
Engineer: Al Pachucki
Guitar: Scotty Moore
Guitar: Chip Young
Guitar: Jerry Reed
Bass: Bob Moore
Drums: D.J. Fontana
Drums: Buddy Harman
Piano: Floyd Cramer
Steel Guitar: Pete Drake
Harmonica: Charlie McCoy
Vocals: Jordanaires

Too Much Monkey Business (Chuck Berry) (Flaming Star movie)
Goin' Home (Joy Byers) (Speedway movie)

January 16, 1967:
RCA Studio B

Producer: Felton Jarvis
Engineer: Bill Vandevort
Guitar: Scotty Moore
Guitar: Chip Young
Guitar: Jerry Reed
Bass: Bob Moore
Drums: D.J. Fontana
Drums: Buddy Harman
Piano: Floyd Cramer
Steel Guitar: Pete Drake
Harmonica: Charlie McCoy
Vocals: Jordanaires

Stay Away (Sid Tepper-Roy C. Bennett)
U.S. Male (Jerry Reed)

September 25, 1969:
RCA Studio B:

Vocal Overdubs:
Let Us Pray
A Little Bit of Green

June 4, 1970:
RCA Studio B

Producer: Felton Jarvis
Engineer: Al Pachucki
Guitar: James Burton
Guitar: Chip Young
Acoustic Guitar: Elvis Presley
Bass: Norbert Putnam
Drums: Jerry Carrigan
Piano: David Briggs

Organ Harmonica: Charlie McCoy
Vocals: Jordanaires
Vocals: Charlie Hodge on "This Is Our Dance" and "Heart of Rome"

Twenty Days and Twenty Nights (Weisman-Westlake)
I've Lost You (Howard-Blaikley)
I Was Born About Ten Thousand Years Ago (adapted Elvis Presley)
The Sound of Your Cry (Giant-Baum-Kaye)
The Fool (Naomi Ford)
A Hundred Years From Now (Lester Flatt-Earl Scruggs)
Little Cabin on the Hill (Bill Monroe-Lester Flatt)
Cindy, Cindy (Kaye-Weisman-Fuller)

June 5, 1970:
RCA Studio B:

Producer: Felton Jarvis
Engineer: Al Pachucki
Guitar: James Burton
Guitar: Chip Young
Acoustic Guitar: Elvis Presley
Bass: Norbert Putnam
Drums: Jerry Carrigan
Piano: David Briggs
Organ Harmonica: Charlie McCoy
Vocals: Jordanaires
Vocals: Charlie Hodge on "This Is Our Dance" and "Heart of Rome"

Bridge Over Troubled Waters (Paul Simon)
Got My Mojo Working/Keep Your Hands Off of It (Foster; Adap E. Presley)
How the Web Was Woven (C. Westlake-M. Most)
It's Your Baby, You Rock It (Milete-Fowler)
Stranger in the Crowd (Winfield Scott)
I'll Never Know (Karger-Wayne-Weisman)
Mary in the Morning (Cymbal-Rashkow)

June 6, 1970:
RCA Studio B

Producer: Felton Jarvis
Engineer: Al Pachucki
Guitar: James Burton
Guitar: Chip Young
Acoustic Guitar: Elvis Presley
Bass: Norbert Putnam
Drums: Jerry Carrigan
Piano: David Briggs
Organ Harmonica: Charlie McCoy
Vocals: Jordanaires
Vocals: Charlie Hodge on "This Is Our Dance" and "Heart of Rome"

I Didn't Make It on Playing Guitar (E. Presley)
It Ain't No Big Thing (But It's Growing) Merritt-Joy-Hall)
You Don't Have to Say You Love Me (Wickham-Napier-Bell-Donaggio-Pallavicine)
Just Pretend (D. Flett-G. Gletcher)
This is Our Dance (Les Reed-Geoff Stephens)
Life (Shirl Milete)
Heart of Rome (Stephens-Blaikley-Howard)

June 7, 1970:
RCA Studio B

Producer: Felton Jarvis
Engineer: Al Pachucki
Guitar: James Burton
Guitar: Chip Young
Acoustic Guitar: Elvis Presley
Bass: Norbert Putnam
Drums: Jerry Carrigan
Piano: David Briggs
Organ Harmonica: Charlie McCoy
Vocals: Jordanaires
Vocals: Charlie Hodge on "This Is Our Dance" and "Heart of Rome"

When I'm Over You (Shirl Milete)
I Really Don't Want To Know (Barnes-Robertson)
Faded Love (B. Wills-J. Wills)
Tomorrow Never Comes (E. Tubb-Bond)
The Next Step is Love (Evans-Parnes)
Make the World Go Away (Hank Cochran)
Funny How Time Slips Away (Willie Nelson)
I Washed My Hand in Muddy Water; (Joe Babcock)
Love Letters (E. Heymann-V. Young)

June 8, 1970:
RCA Studio B

Producer: Felton Jarvis
Engineer: Al Pachucki
Guitar: James Burton
Guitar: Chip Young
Acoustic Guitar: Elvis Presley
Bass: Norbert Putnam
Drums: Jerry Carrigan
Piano: David Briggs
Organ Harmonica: Charlie McCoy
Vocals: Jordanaires
Vocals: Charlie Hodge on "This Is Our Dance" and "Heart of Rome"

There Goes My Everything (Dallas Frazier)
If I Were You (G. Nelson)
Only Believe (Paul Rader)
Sylvia (Geoff Stephens-Les Reed)
Patch It Up (E. Rabbitt-R. Burke)

September 22, 1970:
RCA Studio B

Producer/A&R: Felton Jarvis
Engineer: Al Pachucki
Guitar: Eddie Hinton
Guitar: Chip Young
Bass: Norbert Putnam
Drums: Jerry Carrigan
Piano: David Briggs
Organ, Harmonica: Charlie McCoy
Vocals: The Jordanaires
Vocals: Millie Kirkham, Mary Green, Mary Holladay, Ginger Holladay

Overdubbed later:
Vocals: The Imperials
Vocals: Millie Kirkham, Dolores Edgin, Sonja Montgomery, June Page
Guitar: Harold Bradley
Piano: David Briggs
Percussion: Farrell Morris
Harmony: Elvis Presley ("Snowbird")

Snowbird (Gene MacLellan)
Where Did They Go, Lord? (Dalas Frazier-A.L. Owens)
Whole Lotta Shakin' Goin' On (Dave Williams-Sunny David)
Rags to Riches (Richard Adler-Jerry Ross)

March 15, 1971:
RCA Studio B

A&R/Producer: Felton Jarvis
Engineer: Al Pachucki
Guitar: James Burton
Guitar: Chip Young
Acoustic Guitar: Charlie Hodge
Bass: Norbert Putnam
Drums: Jerry Carrigan
Piano: David Briggs

Harmonica: Charlie McCoy
Vocal: The Nashville Edition
Vocals: Mary & Ginger Holladay, Millie Kirkham

The First Time Ever I Saw Your Face (Ewan McColl)
Amazing Grace (arr Elvis Presley)
Early Morning Rain (Gordon Lightfoot)
That's What You Get For Lovin' Me (Gordon Lightfoot)

May 15, 1971:
RCA Studio B

A&R/Producer: Felton Jarvis
Engineer: Al Pachucki
Electric Guitar:James Burton
Guitar: Chip Young
Acoustic Guitar: Charlie Hodge
Bass: Norbert Putnam
Drums, Percussion: Jerry Carrigan
Piano: David Briggs
Vocals: June Page, Millie Kirkham, Ginger Hollady

Miracle of the Rosary (Lee Denson)
It Won't Seem Like Christmas (J.A. Balthrop)
If I Get Home on Christmas Day (Tony McCaulay)
Padre (LaRue-Hebster-Romans)
Holly Leaves and Christmas Trees (Red West-Glen Spreen)
Merry Christmas, Baby (L. Baxter-J. Moore)
Silver Bells (R. Evans-J. Livingston)

May 16, 1971:
RCA Studio B

A&R/Producer: Felton Jarvis
Engineer: Al Pachucki
Electric Guitar: James Burton
Guitar: Chip Young
Acoustic Guitar: Charlie Hodge
Bass: Norbert Putnam
Drums: Kenneth Buttrey
Piano: David Briggs
Organ: Glen Spreen
Organ, Percussion, Harmonica: Charlie McCoy
Vocals: June Page, Millie Kirkham, Ginger Holladay

The Lord's Prayer (arr Elvis Presley)
I'll Be Home on Christmas Day (Michael Jarrett)
On a Snowy Christmas Night (S. Gelber)
Winter Wonderland (D. Smith-F. Bernard)
Don't Think Twice, It's All Right (Bob Dylan)
O Come, All Ye Faithful (arr Elvis Presley)
The First Noel (arr Elvis Presley)
The Wonderful World of Christmas (Tobias-Frisch)

May 17, 1971:
RCA Studio B

A&R/Producer: Felton Jarvis
Engineer: Al Pachucki
Electric Guitar: James Burton
Guitar: Chip Young
Acoustic Guitar: Charlie Hodge
Bass: Norbert Putnam
Drums, Percussion: Jerry Carrigan
Drums: Kenneth Buttrey
Piano: David Briggs
Organ, Percussion, Harmonica: Charlie McCoy
Vocals: The Imperials
Vocals: June Page, Kirkham, Ginger Holladay

Help Me Make It Through the Night (Kris Kristofferson)
Until It's Time for You to Go (Buffy Sainte-Marie)
Lady Madonna (John Lennon-Paul McCartney)
Lead Me, Guide Me (D. Akers)

May 18, 1971:
RCA Studio B

A&R/Producer: Felton Jarvis
Engineer: Al Pachucki
Electric Guitar: James Burton
Guitar: Chip Young
Acoustic Guitar: Charlie Hodge
Bass: Norbert Putnam
Drums: Kenneth Buttrey
Piano: David Briggs
Piano: Joe Moscheo
Organ, Percussion, Harmonica: Charlie McCoy
Vocals: The Imperials
Vocals: June Page, Millie Kirkham, Ginger Holladay

Fools Rush In (R. Bloom-J. Mercer)
He Touched Me (Bill Gaither)
I've Got Confidence (Andre Crouch)
An Evening Prayer (Battersby-Gabriel)

May 19, 1971:
RCA Studio B

A&R/Producer: Felton Jarvis
Engineer: Al Pachucki
Electric Guitar: James Burton
Guitar: Chip Young
Acoustic Guitar: Charlie Hodge
Bass: Norbert Putnam
Drums: Kenneth Buttrey
Piano: David Briggs
Piano: Joe Moscheo

Piano: Elvis Presley ("It's Still Here," "I'll Take You Home Again Kathleen," "I Will Be True")
Organ, Percussion, Harmonica: Charlie McCoy
Vocals: June Page, Millie Kirkham, Ginger Holladay

Miracle of the Rosary (vocal overdub);
Seeing is Believing (Red West-Glen Spreen)
A Thing Called Love (Jerry Reed)
It's Still Here (Ivory Joe Hunter)
I'll Take You Home Again, Kathleen (arr. Elvis Presley)
I Will Be True (Ivory Joe Hunter)

May 20, 1971:
RCA Studio B

A&R/Producer: Felton Jarvis
Engineer: Al Pachucki
Electric Guitar: James Burton
Guitar: Chip Young
Acoustic Guitar: Charlie Hodge
Bass: Norbert Putnam
Drums, Percussion: Jerry Carrigan (5/15, 17)
Drums: Kenneth Buttrey (5/16-21)
Piano: David Briggs
Organ, Percussion, Harmonica: Charlie McCoy
Vocals: June Page, Millie Kirkham, Ginger Holladay

I'm Leavin' (Michael Jarrett-Sonny Charles)
We Can Make the Morning (Jay Ramsey)
I Shall Be Released (Bob Dylan)
It's Only Love (Mark James-Steve Tyrell)

May 21, 1971:
RCA Studio B

Love Me, Love the Life I Lead (Tony Macaulay-Roger Greenaway)
June 8, 1971: RCA Studio B:

A&R/Producer: Felton Jarvis
Engineer: Al Pachucki
Electric Guitar: James Burton
Guitar: Chip Young
Acoustic Guitar: Charlie Hodge
Bass: Norbert Putnam
Drums: Jerry Carrigan
Drums: Kenneth Buttrey
Piano: David Briggs
Piano: Joe Moscheo ("Reach Out To Jesus"?)
Organ: Charlie McCoy
Organ: Glen Spreen ("Until It's Time For You to Go")
Vocals: The Imperials
Vocals: June Page, Millie Kirkham, Sonja Montgomery, Dolores Edgin

Until It's Time For You to Go (remake) (Buffy Sainte-Marie)
Put Your Hand in the Hand (Gene Maclellan)
Reach Out to Jesus (Ralph Carmichael)

June 9, 1971:
RCA Studio B

A&R/Producer: Felton Jarvis
Engineer: Al Pachucki
Electric Guitar: James Burton
Guitar: Chip Young
Acoustic Guitar: Charlie Hodge
Bass: Norbert Putnam
Drums: Jerry Carrigan
Drums: Kenneth Buttrey
Piano: David Briggs
Piano: Joe Moscheo ("Reach Out To Jesus"?)

Organ: Charlie McCoy
Organ: Glen Spreen ("Until It's Time For You to Go")
Vocals: The Imperials
Vocals: June Page, Millie Kirkham, Sonja Montgomery, Dolores Edgin

He Is My Everything (Dallas Frazier)
There is No God But God (Bill Kenny)
I John (Johnson-McFadden-Brooks)
The Bosom of Abraham (Johnson-McFadden-Brooks)

June 10, 1971:
RCA Studio B

A&R/Producer: Felton Jarvis
Engineer: Al Pachucki
Electric Guitar: James Burton
Guitar: Chip Young
Acoustic Guitar: Charlie Hodge
Bass: Norbert Putnam
Drums: Jerry Carrigan
Drums: Kenneth Buttrey
Piano: David Briggs
Piano: Joe Moscheo ("Reach Out To Jesus"?)
Organ: Charlie McCoy
Organ: Glen Spreen ("Until It's Time For You to Go")
Vocals: The Imperials
Vocals: June Page, Millie Kirkham, Sonja Montgomery, Dolores Edgin

My Way (Anka-Reveaux-Francois)
I'll Be Home on Christmas Day (remake) (Michael Jarrett)

SONGS ELVIS RECORDED IN NASHVILLE
AND THE DATE OF RECORDING

Ain't That Loving You Baby?
(6/10/58)
All I Needed Was the Rain
(10/1/67)
Amazing Grace (3/15/71)
An Evening Prayer (5/18/71)
Angel (7/2/61)
Animal Instinct (2/26/65)
Anyone (Could Fall In Love With
You) (9/29/63)
Anything That's Part of You
(10/15/61)
Are You Lonesome Tonight?
(4/3/60)
Ask Me (1/12/64)
Ask Me (5/27/63)
Barefoot Ballad (9/29/63)
Beyond the Reef (5/26/66)
Big Boss Man (9/10/67)
Big Hunk o' Love, A (6/10/58)
Blue River (5/27/63)
Bosom of Abraham, The (6/9/71)
Bridge Over Troubled Waters
(6/5/70)
By and By (5/26/66)
Catchin' On Fast (9/29/63)
Cindy, Cindy (9/25/69)
Clambake (2/22/67)
Clambake (reprise) (2/23/67)
Come What May (5/28/66)
Confidence (2/22/67)
Crying in the Chapel (10/30/60)

Devil in Disguise, (You're the)
(5/26/63)
Dirty, Dirty Feeling (4/3/60)
Dominick (10/1/67)
Don't Think Twice, It's All Right
(5/16/71)
Down in the Alley (5/25/66)
Early Morning Rain (3/15/71)
Easy Question (3/18/62)
Echoes of Love (5/26/63)
Faded Love (6/7/70)
Faded Love (9/25/69)
Fame and Fortune (3/20/60)
Farther Along (5/26/66)
Fever (4/3/60)
Finder Keepers, Loser Weepers
(5/26/63)
First Noel, The (5/16/71)
First Time Ever I Saw Your Face,
The (3/15/71)
Follow That Dream (7/2/61)
Fool, The (9/25/69)
Fool Such as I, A (6/10/58)
Fools Fall in Love (5/28/66)
Fools Rush In (5/18/71)
For the Millionth and the Last
Time (10/15/61)
Fountain of Love (3/18/62)
Funny How Time Slips Away
(6/7/70)
Gently (3/12/61)
Girl I Never Loved, The (2/21/67)

Girl Next Door Went A' Walking, The (4/3/60)

Girl of My Best Friend, The (4/3/60)

Give Me the Right (3/12/61)

Go East, Young Man (2/26/65)

Goin' Home (1/15/68)

Golden Coins (2/26/65)

Gonna Get Back Home Somehow (3/18/62)

Good Luck Charm (10/15/61)

Got My Mojo Working/Keep Your Hands Off of It (6/5/70)

Guitar Man (9/10/67)

Harem Holiday (2/26/65)

He Is My Everything (6/9/71)

He Knows Just What I Need (10/30/60)

He Touched Me (5/18/71)

Heart of Rome (6/6/70)

Heartbreak Hotel (1/10/56)

Help Me Make It Through the Night (5/17/71)

Hey Little Girl (2/25/65)

Hey, Hey, Hey (2/22/67)

Hi-Heel Sneakers (9/11/67)

His Hand in Mine (10/30/60)

Holly Leaves and Christmas Trees (5/15/71)

House That Has Everything, A (2/21/67)

How Can You Lose What You Never Had (2/21/67)

How Great Thou Art (5/25/66)

How the Web Was Woven (6/5/70)

Hundred Years From Now, A (9/25/69)

I Believe in the Man in the Sky (10/30/60)

I Didn't Make It on Playing Guitar (6/6/70)

I Feel So Bad (3/12/61)

I Feel That I've Known You Forever (3/18/62)

I Got a Woman (1/10/56)

I Got Stung (6/10/58)

I Gotta Know (4/3/60)

I John (6/9/71)

I Met Her Today (10/15/61)

I Need Your Love Tonight (6/10/58)

I Really Don't Want To Know (6/7/70)

I Shall Be Released (5/20/71)

I Want You With Me (3/12/61)

I Want You, I Need You, I Love You (4/13/56)

I Was Born About Ten Thousand Years Ago (9/25/69)

I Was the One (1/11/56)

I Washed My Hand in Muddy Water (6/7/70)

I Will Be Home Again (4/3/60)

I Will Be True (5/19/71)

I'll Be Home on Christmas Day (5/16/71)

I'll Be Home on Christmas Day (remake) (6/10/71)

I'll Never Know (6/5/70)

I'll Remember You (Kuiokalani Lee) (VOCAL) (6/12/66)

I'll Remember You (KuiokalaniLee) (TRACKS) (6/10/66)

I'll take You Home Again
(5/19/71)
I'm Coming Home (3/12/61)
I'm Counting on You" (1/11/56)
I'm Gonna Walk Dem Golden
Stairs (10/30/60)
I'm Leavin' (5/20/71)
I'm Not the Marrying Kind
(7/2/61)
I'm Yours (6/25/61)
I've Got Confidence (5/18/71)
I've Lost You" (9/25/69)
If Every Day Was Like Christ-
mas (Red West) (TRACKS)
(6/10/66)
If Every Day Was Like Christmas
(Red West) (VOCAL) (6/12/66)
If I Get Home on Christmas Day
(5/15/71)
If I Were You (6/8/70)
If the Lord Wasn't Walking By
My Side (5/27/66)
If We Never Meet Again
(10/30/60)
In My Father's House (10/30/60)
In the Garden (5/26/66)
In Your Arms (3/12/61)
Indescribably Blue (TRACKS)
(6/10/66)
Indescribably Blue (VOCAL)
(6/12/66)
It Ain't No Big Thing (But It's
Growing) (6/6/70)
It Feels So Right (2/20/60)
It Hurts Me (1/12/64)
It Won't Seem Like Christmas

(5/15/71)
It's a Sin (3/12/61)
It's Now or Never (4/3/60)
It's Only Love (5/20/71)
It's Still Here (5/19/71)
It's Your Baby, You Rock It
(6/5/70)
Joshua Fit the Battle (10/30/60)
Judy (3/12/61)
Just Call Me Lonesome (9/10/67)
Just for Old Time's Sake (3/18/62)
Just Pretend (6/6/70)
Just Tell Her Jim Said Hello
(3/18/62)
Kissin' Cousins No. 2 (9/29/63)
Kismet (2/25/65)
Kiss Me Quick (6/25/61)
Kissin' Cousins (9/29/63)
Known Only to Him (10/30/60)
Lady Madonna (5/17/71)
Lead Me, Guide Me (5/17/71)
Life (6/6/70)
Like a Baby (4/3/60)
Little Bit of Green, A
Little Cabin on the Hill (9/25/69)
Little Sister (6/25/61)
Long Lonely Highway, (It's a)
(5/27/63)
Lord's Prayer, The (5/16/71)
Love Letters (5/26/66)
Love Letters (6/7/70)
Love Me Tonight (5/26/63)
Love Me, Love the Life I Lead
(5/21/71)
Make Me Know It (3/20/60)
Make the World Go Away (6/7/70)

Mansion Over the Hilltop (10/30/60)
Marie's The Name Of His Latest Flame (6/25/61)
Mary in the Morning (6/5/70)
Memphis Tennessee (5/27/63)
Memphis, Tennessee (1/12/64)
Merry Christmas, Baby (5/15/71)
Mess of Blues, A (3/20/60)
Milky White Way (10/30/60)
Mine (9/10/67)
Miracle of the Rosary (5/15/71)
Mirage (2/26/65)
Money Honey (1/10/56)
My Desert Serenade (2/25/65)
My Way (6/10/71)
Never Ending (5/26/63)
Next Step is Love, The (6/7/70)
Night Rider (10/15/61)
Night Rider (3/18/62)
O Come, All Ye Faithful (5/16/71)
On a Snowy Christmas Night (5/16/71)
Once Is Enough (9/29/63)
One Boy, Two Little Girls (9/29/63)
Only Believe (6/8/70)
Padre (5/15/71)
Patch It Up (6/8/70)
Put the Blame on Me (3/12/61)
Put Your Hand in the Hand (6/8/71)
Rags to Riches (9/22/70)
Reach Out to Jesus (6/8/71)
Reconsider Baby (4/3/60)
Run On (5/25/66)

Seeing is Believing (5/19/71)
Sentimental Me (3/12/61)
Shake That Tambourine (2/24/65)
She's Not You (3/18/62)
Silver Bells (5/15/71)
Singing Tree (9/10/67)
Singing Tree (9/11/67)
Slowly But Surely (5/27/63)
Smokey Mountain Boy (9/29/63)
Snowbird (9/22/70)
So Close, Yet So Far (From Paradise) (2/25/65)
So High (5/26/66)
Soldier Boy (3/20/60)
Somebody Bigger Than You and I (5/27/66)
Something Blue (3/18/62)
Sound Advice (7/2/61)
Sound of Your Cry, The (9/25/69)
Stand By Me (5/25/66)
Starting Today (3/12/61)
Stay Away (1/16/67)
Stay Away Joe (10/1/67)
Stranger in the Crowd (6/5/70)
Stuck on You (3/20/60)
Such a Night (4/3/60)
Suppose (2/23/67)
Surrender (10/30/60)
Suspicion (3/18/62)
Swing Down, Sweet Chariot (10/30/60)
Sylvia (6/8/70)
Tender Feeling (9/29/63)
That's Someone You Never Forget (6/25/61)
That's What You Get For Lovin'

Me (3/15/71)
There Goes My Everything (6/8/70)
There is No God But God (6/9/71)
There's Always Me (3/12/61)
There's Gold In the Mountains
 (9/29/63)
Thing Called Love, A (5/19/71)
This is Our Dance (6/6/70)
Thrill of Your Love (4/3/60)
Tomorrow Is a Long Time
 (5/25/66)
Tomorrow Never Comes (6/7/70)
Too Much Monkey Business
 (1/15/68)
Twenty Days and Twenty Nights
 (9/25/69)
U.S. Male (1/16/67)
Until It's Time for You to Go
 (5/17/71)
Until It's Time For You to Go
 (remake) (6/8/71)
We Call On Him (9/11/67)
We Can Make the Morning
 (5/20/71)
Western Union (5/27/63)
What a Wonderful Life (7/2/61)
What Now, What Next, Where To
 (5/26/63)
When I'm Over You (6/7/70)
Where Could I Go But To The
 Lord (5/27/66)
Where Did They Go, Lord?
 (9/22/70)
Where No One Stands Alone
 (5/25/66)
Whistling Tune, A (7/2/61)

Who Needs Money? (2/22/67)
Whole Lotta Shakin' Goin' On
 (9/22/70)
Winter Wonderland (5/16/71)
Wisdom of the Ages (2/25/65)
Witchcraft (5/26/63)
Without Him (5/27/66)
Wonderful World of Christmas,
 The (5/16/71)
Working on the Building
 (10/30/60)
You Don't Have to Say You Love
 Me (6/6/70)
You Don't Know Me (2/21/67)
You Don't Know Me (9/11/67)
You'll Be Gone (3/18/62)
You'll Never Walk Alone
 (9/11/67)

INDEX

INDEX

INDEX

INDEX

INDEX

INDEX

INDEX

INDEX

INDEX

INDEX

INDEX

INDEX

INDEX

INDEX

INDEX

INDEX

INDEX

INDEX

INDEX

INDEX

INDEX

INDEX

INDEX

INDEX

41682161R00181

Made in the USA
Charleston, SC
05 May 2015